Hermias

*On Plato
Phaedrus 257C–279C*

with

'Syrianus'

Introduction to Hermogenes On Styles

Ancient Commentators on Aristotle

GENERAL EDITORS: Richard Sorabji, Honorary Fellow, Wolfson College, University of Oxford, and Emeritus Professor, King's College London, UK; and Michael Griffin, Professor, Departments of Philosophy and Classics, University of British Columbia, Canada.

This prestigious series translates the extant ancient Greek philosophical commentaries on Aristotle. Written mostly between 200 and 600 AD, the works represent the classroom teaching of the Aristotelian and Neoplatonic schools in a crucial period during which pagan and Christian thought were reacting to each other. The translation in each volume is accompanied by an introduction, comprehensive commentary notes, bibliography, glossary of translated terms and a subject index. Making these key philosophical works accessible to the modern scholar, this series fills an important gap in the history of European thought.

A webpage for the Ancient Commentators Project is maintained at ancientcommentators.org.uk and readers are encouraged to consult the site for details about the series as well as for addenda and corrigenda to published volumes.

Hermias

*On Plato
Phaedrus 257C–279C*

with

'Syrianus'

Introduction to Hermogenes On Styles

Translated by
Dirk Baltzly and Michael Share

BLOOMSBURY ACADEMIC
LONDON • NEW YORK • OXFORD • NEW DELHI • SYDNEY

BLOOMSBURY ACADEMIC
Bloomsbury Publishing Plc, 50 Bedford Square, London, WC1B 3DP, UK
Bloomsbury Publishing Inc, 1385 Broadway, New York, NY 10018, USA
Bloomsbury Publishing Ireland, 29 Earlsfort Terrace, Dublin 2, D02 AY28, Ireland

BLOOMSBURY, BLOOMSBURY ACADEMIC and the Diana logo are trademarks of
Bloomsbury Publishing Plc

First published in Great Britain 2025

Copyright © Dirk Baltzly and Michael Share, 2025

Dirk Baltzly and Michael Share have asserted their rights under the Copyright, Designs and
Patents Act, 1988, to be identified as Author of this work.

Cover design: Terry Woodley

All rights reserved. No part of this publication may be: i) reproduced or transmitted in any form, electronic or mechanical, including photocopying, recording or by means of any information storage or retrieval system without prior permission in writing from the publishers; or ii) used or reproduced in any way for the training, development or operation of artificial intelligence (AI) technologies, including generative AI technologies. The rights holders expressly reserve this publication from the text and data mining exception as per Article 4(3) of the Digital Single Market Directive (EU) 2019/790.

Bloomsbury Publishing Plc does not have any control over, or responsibility for, any third-party websites referred to or in this book. All internet addresses given in this book were correct at the time of going to press. The author and publisher regret any inconvenience caused if addresses have changed or sites have ceased to exist, but can accept no responsibility for any such changes.

A catalogue record for this book is available from the British Library.

A catalog record for this book is available from the Library of Congress.

ISBN: HB: 978-1-3503-6376-2
ePDF: 978-1-3503-6378-6
eBook: 978-1-3503-6379-3

Series: Ancient Commentators on Aristotle

Typeset by RefineCatch Limited, Bungay, Suffolk
Printed and bound in Great Britain

For product safety related questions contact productsafety@bloomsbury.com.

To find out more about our authors and books visit www.bloomsbury.com
and sign up for our newsletters.

Acknowledgements

The present translations have been made possible by generous and imaginative funding from the following sources: the National Endowment for the Humanities, Division of Research Programs, an independent federal agency of the USA; the Leverhulme Trust; the British Academy; the Jowett Copyright Trustees; the Royal Society (UK); Centro Internazionale A. Beltrame di Storia dello Spazio e del Tempo (Padua); Mario Mignucci; Liverpool University; the Leventis Foundation; the Arts and Humanities Research Council; Gresham College; the Esmée Fairbairn Charitable Trust; the Henry Brown Trust; Mr and Mrs N. Egon; the Netherlands Organisation for Scientific Research (NOW/GW); the Ashdown Trust; the Lorne Thyssen Research Fund for Ancient World Topics at Wolfson College, Oxford; Dr Victoria Solomonides, the Cultural Attaché of the Greek Embassy in London; and the Social Sciences and Humanities Research Council of Canada. The editors wish to thank John Dillon, David Mirhady, Harold Tarrant, and Sarah Wear for their comments; Dawn Sellars for preparing the volume for press; and Alice Wright, Commissioning Editor at Bloomsbury Academic, for her diligence in seeing each volume of the series to press.

Contents

Hermias: *On Plato Phaedrus 257C–279C*

Conventions	3
Abbreviations	4
Introduction	7
Departures from Lucarini and Moreschini's Text	29
Translation	31
Notes	103
Bibliography	129
English–Greek Glossary	133
Greek–English Index	137
Subject Index	147

'Syrianus': *Introduction to Hermogenes On Styles*

Conventions	153
Abbreviations	154
Introduction	155
Translation	173
Notes	185
Bibliography	191
English–Greek Glossary	195
Greek–English Index	197
Subject Index	202

Hermias

On Plato Phaedrus 257C–279C

Conventions – Hermias

[...]   Square brackets enclose words or phrases that have been added to the translation for purposes of clarity and to our expansions of Hermias' lemmata.

(...)   Round brackets, besides being used for ordinary parentheses, contain transliterated Greek words or references to the text of the *Phaedrus* or of Hermias' commentary itself.

<...>   Angle brackets enclosing text contain additions to Lucarini and Moreschini's text. Those enclosing three stops indicate points at which they assume a lacuna in the Greek text.

In addition to their normal uses, italics are used to identify direct quotation of the *Phaedrus*.

The page and line numbers of Lucarini and Moreschini's edition are printed in the margins of the translation and the page numbers of Couvreur's edition are printed in bold and in round brackets in the text.

Abbreviations – Hermias

Ast	Friedrich Ast (ed.), *Platonis Phaedrus recensuit Hermiae scholiis e Cod. Monac. XI. suisque commentariis illustravit*, Leipzig: Schwickert, 1810.
Bernard	Hildegund Bernard (tr.), *Hermeias von Alexandrien, Kommentar zu Platons* Phaidros, Tübingen: Mohr Siebeck, 1997.
Couvreur	P. Couvreur (ed.), *Hermiae Alexandrini in Platonis Phaedrum scholia*, Paris: Librairie E. Bouillon, 1901.
DK	H. Diels, *Die Fragmente der Vorsokratiker, Griechisch und Deutsch*, 6th edn, ed. W. Kranz, 3 vols, Berlin: Weidmann, 1951–2.
Dillon	John Dillon (ed.), *Iamblichi Chalcidensis in Platonis dialogos commentariorum fragmenta*, Leiden: Brill, 1973.
Hackforth	R. Hackforth (tr.), *Plato's* Phaedrus, Cambridge: Cambridge University Press, 1952.
Lampe	G. W. H. Lampe (ed.), *A Patristic Greek Lexicon*, Oxford: Clarendon Press, 1961.
LCL	Loeb Classical Library
LSJ	H. G. Liddell and R. Scott (comps), *A Greek-English Lexicon*, rev. H. Jones, with a New Supplement, 9th edn, Oxford: Clarendon Press, 1996.
Lucarini and Moreschini	C. M. Lucarini and C. Moreschini (eds), *Hermias Alexandrinus: in Platonis Phaedrum scholia*, Berlin and Boston: De Gruyter, 2012.
OCT	Oxford Classical Texts
Perry	Ben Edwin Perry (comp.), *Aesopica*, New York: Arno Press, 1980.
PT	H. D. Saffrey and L. G. Westerink, *Proclus: Théologie platonicienne*, 6 vols, Paris: Les Belles Lettres, 1968–97.
TLG	*Thesaurus Linguae Graecae* (CD ROM and online at https://stephanus.tlg.uci.edu)

West	M. L. West, *Iambi et elegi Graeci ante Alexandrinum cantati: Vol. 2*, 2nd edn, Oxford: Oxford University Press, 1992.
Yunis	Harvey Yunis, *Plato*, Phaedrus, Cambridge: Cambridge University Press, 2011.

Any otherwise unattributed references to volume 1 or volume 2 refer to the first and second volumes of the translation of Hermias' commentary in Baltzly and Share 2018 and 2023 respectively.

Introduction

1. Hermias' uneven commentary

As we noted in the second volume of our translation, Hermias' commentary does not devote the same level of attention to all parts of Plato's dialogue. The palinode (243E9–257B6) takes up about a quarter of Plato's *Phaedrus*, but Hermias devotes almost half the pages in his commentary to this part of the dialogue. Moreover, even within the section of Hermias' commentary that concerns the palinode, the depth and thoroughness of his attention to Plato's text differs. Once he has concluded his discussion of the periods of the soul's incarnation at 249D, the numbered sections dealing with individual lemmata become much briefer and, often, much more superficial. Thus Book 2 §§ 10–49 deals with 246A3–249D3 – a bit over 3 Stephanus pages. It takes Hermias roughly 58 pages in his commentary to cover this material. But Book 3 deals with 249D4–257C1 (roughly 11 Stephanus pages) in 98 sections and the sections are so much briefer that he covers this portion of Plato's text in 32 pages. The different levels of exegetical engagement are perhaps unsurprising when we consider the role of the *Phaedrus* in the Platonic curriculum. It was regarded as a 'theological' dialogue (along with the *Symposium*) and the part of the text that Hermias expends the most effort over concerns Socrates' description of *divine souls* and the manner in which they guide human souls to a vision of the intelligibles.

Hermias' thoroughness in the treatment of the lemmata from the end of the palinode at 257C1 declines even more dramatically. This volume of our translation begins with Book 3 § 99 and concludes with § 308. The commentary discusses just over 40 per cent of Plato's dialogue (257C–279C) but does so in the space of only 61 pages, so the sections tend to be correspondingly shorter. But they are not uniformly short: Hermias takes more time over some parts of the text than others. Some of the longer discussions, as one might expect, concern the digression that Socrates takes in the myth of the cicadas (258E6–259D7) and on the transition to the discussion of writing (257C ff.). Platonic myths tend to call forth extensive discussion in the Neoplatonic commentary tradition. So too do questions about the structure of the text and its overall unity. Given the attention that Platonist commentators normally dedicate to myths, one might expect, then, that Socrates' account of the genesis of writing with Theuth and Thaumas (274C1–275B2) would be treated at length by Hermias. But Hermias regards this myth as 'clear' (267,9 and 268,29) and his comments on it serve principally to explicate the meaning or significance of individual words and phrases. Perhaps this is because Hermias takes seriously Phaedrus' remark that Socrates has just made the whole story up on the spot (275B3). This myth is thus unlike the myth spoken in the palinode where Hermias regards Socrates as divinely inspired, so that his words come as a kind of divine revelation. Whatever the reason, then, Hermias' explication of the story of Theuth and Thaumas concentrates on matters of detail, like the symbolic significance of the ibis as a sacred bird (274C6–7).

In our previous volume 2, Hermias spent time showing the consistency of Socrates' theological account with that of Orpheus, as well as showing how what the *Phaedrus* tells us agrees with other Platonic dialogues. In the present volume, we still see *Platonic* intertextuality. In particular, Hermias notes the agreement of the *Phaedrus* with the *Sophist*, *Symposium* and, especially, the *Gorgias*, but we no longer see Hermias working to establish the consistency of Plato's remarks with Orphic ideas or with the 'theology' of Homer. This is, in all likelihood, simply a result of the fact that the material in *Phaedrus* 257C–279C does not offer many opportunities for discovering such parallels with non-Platonic sources of authority since its subject matter concerns beauty at the level of language rather than the divine, super-sensible principles of beauty.

Another common theme across all three volumes of this translation is Hermias' concern with the unity and structure of the *Phaedrus*. We shall turn to this attempt to discover a unity in the case of the conclusion of the palinode and the discussion of rhetoric and writing in section 2 of the Introduction. We shall take up Platonic intertextuality in section 4 and Hermias' treatment of the cicada myth in section 3.

But let us first consider one hypothesis as to why Hermias' treatment of the latter part of the *Phaedrus* seems so superficial in relation to his treatment of the palinode. Let us call this hypothesis 'the Neoplatonic rejection of rhetoric'. On this hypothesis, Hermias' commentary on the latter parts of the dialogue is relatively superficial because *the Neoplatonic philosophers were not particularly interested in, or positively disposed towards, rhetoric*.

Such a hostile attitude towards rhetoric could easily be regarded as true to Plato. After all, Plato's depiction of Gorgias, Polus, and Callicles in conversation with Socrates in the *Gorgias* stands out as among the most polemical of Plato's dialogues. By the time that Callicles enters the conversation in that dialogue, philosophy and rhetoric have expanded to the role of diametrically opposed, totalising ethical visions. Callicles rejects as signs of weakness or stupidity the commitment to the virtues of justice and self-control that Socrates regards as necessary (and perhaps sufficient) conditions of human well-being. Callicles also denigrates philosophy as a childish waste of time that risks leaving the philosopher open to shameful abuse by those who have the power of persuasion. Socrates, for his part, characterises rhetoric as a non-art that yields no genuine benefit to its practitioners. If the *Phaedrus* attenuates this hostile and negative portrait of rhetoric and rhetoricians, it is only by holding out the ideal of a 'true rhetoric' that no actual rhetorician seems to have achieved. So one might suppose that if the Neoplatonists in the Athenian school were hostile towards, or at least dismissive of, rhetoric, they had ample Platonic authority for such an attitude.

In addition to this Platonic warrant for hostility to rhetoric, members of the school of Syrianus at Athens might well have resented the fame and wealth of the schools of rhetoric in their city. In the fourth century, Athens was famous as a destination for study, but this fame was built on the notable teachers of *rhetoric* who made the city their home and who offered instruction. While there were Platonic philosophers who taught in Athens after Longinus (d. 273), the first teacher of Porphyry, none of them enjoyed the same repute. From Longinus to Plutarch of Athens (d. 432), we know little about Platonic philosophers in Athens. By contrast, thanks to works like Philostratus' *Lives of the Sophists*, we have a vivid picture of many of the rhetoricians at Athens in the third and fourth centuries.[1] By the early fifth century, the reputation of Platonic philosophers at Athens was well established as evidenced by the fact that young men like Hermias and Proclus came to study with Plutarch and Syrianus. But it is also true that by the early fifth century the political influence of both the pagan teachers of rhetoric and of philosophy on civic affairs in Athens was diminished relative to their power in the fourth century.[2] Even so, the Athenian Platonists might have had reasons of their own – apart from the authority of Plato's depictions of rhetoric as philosophy's debased and wicked rival – to resent the other, more numerous, providers of education in Athens.

In fact, however, both rhetoric and philosophy had changed significantly since the composition of Plato's *Gorgias*. Rhetoric in late antiquity was much more philosophical than the activity that Plato criticised. Similarly, nearly all the

Platonic philosophers in late antiquity came to philosophy by way of a prior education in rhetoric. It is certainly true that part of the hagiography of nearly every Platonic philosopher was that the subject turned his back on rhetoric at the point at which he was 'converted' to philosophy. But it is equally true that Platonist philosophers regularly defended Plato as a master stylist and that they evince a good understanding of the theoretical concepts in late antique rhetoric.[3] In fact, in the latter third of this volume we translate the introduction to a commentary on a work of rhetorical theory that was attributed to Hermias' teacher, Syrianus. The engagement of Platonic philosophers with rhetoric and its teaching may also reflect the fact that jobs teaching rhetoric were more numerous than those teaching philosophy. So, the relation between philosophy and rhetoric in late antiquity was complex and is perhaps best glossed with the twentieth-century portmanteau: 'frenemies'. We therefore think that 'Neoplatonic rejection of rhetoric' is not a good explanation for the fact that Hermias' commentary on the latter part of the *Phaedrus* is relatively brief and relatively shallow.

So why *is* the final section of Hermias' commentary on the *Phaedrus* relatively superficial compared to the earlier parts? There may be no good answer to this question apart from the observation that it was not unusual for Neoplatonist commentaries on Plato's works to become less detailed as they went along. Some of our most extensive Plato commentaries – those of Proclus on *Alcibiades I*, *Parmenides*, and *Timaeus* are incomplete. Each of these breaks off and, at least in the case of *Alcibiades I* and *Parmenides*, we know that this was because, at some point, a copyist didn't finish the monumental task before him. In the case of the *Timaeus*, Tarrant has suggested that Proclus' missing original abandoned the method of detailed, line-by-line commentary and addressed various topics in a manner not unlike Proclus' *Republic Commentary*.[4] But where we *do* have complete commentaries on Plato's dialogues, as in the case of Olympiodorus on *Alcibiades I* and on *Gorgias*, the commentary gets briefer and more superficial towards the end. (This is rather surprising in the case of the *Alcibiades I*, since it is at the end that things get really interesting.) Now, both the Olympiodorus commentaries just mentioned are *apo phonês* – accounts of lectures by Olympiodorus recorded by some student. (Though it is, of course, possible that Olympiodorus reviewed the content of the work, suggesting additions or corrections. We simply don't know.) We noted in volume 1 that remarks in Hermias' commentary on the *Phaedrus* like 'then my companion Proclus asked …' show that his commentary owes *something* to lectures by Syrianus. We urged agnosticism about how much is owed to Syrianus and how much might represent a reworking of notes from those lectures by Hermias. But *somewhere* in the genesis of Hermias' work, there were lectures by Syrianus and notes on them. Now we cannot know whether there were regular schedules of teaching in the Platonic schools – much less given timeframes like semesters. But it is not uncommon for contemporary academics to begin a post-graduate seminar with ambitions to study carefully, say, three books in thirteen weeks. But then the class becomes absorbed in the detail of the first and one doesn't quite get to the second and third books as one had hoped. It is not hard to imagine that in the schools of Athens or Alexandria a series of lectures on a Platonic work might similarly run short of time, or perhaps that the lecturer and the class might run short of the energy needed to engage with the text at the same level of detail throughout.

Whatever the reason, we can say that the trajectory of engagement with Plato's text that we observe in Hermias' *Phaedrus Commentary* is not uncommon among the few remaining full commentaries on Plato's works that we possess from the Platonists of late antiquity. Thus we think it calls for no special explanation. Any such explanation would have to be speculative. The idea of a fundamental opposition between philosophy and rhetoric is not only speculative, but a speculation that does not comport well with the extent to which Platonist philosophers engaged with the business of rhetorical theory – an engagement we shall discuss in more detail in our Introduction to the second translation in this volume.

2. The unity of the dialogue: Hermias on the transition at 257C

Given Socrates' remarks at 264C2–5 about the unity of good writing resembling the unity of a living animal, it is important to Hermias to show that the *Phaedrus* itself obeys this rule and has the unity of a living creature.[5] But the transition from the palinode to the discussion of speech-writing looks a bit artificial. It *seems* like a change of subject and while such changes in subject are not unusual for conversations among friends – even philosophical conversations – the Neoplatonists' commitment to the claim that every dialogue possesses a unifying *skopos* that determines its decomposition into parts seems threatened by this. After all, Platonic dialogues are not mere reports of philosophical conversations.

Hermias claimed at the beginning that the unifying theme of the *Phaedrus* was 'beauty at every level'. As he sees it, the dialogue moves from (i) visible beauty (in the physical form of Phaedrus, a beauty loved by Lysias) to (ii) beauty in *logoi* (since Lysias' speech is the object of Phaedrus' love) to (iii) beauty of souls (since this is supposedly the subject of Socrates' first speech since it deals with virtue and the distinction between licentious and rational love). From the beauty in souls, the dialogue moves to (iv) beauty of the encosmic gods in the first part of the Socratic palinode, and then finally to (v) the very source of beauty in Socrates' description of the super-celestial place – 'the very source of beauty and the god Love and the beautiful itself' (13,2–3). Hermias claims that the dialogue then descends back through each of these levels of beauty 'by means of [the method of] division to the beauty of souls and the beauty of the virtues and the sciences, then back once more to the beautiful in speeches, joining the end to the beginning' (13,3–5).

If we attempt to pursue this ring structure through Hermias' commentary, then it is perhaps noteworthy that at 197,6 (on *Phaedrus* 252C3-4) and at 201,17 (on 253C6–D2) he speaks first of the *telos* of 'the erotic enterprise' and then of 'the *telos* of the erotic art'. The two Platonic passages seem to mark a return to the level of (iv) the encosmic gods and then to (iii) the level of the beauty of souls. The first part describes the kinds of lovers who would ideally correspond to those who followed upon Zeus, Ares, etc. But at 201,17 we return to the image of the soul as a winged chariot and driver. This seems, then, to correspond to the virtues and sciences in the soul, since 253D2–3 concerns the virtues of the good horse and the vices of the bad one. So the next stage should be to consider (ii) beauty in *logoi*.

Now, it must be said that Plato's dialogue does not make this transition as seamless as would be convenient for Hermias' view of its unity and structure. The hinge point seems to be Phaedrus' observation about Lysias' speech-writing at 257C1–7. Here Phaedrus suggests that the speech of Lysias looks poor in comparison to the palinode just delivered by Socrates and, moreover, that Lysias might be reluctant to write in competition with it. Almost as an aside (*kai gar*, 257C4), Phaedrus observes that a certain politician recently abused Lysias for writing speeches. In light of this event, Phaedrus suggests that Lysias might well give up writing out of concern for how he will *look* in the public eye. If we take Hermias' ring structure of the dialogue seriously, this is not quite a sudden descent to physical beauty in the ordinary sense – that is to say, back to the level from which the dialogue began – but it is certainly concern for what we might call 'apparent' or 'phenomenal beauty/nobility'. But Socrates seems to think better of Lysias and rebukes Phaedrus for supposing that the speech-writer will be concerned with such superficial matters as what people say of him (257C8–D2).

Hermias engineers for Plato a more subtle transition from (iii) the level of beauty in souls to (ii) beauty in *logoi* by appeal to the idea that *the soul is itself a logos* (222,16–19). This is a consequence of the fact that the rational soul has its substantial being and its activity after the manner (*kata*) of the intellectual element *in* it and it is by virtue of this fact that the soul wishes to produce *speeches*. Hermias pulls this transitional rabbit out of the hat of Phaedrus' enthusiasm for asking the question 'What is the way of writing appropriately?' In Plato's dialogue, Phaedrus has responded to Socrates' proposal to pose this question with the remark, 'What else should one *live for* than pleasures of this sort?' (258E1–2). Hermias takes this remark to point towards the soul's life or activity and to indicate that this involves the production of *logoi*, since the soul is itself a *logos*. Thus, in Hermias' eyes at least, the transition between the virtues of the soul in love at the end of the palinode and the discussion of speech-writing has the organic connection of one part of a living creature to another part. The life of the soul as a kind of *logos* oils what would otherwise seem to be a creaky hinge as the dialogue turns from the virtuous lover's *soul* to the question of *speeches*. This, of course, complicates how the translator must handle '*logos*' in this context, since Hermias is relying on its multiple meanings in his account of the connections among the dialogue's parts. This is also true of his integration of the next apparent digression – the story of the cicadas.

3. The allegorising of Plato's myths: listening to the cicadas

One commonly finds that the Neoplatonists expend significant exegetical effort over Plato's myths and the digression on the cicadas (258E6–259E1) and the proper use of midday leisure is no exception. Hermias' allegorical treatment of this passage is not too wild, though some features of it need to be understood in relation to associations between Muses and Sirens in the work of his classmate, Proclus.

Unlike the transition between the palinode and the discussion of writing, the connection between the myth of the cicadas and what comes before and after in Plato's text feels less adventitious. After all, it is writing and speaking that is the subject matter and the Muses are individually associated with various genres of writing or, more generally, with activities like dance that have strong historical connections with poetic performance. Hermias' contribution to enhancing the audience's appreciation of this unity is relatively modest. In his treatment of the passage, the Muses are not merely associated with writing, but are described as the overseeing gods and causes of *logos* (223,13–14). The generality of their oversight regarding all aspects of *mousikê* is mirrored in Hermias' frequent reminders that, although the individual speeches of Lysias and Socrates are to be contrasted, these are but examples. The subject under discussion is good writing and speaking *in general* and such an insistence on generality is not perhaps unreasonable in view of *Phaedrus* 259E1–2.

Much of Hermias' exegetical energy in his discussion of the myth of the cicadas is invested in pre-empting misleading appearances of temporality. Socrates' story concerns humans who seemingly *pre-dated* the existence of the Muses and *subsequently* became entranced by the song of the Muses. As with the temporal language in the *Timaeus* (which might be taken to suggest that the sensible cosmos came into existence at some point in time), the seemingly temporal narrative structure of the *Phaedrus*' account of the Muses and humans needs to be understood differently. Apparent temporal priority is translated into causal priority. Hermias credits Iamblichus for the general strategy here (225,21–226,4).[6] Thus the human souls who became absorbed by the arts of the Muses 'after' the Muses came into being point towards human souls in the company of the hypercosmic gods – presumably those hypercosmic gods who lead the procession of souls up to the intelligible in the palinode. The Muses, in turn, are identified with the spheres of the heavens and the sensible cosmos. When the human souls become infatuated with the songs of the Muses, then, this indicates their descent into Becoming generally. Yet because these souls are newly initiated (*neotelês*, cf. *Phaedrus* 250E1), they remember the intelligible realm and thus do not seek nourishment from Becoming and so are said to 'starve'. That is to say, they pursue the recollection of the intelligible world and do not 'participate in perceptual opinion'. For their devotion to the higher life, these starved souls have become intermediaries between gods and humans. They report to the gods how human souls down here conduct themselves in relation to the temptations of matter as symbolised by the cicadas' own sounds which lull people to sleep at midday. When Socrates alludes again to the cicadas later in the dialogue (262D2–4), Hermias takes this to refer to the orders of local gods and daemons that sometimes mediate the gods' providence to human souls (238,27–239,3).

Hermias connects this episode explicitly or implicitly to other dialogues. Explicitly, the idea that the cicadas play a role as intermediaries between gods and humans is compared with the role of daemons in the *Symposium* (226,23). In this context, it is worth remembering that the *Symposium* was grouped with the *Phaedrus* in the Iamblichean curriculum as a 'theological' dialogue. Hermias also implicitly connects the Muses with the music of the celestial spheres with which they are identified and this doubtless reflects the role played by the Muses

Introduction 15

in the Myth of Er at the end of the *Republic*. In that myth, Muses sit on the edge of each of the whorls and each sings a single note, their collective singing forming a harmony. Hermias observes that Pythagoras heard these celestial voices and that musical notes are named after them.

4. Intertextuality: *Phaedrus* and *Gorgias* on rhetoric

The proper definition of rhetoric was a concern for both philosophers and rhetoricians in late antiquity. We know this from the various introductions to the canonical works of rhetorical theory for the period.[7] In one of these introductions, credited (probably falsely) to Marcellinus, the author examines definitions of rhetoric drawn from both the *Gorgias* and the *Phaedrus*.[8] He takes these definitions to be inconsistent if they concern one and the same rhetoric. After all, it is clear from the *Phaedrus* that there is a true rhetoric that is theoretically possible and it – if anyone could possess it – would be an art or *tekhnê*. But the *Gorgias* famously insists that what Gorgias and Polus practise is not a *tekhnê* but a mere knack or *empeiria*. So [Marcellinus] claims that if Plato did indeed posit two or more kinds of rhetoric, it is not the false and sycophantic kind of rhetoric that *we* – i.e. respectable rhetoricians like himself – teach. Nor is such a false rhetoric that with which Hermogenes' canonical works deal. So even if the *Gorgias* is consistent with the *Phaedrus* because Plato's real view is that 'rhetoric is many', this in no way impugns what is taught and practised by contemporary rhetoricians ([Marcellinus] *Introduction*, 281,17–18).

Hermias in his *Phaedrus Commentary* and Olympiodorus in his *Gorgias Commentary* agree: the condemnation of rhetoric as a mere knack in the *Gorgias* is consistent with the vision of the true rhetoric articulated in the *Phaedrus*. Olympiodorus initially makes a division between only two kinds of rhetoric:

> Note that rhetoric is of two kinds, one kind true and scientific (*technikê*), the other false and [based on] experience (*empeiria*). That which is subordinate to the statesman is scientific, that which aims at pleasure is false.
> (*in Gorg.* 1.13,4–7, trans. Jackson, Lycos, and Tarrant 1998)

But Olympiodorus goes on to make further divisions among the kinds of rhetoric – or perhaps the kinds of orators – whose relation to this initial dichotomy is not entirely clear. So, *between* those who practise the true and false rhetorics, we find orators who are said to be of the *intermediate* kind: Pericles, Themistocles, Miltiades, and Cimon. Unlike practitioners of the false rhetoric, Olympiodorus says, these men were not flatterers. But they are still distinct from the true rhetoric which is 'the servant of statesmanship'. These intermediate orators did not aim at the truth and merely saved the *bodies* of their fellow citizens by preserving public safety, without doing what was truly beneficial – saving their *souls* (*in Gorg.* 32.3,8–20). But Olympiodorus also explains, albeit too briefly, another division into five kinds of rhetoric, each corresponding to the different kinds of civic and psychic constitutions discussed in the *Republic*: aristocracy, timocracy, oligarchy, democracy, and tyranny.

> Note that each of these kinds has its own rhetoric, and so there are *five rhetorics*. The true rhetoric is that of aristocracy, over which the statesman presides. For in that case the rhetor serves the statesman by way of recommending whatever he commands, for example, 'Persuade them that there should be a doctor in the city', 'Persuade them that there should not be comedy'. And just as the doctor looks to a single end, healing all who suffer, making use of a variety and not the same kind of remedies, so too the rhetor should persuade by every means, using different arguments, one kind for the doctor, another for the military, and another for the labourer. Such is the true rhetoric, the others being falsely so-called.
>
> (*in Gorg.* 1.13,22–33, trans. Jackson, Lycos, and Tarrant)

Olympiodorus is clear that the kind of rhetoric practised by orators in the service of tyrants is the worst: a base form of flattery that is analogous to a doctor who prescribes a deliciously rich diet for his patient out of a desire to share his table. Python, a student of Isocrates who served Philip of Macedon, is Olympiodorus' example here. He contrasts Python with Themistocles who is likened to a doctor who prescribes a strict diet for a patient who won't stick to it. Such doctors 'do not abandon them when they break it, nor even turn a blind eye, but take a stand against each deviation from their prescription' (*in Gorg.* 1.13,63–5). Olympiodorus claims that although the four democratic rhetoricians were not flatterers, they did nothing useful, as one can see from the fact that they did not create an aristocracy from a democracy (32.3,20–1). One does not know exactly how much weight to hang on Olympiodorus' advice to his audience that immediately follows (32.4): if *we* lack the power to put those who are ruled in good order, we should retreat and not remain with them. Doing so would be as foolish as trying to pet wild animals! *If* – and this is speculative – Olympiodorus addresses his audience as 'we who aspire to practise the true rhetoric', then this would imply that the true rhetoric cannot be practised anywhere except in the ideal city where the education of all the citizens makes them amenable to being put in order (*rhuthmizein*) by the servant of the statesman – the true orator. If that is correct, then it would seem that the true rhetoric is inseparable from philosophy in this sense: it cannot be successfully practised in any city that is not ruled by philosophers.

Hermias similarly distinguishes between true and false rhetoric and thus treats the *Gorgias* as fully consistent with the *Phaedrus*. Like Olympiodorus, he also places Pericles, Themistocles, and Demosthenes in an intermediate category between the true and false rhetoric. But he is much more explicit than Olympiodorus in *identifying* the true rhetoric with philosophy.[9] Thus he says at 1,11 'he is now elevating Phaedrus, who is passionate about rhetoric, [to an appreciation of] the *true* rhetoric, i.e. philosophy.'[10] Just a bit later he provides an overview of the difference between the false or popular rhetoric and the true one.

> Anyone, then, who is going to write well must know the truth of things. And this is how the true and the popular rhetoric are distinguished: the former is acquainted with truth, is a knowledge of what is just and what not just, is an attendant (*opados*) of philosophy, *belongs to the philosopher alone*, and creates and delivers content that is *pleasing to gods* (273E7) and men; the popular kind, on the other hand, produces a kind of allurement or charming of the soul and is a sort of *knack that lacks all art* (260E5) and is without any science.
>
> (*in Phaedr.* 7,2–9)

The idea that the philosopher alone has the genuine *tekhnê* of the true rhetoric is one that emerges naturally enough from Socrates' insistence that a genuinely artful or scientific rhetoric must know the truth of things through *dialectic* (266B8–D2). This knowledge of the subject matter, achieved by the mastery of dialectic, conjoined with both an understanding of the nature of the souls of the audience (270C1–271A2) and an understanding of the kinds of speeches and their effects upon such souls (271B1–5), is the content of the true rhetoric. What those who practise the false or popular rhetoric teach and the techniques they pride themselves on are merely the preliminaries for rhetoric (269B7–8).

Following Plato, Hermias insists that rhetoric is not really these preliminaries, but the capacity to use them *well* (249,16–19). Moreover, one cannot use them well unless one knows, not only the nature of the souls being addressed and the effects of the various kinds of speeches upon them, but the truth of the matter under discussion (252,22–8). At 255,1–2, however, Hermias makes the further claim: that it is *not possible* to speak persuasively without *speaking the truth*. This is not a thesis that Socrates commits himself to in Plato's dialogue. He says at 259E4–6 that the person who is going to speak well and nobly (*kalôs*) must *have in mind the truth* concerning the subject he is addressing. That is a different matter, of course, from speaking that truth. Moreover, Hermias' claim seems empirically doubtful, to put it politely. After all, about a third of US voters believe that Joe Biden did not really win the 2020 Presidential election. They have seemingly been persuaded by the speech of Mr Trump or of the hosts on Fox News, but they were not speaking the truth – not even the truth as they saw it. As the e-mail and texts that were made public prior to the settlement with Dominion, the manufacturer of electronic voting machines that were baselessly alleged to have changed vote totals to favour Mr Biden show, many of the Fox News hosts knew they were not speaking the truth. Yet their speech, though untrue, seems to have been persuasive.

Perhaps it is better to see Hermias' off-hand remark in the context of his insistence that rhetoric is the capacity to lead souls *successfully* – that is to say, to make them noble/beautiful (*kalos*) and good (264,20–2). Thus we might treat the claim that 'it is not possible to speak persuasively without speaking the truth' as tantamount to the claim that 'one cannot lead souls to a condition that is noble and good without speaking the truth.' So, 'speaking persuasively' would be what philosophers sometimes call a 'success term': just as you can't *recognise* the man at the bar unless he's someone you've actually seen before, so too the orator can't *speak persuasively* – at least as Hermias understands the phrase – without morally improving his audience.

Nonetheless, we are still left to wonder whether the moral improvement of some audiences might best be accomplished by telling them lies – albeit noble ones, as Socrates suggests in one of the more notorious passages in the *Republic* (414B8). One might try to defend the 'success term' reading of speaking persuasively and the insistence that truth is a necessary condition for this by distinguishing speech that makes an audience *better* than they were before from speech that makes them *fully and truly* noble-and-good (*kalos*). But this seems like a pretty desperate strategy. Has Hermias created a problem for himself by his insistence not merely that the true orator must have *knowledge* of his subject matter, but that he must *speak* the truth about it?

5. Deus ex machina: Hermias on the success of the true rhetoric

Let us take stock. We think that one ought to grant that Olympiodorus and Hermias are right to oppose critics who take the *Gorgias* and the *Phaedrus* to be inconsistent on the subject of rhetoric. What is condemned in the *Gorgias* as mere knack is similar to what the *Phaedrus* treats as the rhetoric taught and practised by non-ideal rhetoricians. So the criticisms of the non-ideal that are offered in the *Gorgias* are consistent with the existence of a true art envisioned in the *Phaedrus*. But one might still object that the status of a genuine *tekhnê* that is attributed to the true rhetoric in the *Phaedrus* comes at too high a price. Arguably it removes the true rhetoric so far from the actual practice of public persuasion as to make it implausible that the one is the ideal form of the other rather than something wholly different and completely irrelevant to the goals of 'popular rhetoric'.

To be fair, Plato's characters in the *Phaedrus* are aware that the true rhetoric that they are discussing is far removed from the practice of actual orators and actual teachers of rhetoric. Socrates and Phaedrus note repeatedly that the kind of rhetoric that combines *dialectic* with psychology is hard to achieve and very different from what Thrasymachus, Gorgias, et al. practise and teach. They consider two reasons why actual rhetoricians should regard knowledge of the subject matter, and thus the art of dialectic through which such knowledge is allegedly gained, to be necessary conditions for the true art of rhetoric.[11] The first of these begins from the assumption that a rhetoric worthy of the status of *tekhnê* is a *benefit* to its possessor. The example of the ignorant orator and his ignorant audience who do not know a donkey from a horse (260B1–D2) is offered to illustrate this point. When the speaker doesn't know what he is talking about, it is not likely that the persuasion he effects upon his equally ignorant audience will be a benefit to either of them. A second argument for knowledge of the truth as a necessary condition for success in public speaking is offered at 261E–262C3 and it concerns the *means* through which the audience's conviction is to be achieved. Deception (*apatê*) is best achieved through disguised progress through a range of similar things – this motion carrying the audience from what they believe at the start of the speech, through considerations similar to other things they believe, and ending in a conclusion different from where they started. But the person who is best able to produce or bring to light similarities through which his audience may be led along this pathway is the person who knows what he is talking about. Such a person can also bring to light the subtle sleights of hand through which the competing speaker seeks to carry the audience smoothly from A to B.

Both the horse and donkey example and the considerations about deception seem to gesture towards familiar settings for the deployment of rhetoric. Though Socrates does not say so explicitly, the potential military value of the horse that is mentioned at 260B8 invites the thought of debate in the Assembly about going to war and what is needed for success in such a war. The deception argument explicitly mentions the opposing views in the law courts about what is just and unjust as well as opposing views in public debate about what is good or beneficial (261C4–D4; cf. *Gorgias* 452E1–4 and 454B5–7). But it is precisely in this context, that Socrates and Phaedrus agree that the practice of speaking on opposite sides (*antilogikê*) occurs not only in the law courts and in the Assembly, but more generally in any context where there is contention on opposite sides (261D10–E4). This significantly expands the scope of rhetoric, as Socrates urges us to understand it, so that it includes far more than speaking publicly in the traditional contexts of juridical, deliberative, and even epideictic rhetoric. This step occurs in the midst of Socrates' argument that knowledge of the truth of what one is talking about is a prerequisite for successful deception.

This expansion of the scope of rhetoric, however, makes the argument about the nexus between truth and the true rhetoric more doubtful because in the wider sense of rhetoric now at issue, it is doubtful whether deception is essential to all of these contexts. So consider the example that Gorgias uses at 454B1–5 of accompanying his brother, the physician Herodicus, to see patients who were unwilling to submit to the treatment his brother deemed best. Knowing nothing of medicine, but being in command of the art of rhetoric, Gorgias persuaded his brother's patients even when Herodicus himself could not. Gorgias' use of his persuasive power in this context escapes the problem of the donkey and the horse: Gorgias himself does not need to know medicine in order to know that the procedure is in the patient's best interest. He can substitute the judgement of his physician brother and so has no need to know the truth of the matter about the things he is speaking about. Nor is it clear that Gorgias needs to engage in any *deception* in this context. It seems likely that all Gorgias needs to do is to appeal in rhetorically compelling ways to things that the patient already values – the nobility of courage, the hope of more time with his family – in order to help him to see that treatment serves his genuine long-term interest. If this is so, then the argument that knowledge of the truth concerning the subject matter is essential to successful deception does not apply.

Now, the true rhetoric as it is described in the *Phaedrus* does have an additional requirement that certainly *does* seem relevant to the example of Gorgias and his brother's patient. The true rhetoric includes knowledge of human psychology and the ways in which various minds are affected by various kinds of speeches (270B1–271B4). It will be knowing how to represent the value of treatment to a patient of this psychological type that permits Gorgias to succeed where Herodicus has failed. But this example seems to show that

Socrates' insistence that the practitioner of the true rhetoric must know the *subject matter* about which he is speaking is mistaken. Moreover, the fact that knowledge of the content is seemingly not a necessary condition is rendered *even more* evident by the expansion of the scope of the genuinely scientific rhetoric beyond the judicial and deliberative contexts characteristic of rhetoric as traditionally understood. Socrates seems to have scored an own goal.

This is not a problem that Hermias confronts directly but we believe that there is an answer implicit in his various remarks on this portion of the *Phaedrus*. Recall that Hermias seems to go a step beyond Socrates' already bold claim that knowledge of the truth is a necessary condition for possession of the true art of rhetoric. Hermias, as we noted above, interprets the isolated phrase 'speaking persuasively' at *Phaedrus* 269C2-3 to mean that it is not possible to speak persuasively without *speaking the truth* and this, of course, means *knowing* the truth – a claim that Socrates *does* seem committed to. Why does Hermias suppose that the truth has such persuasive power? We take the answer to this question to lie in his account of the nature of 'the probable' (*to eikos*). At 273D–E Socrates addresses himself as if to Tisias and summarises his case for the necessity of mastery of dialectic to the true art of rhetoric. Tisias was right to insist that 'the probable' is important to the true rhetoric, but wrong in his understanding of what 'the probable' actually consists in. It is *not* to be identified with 'what appears [to be the case] to the many' (273B1). Hermias takes the real probable to consist simply in 'resemblance to the truth' and it is in virtue of being like the truth that 'the probable' has its persuasive power:

> So since all the writers on the art of rhetoric say that probabilities (*ta eikota*) and plausibilities (*ta pithana*) are the subject matter of rhetoric and that a juror is persuaded by means of these but do not give the reason why these persuade [him], the philosopher has also given the reason for these [being persuasive], stating that it is *because of their resemblance to the truth that probabilities are persuasive*. Hence truth is the first principle (*arkhê*) of all things and the speaker persuades by knowing what is true.
>
> (237,23–8)

A bit further on, Hermias makes the point again:

> And he briefly summarises the rest of what he said about the true rhetoric, [namely,] that this probability (*eikos*), by being like (*eoikenai*) the truth, convinces souls and the many thanks to its resemblance to the truth, so that someone who knows the truth knows the probability.
>
> (264,7–11)

This idea that the true art of rhetoric concerns itself with a notion of probability that consists simply in likeness to the truth is puzzling. After all, isn't 'the probable' always what seems likely *to some audience*? And isn't resemblance always a matter of what seems like what *to someone* – even if the identity of the someone in question is somewhat vague? Fool's gold resembles gold *to* most people who aren't experienced gold prospectors. *For whom* does 'the probable', properly understood, resemble the truth?

We think it likely that 'the probable' which is the proper concern of the true rhetorician is what seems like the truth *to the gods*. They matter in this context for it is gods, not humans, who are the real audience to whom the true rhetorician addresses himself. In the continuation of his hypothetical address to Tisias, Socrates grants the difficulty of mastering dialectic – a method through which the genuine rhetorician comes to know the truth. This task, Socrates continues, is not something that a wise person ought to undertake merely for the sake of speaking or acting well before *men*, but rather in order that he might speak and do everything, as far as possible, in a manner that is *pleasing to the gods*. This is a key passage for Hermias. At 264,20–6 he comments that Socrates appropriately includes 'acting well' alongside 'speaking well' and that in this passage he gives us the goal or *telos* of the true art of rhetoric: to speak and to write things that are pleasing to the gods (273E7) and he gives as examples hymns, dances and the like. But the only subject matter worthy of the attention of the gods is itself divine. Mere words, however, cannot express the full truth of the gods. Their full nature is beyond discursive thought or speech, but with proper attention to likenesses of the truth (i.e. 'the probable' properly understood), the genuine rhetorician can speak and act in ways that are pleasing to them – that is to say, in ways that discursively approximate their ultimately ineffable nature.

But what then of the normal uses of rhetoric in deliberation or in juridical settings before a human audience? Hermias seems to think that success in the mundane human realm will almost inevitably accompany the kinds of pious speech and action that please the gods. At 264,28–265,1 he continues that someone who is doing things that are pleasing to human beings need not be doing things that are pleasing to the gods, but contrariwise 'the person who does things that are pleasing to the gods is also doing them for human beings, for that which is worse follows the one who hymns the divine.' When the gods enjoy what we say and do, Hermias claims, 'all goes smoothly with us' (265,20). Even if we do not enjoy success in relation to a human audience, to act or speak in ways that are pleasing to the gods is a beautiful thing – something *kalos*. Hermias assures us that 'the attempt, then, at fine actions is to be praised, even if the person is doomed to fail or to suffer something, whatever it may be, on account of that very [attempt]' (265,24–5).

In Plato's dialogue, Socrates insistence on knowledge of the truth as a necessary condition for the true art of rhetoric seems open to certain objections. These objections are made more obvious by the fact that Socrates extends the scope of the true rhetoric beyond public speaking in the law courts or deliberative contexts like the Assembly. Hermias has answers of a sort to these objections, but they involve a further and more radical re-imagining of the nature and purpose of the genuinely artful kind of rhetoric. It becomes the employment of speech or writing *with the goal of pleasing the gods*. Given that goal, it is unsurprising and uncontroversial that an *understanding* of the truth is a necessary condition for possessing the true art of rhetoric. It is perhaps also unsurprising that *speaking* the truth is a necessary condition for persuasion. But this is not persuasive success as ordinary rhetoricians understand it. It is, instead, the manifestation of a uniquely *discursive form of piety*. This is perhaps unsurprising from Hermias. After all, his commentary takes every opportunity to note the pious manner in which Socrates speaks: the fact that he delivers his speech with his head covered (51,15–22); in connecting his awareness of his sin against the divine at 242C3 with the passage in *Philebus* (12C2) where Socrates expresses his awe over the proper names of the gods (74,24); as well as all his comments on Socrates' various prayers. Given what has come before, it should come as no surprise that Hermias' conception of the genuine art of rhetoric should turn out to be a distinctively discursive expression of piety. It turns out that the *Phaedrus* is a 'theological' dialogue in Hermias' view, not merely because of the divine things described in Socrates' palinode, but because of the way in which the point and purpose of writing and speaking is reconfigured in the true rhetoric that is described following the palinode.

6. Writing and piety

The discussion of writing at the end of the *Phaedrus* has figured prominently in one of the deepest scholarly divisions over the proper approach to Plato's dialogues in the twentieth century: the question of 'Plato's esotericism'.[12] In the context of these disputes, 'esotericism' came to have two distinct, but easily conflated, meanings. On the one hand, it came to connote a deliberate tendency on Plato's part to conceal, within his writings, some of his thoughts from those deemed unfit to receive them. This is the kind of esotericism one associates with

Leo Strauss and the Straussian tradition. On the other hand, the tradition of the so-called Tübingen school involves a different kind of esotericism. According to them, Plato did not seek to conceal some of his philosophical views *within* his dialogues, but instead declined to commit these views to writing *at all*. Both approaches to understanding Plato's philosophy utilise Plato's critique of writing in the *Phaedrus* to motivate their preferred approach. For Strauss, the *Phaedrus* pointed to Plato's awareness of the 'essential defect of writing': writings are equally accessible to all readers and say the same things to everyone.[13] This essential defect Strauss took to be overcome by Plato's dialogic form:

> We may conclude that the Platonic dialogue says different things to different people – not accidentally, as every writing does, but that it is so contrived as to say different things to different people, or that it is radically ironical. The Platonic dialogue, if properly read, reveals itself to possess the flexibility or adaptability of oral communication.
>
> (Strauss 1964, 52–3)

By contrast, the Tübingen approach takes the critique of writing in the *Phaedrus*, along with the disputed *Seventh Letter*, as evidence that one must supplement one's understanding of Plato's thought by seeking the clues left in our accounts of his oral teachings. Krämer, for instance, claimed that these two sources showed that Plato purposefully and deliberately avoiding fixing certain aspects of his philosophy in written form. Thus the unwritten doctrines were not merely doctrines he failed to get around to writing about in his dialogues. They were deliberately not communicated in the dialogues or in any other written form because of the alleged limitations of writing. Moreover, Krämer argued that these unwritten doctrines were, in fact, more important than what one finds in Plato's written works on the basis of Socrates' remark at 278D8 about the writer as one who has nothing more valuable (*timiôteros*) to spend his time on.[14]

Esotericists of either stripe have had little to say about Hermias and the reasons for this are pretty obvious. Proponents of Plato's unwritten doctrines have noted the similarity between Neoplatonic metaphysics and the system that derives all things from the One and the Indefinite Dyad (or the 'great and the small'). So, one might expect them to share other common ground with esotericism as well. But, as Rogério De Campos puts it, 'Hermias shows a Plato who does not refuse the written word and reconciles in a harmonious manner the superiority of the oral tradition in his philosophy with his activity as a writer.'[15]

Now, it is not as if the Platonists of antiquity were unaware of the need to say something about the fact that Plato both criticises the activity of writing and does so in writing. The *Anonymous Prolegemenon to Platonic Philosophy* (13.6–14) reports that critics had accused Plato of slandering the authors of written works, or *sungrammata*, on the grounds that these were lifeless and incapable of giving an answer. Why then, a critic might ask, did he not simply leave behind pupils as 'living writings', as Socrates and Pythagoras were alleged to have done? Hermias, however, insists that a philosopher, qua philosopher, *can* write *if* he or she enters into the activity with the right aims and a suitable attitude (277,28–278,1). Hermias lists a number of limitations on the proper approach to writing at 271,10–18. The one who writes in a manner that will please the gods must (a) know the truth about the subject he writes about; (b) write for the purpose of reminding himself as proof against the forgetfulness of old age or for the benefit of pupils; and (c) not take it seriously, but as a bit of fun. The benefit to learners, however, Hermias seems to regard as contingent upon supplementation with opportunities for question and answer (270,11–12). But such an insistence upon the necessity for written philosophy to be supplemented with discussion is a very far cry from an insistence that some doctrines are not appropriately communicated in writing at all. So Hermias' view seems very far indeed from the manner in which the Tübingen school regards the limitations on writing in the last part of the *Phaedrus*.

Hermias does not seem to be concerned with the universal accessibility of writing to any reader as a serious problem, in the manner in which Strauss did. He certainly distinguishes between the surface meaning of, say, Socrates' first speech and 'the secret doctrine that it enigmatically imparts' (69,3–4). But Hermias also takes seriously the idea that in uttering this speech Socrates is in the early stages of being possessed by the Nymphs. All communications from the divine – even if they be via theological poets like Orpheus or Homer – demand a distinction between the surface meaning and the underlying allegorical meaning. Plato is not, in this case, utilising the dialogic form as a means to evade the problem that writing speaks to any reader. Rather, by Hermias' lights, Plato's dialogue channels a divine communication which, by its very nature, demands different levels of interpretation. Hermias' friend, Proclus, is more forthcoming about the many modes through which Plato communicates in his written works.[16] But Plato's various modes of communication are not necessitated by the ever-present threat of persecution, given philosophy's intimate connection to politics.

In short, there is little in Hermias' discussion of writing to give aid and comfort to esotericists of either the unwritten doctrines sort or of the Straussian sort. This is not to say that Hermias' interpretation of the *Phaedrus* on writing is not pregnant with a broader theory about philosophy and writing. It just isn't a theory that will strike most modern readers as plausible.

As in the case of the true art of speaking, Hermias' eye is fixed on the divine in the case of writing. Socrates' question to Phaedrus at 274B9 about whether he knows how to please god in the matter of discourse (*logos*) affords Hermias the opportunity to observe that:

> Writing (*graphein*) in a seemly manner is this: saying things that are pleasing to the gods; for since they have gifted us with *logos* itself, one should raise propriety of *logos* to [the level of] the gods and use this instrument for the contemplation (*theôria*) of them.
>
> (266,11–14)

Thus it would seem that the principal audience for any act of writing is the gods. Writing may have secondary mundane effects: it can assist the person who already knows to remember what he knew before. Or it may assist – in some manner whose details are left unexplored by Hermias – students in coming to grasp important truths (provided that this impetus is properly supplemented with discussion of the appropriate sort). But these mundane purposes are subordinate to the primary goal of writing: to please the very gods from whom all *logos* comes and to use it as an instrument for contemplating them. Unsurprisingly, writing – like rhetoric – turns out to be a discursive form of piety according to Hermias. With that thought, we bring this Introduction to a close. Amen.

Notes

1 Miles and Baltussen 2023.
2 Watts 2006, 79–87.
3 On the complex relation between the Platonist philosophers of the Athenian school and rhetoric, see Caluori 2014.
4 Tarrant 2017, 1–7.
5 cf. Gardiner and Baltzly 2020.
6 This passage is fr. 7 from Iamblichus' *Phaedrus* commentary in Dillon 1973.
7 The introductions are collected in Rabe 1931.
8 *Introductio in prolegomena Hermogenis artis rhetoricae fort. auctore Marcellino*, 281,17–283,10 in Rabe 1931; cf. Kennedy 1983, 113.
9 Bohle 2021,151 suggests that there is no real difference between Olympiodorus and Hermias on this point: being a (true!) rhetorician would be a skill of the philosopher-statesman.

10 *tên alêthê rhetorikên, toutesti philosophian*. Philosophy is similarly the true and highest form of *mousikê*; cf. Proclus' discussion in the fifth question of Essay 5 in his *Republic* commentary with reference to *Phaedo* 61A.
11 On dialectic in Hermias' *Phaedrus* commentary, the only sustained study is Gabor 2020. We think that Hermias' relatively few remarks on the subject are not entirely sufficient to support all of Gabor's conclusions. In particular, we find we are unpersuaded of his claim that 'dialectic is identical to and constitutive of the activity of philosophy' (p. 50). Proclus' more substantial body of work provides richer evidence for the views of the Athenian school on dialectic and the method of division. cf. Tresnie 2020 and Baltzly 2023.
12 This section expands on some of the arguments put forward in Tarrant & Baltzly 2018.
13 Strauss 1964, 52.
14 Krämer 2012, 66, which offers a translation of Krämer 1996 along with other important essays from Tübingen school writers.
15 De Campos 2022, 186.
16 cf. *PT* 1.4,17,18–23.

Departures from Lucarini and Moreschini's Text

219,6   Changing the first *ei* to *hoti*.

224,28   Filling the lacuna with *ton Odussea*, as suggested by Couvreur.

226,14   Omitting *dêlon* but translating the other obelised words.

231,4   Emending *to de* to *tou* and removing the full stop.

236,4   Adding *tôn de brakheôn ou* after *akêkoas*, as suggested by a reader.

236,11   Emending *tês rhetorikês* to *têi rhetorikêi*, and emending *touto* to *toutôi*, as suggested by a reader.

237,6   Adding *epi* before *epitêdeumatôn*, as suggested by Lucarini in the apparatus.

245,6–7   Translating *êgoun dia touto apeikazontes ho isôs eipen*, the reading of manuscript A, rather than *êgoun dia touto to apeikazontes to isôs eipen*, as printed by Lucarini and Moreschini.

249,30   Following Bernard in rejecting a lacuna.

251,20   Adding *katomosanta* after *homoia*, as suggested by Lucarini in the apparatus.

254,20   Like Bernard, rejecting a lacuna.

259,10   Rejecting Lucarini and Moreschini's obelising of *houtôs tekhnên*, accepting Couvreur's emendation of *endeiknumenên* (or *endeiknumenê*) to *endeiknumenon*, and retaining *tekhnê*, the reading of most of the manuscripts, in preference to *tekhnên*.

268,23   Preferring *paideia*, the reading of some manuscripts, to *paidia*, as printed by Lucarini and Moreschini.

Hermias

*On Plato
Phaedrus 257C–279C*

Translation

99. [*I have long been marvelling*] *at your speech*, etc. (257C1–2)

He is amazed by the philosopher's speech – the one of recantation (*palinôidia*) – because it is more beautiful than the previous one. And indeed it surpasses it by far. For here he has spoken of intelligible being and of the immortality of the soul and of Zeus, the leader, [telling] how he brings all things together, and of the nine ways of life and of the other things he recently mentioned [in it].[1]

219,1

100. *And so I hesitate* [*lest Lysias should seem to me to be humbled should he even be willing to pit another* [speech] *against this one*] (257C2–4)

Since Socrates prayed, asking that Lysias should, as Polemarchus had,[2] turn to philosophy, on account of this Phaedrus says: 'I don't think that[3] Lysias would be able to pit an equivalent speech against this speech even if he wanted to.'

5

101. *And in fact, my remarkable friend, a certain* [*politician was recently reviling* [him], *rebuking* [him for] *this very thing, and through all of* [his] *railing kept calling him a speech-writer*] (257C4–6)

The philosopher is to be considered remarkable in all things, but above all for the density and continuity and unity of his discourse. For he writes in such a way that the entire discourse is rendered (*apoteleisthai*)[4] a single living being; for just as a living being has parts that are united and [yet] distinct, so too does the discourse of Socrates.[5] Therefore, since he now intends to proceed to the discourse about rhetoric, from which the dialogue also took its origin – for because Phaedrus marvelled at the phenomenal beauty and the composition of the speech [of Lysias][6] the philosopher arrived at all the discourses that have been delivered thanks to Phaedrus – observe, then,[7] how harmoniously he proceeds to the discourse on rhetoric: for Phaedrus says that 'Lysias would not be willing *to compete* with your speech, since *someone* once *reproached* him as being a speech-writer (257C4–7)', and [starting out] from this statement the philosopher begins his discourse on rhetoric, saying that speech-writing [itself] is not bad, but writing badly *is* bad – writing fine and good things is, of course, a fine thing. In fact fineness and badness depend on the intention of the writer, since, as he says elsewhere (*Symposium* 180E4–5), 'every action taken by itself is neither fine nor bad'.

10

15

20

The ancients called those who wrote speeches for a fee **(210)** 'speech-writers', for there were some among the orators (*rhêtôr*)[8] who sold speeches to those who spoke in the courts; they [only] called those who spoke on their own behalf orators.[9]

220,1 102. *So perhaps [we shall find he may refrain from writing out of concern for his reputation]* (257C7)

For we often refrain from shameful things so as to be held in good repute (*timasthai*). Hence Lysias too, he says, would refrain from writing so as to be held in good repute, avoiding reproach and eager for esteem (*timê*).[10]

103. *[The view you express], young man, is ridiculous [and you are much mistaken about your friend if you really think he's someone who's frightened of* [a bit of] *noise]* (257C8–D2)

For, he says, Lysias will want to write, and moreover those who condemn speech-writing take pleasure in writing speeches because, by leaving behind writings, they leave behind children who are more nobly born than themselves, as he says in the *Symposium* (209C5–7).[11]

Those who are frightened by the sounds of flies and anything else that comes along are called 'phonophobic' (*psophodeês*).[12]

104. *[But perhaps] you actually think [the person who was reviling him said what he said] believing (nomizonta) [it to be so]* (257D2–3)

Equivalent to 'said [what he said] thinking [it to be so]'; that is to say, not even the very person who is reviling speech-writing is attacking it out of a conviction that it is a bad thing.

105. *[He did seem to, Socrates.] And you [yourself] are aware, I imagine, [that the most powerful and respected men in cities are ashamed to write speeches or leave behind writings of theirs, fearing the opinion of later time, lest they be called sophists]* (257D4–8)

Phaedrus wants to argue on the basis of common opinion (*endoxôs*). (An argument based on common opinion is one that comes from the many.) Since, then, people have reviled speech-writing on the basis of prevailing custom, on account of this he too says that people with great *power* (257D5), such as Themistocles and Pericles, have avoided writing speeches, although they were good enough speakers [to have done so], as have other cultivated men such as Pythagoras and Socrates himself. Hence Plato, himself, also arguing on the basis of common opinion, adduces as counter-examples those who *have* written.

106. [*It has escaped you, Phaedrus, that*] '*sweet bend*' [*has been named from the long bend of the Nile. And as well as the bend, it is escaping you that the proudest of the politicians most of all love writing speeches and leaving writings behind* [*them*] . . .] (257D9–E4)

This is a proverb. There is a spot in Egypt thus named where there is much difficulty. So, by antiphrasis, the spot is said to be sweet on account of the difficulty (**211**) of the spot. So here too, [although] in the opposite [sense] to the proverb, it [*sc.* speech-writing] is said to be the opposite [of what it is]; for although it is a fine thing, speech-writing is said to be shameful. So the proverb is used of those who say the opposite of what they mean. For *they* both *love* speech-writing and want to undertake it and, although it is praiseworthy, say that it is shameful and blameworthy when they are not really of this view. What he [*sc.* Socrates] is saying, then, is this: just as the reason why the spot, although it is difficult and bitter, has been called '*sweet bend*' has escaped Phaedrus, so too has it escaped him that speech-writing has been called shameful in spite of its being praiseworthy and fine.

And as well as the bend, it is escaping you: for Plato tries to demonstrate, also on the basis of common opinion (*endoxôs*), that speech-writing is not bad, and adduces as counter-examples [to Phaedrus' claim] the people of great power themselves,[13] who have written laws and decrees and the like.

107. . . . *at any rate, whenever they write a* [*speech, they are so pleased with those who praise* [*them*] *that they write in at the beginning* [*the names of*] *those who praise them on any occasion*] . . . (257E4–6)

[That is,] those who swagger about and pride themselves on their work as though it were a fine thing, and accordingly say: 'The Council and the People have decided that such and such a person from such and such a deme should do this or that' and inscribe[14] themselves and those to whom they are making the speeches.[15]

108. ... *[the writer mentioning] his own self, of course, [with great solemnity]* ... (258A5-6)

He has added 'his own'[16] due to their having a high opinion of themselves.

Should [this speech] stand (258B2): that is, should the speech be accepted and not voted down.

109. *Well then – when [he becomes a] good enough [speech-maker or king to acquire the power of a Lycurgus or a Solon or a Darius and become an immortal speech-writer in a city, doesn't he think himself equal to the gods ...]?*(258B10-C3)

Because he [sc. Phaedrus] has said that there were some people in the city with great power who avoided writing speeches, on account of this he [sc. Socrates] adduces as counter-examples certain powerful lawgiver-kings[17] who have left behind their writings.

Of such people (258C7): [that is,] of those who criticise the writing of speeches.

What, then, is the way (tropos) [to write well – and not [well]?] (258D7) <...>[18] talking (*dialegesthai*)[19] about (*peri*) rhetoric but also about the poetic art and about speaking in general; and he carries the account back to first principles, making the question (*skemma*) a philosophical and scientific one; for while scientific knowledge (*epistêmê*) is of universals, it also encompasses particulars.[20] So he carries back to its first principle and cause the entire discourse as to when it is possible to write and to speak appropriately. What he says then is this: a person who is going to write ought to have knowledge of the facts (*pragmata*), for written characters are images of the spoken word (*ta legomena*), but it is not possible to know the **(212)** images unless one knows the archetypes.[21] He draws motivation for scrutinising the speech of Lysias from this, [namely,] that he wrote unsystematically and in an unstructured way. For if we learn the way to write appropriately in general, we can work out the details using this as a standard.

110. *[Is there any need, Phaedrus, for us to examine] Lysias [or anyone else who has ever written or will write anything] about these matters?* (258D8-9)

That is to say, [to examine] Lysias' speech.

... or anyone else who [has] ever [written or will write anything]: observe how he makes the account general, for he not only talks about Lysias but [says] *whether a political or a private* [composition], whether *metrical or non-metrical* (258D9-11). It is thus obvious that the present account concerns speeches and writings in general.

By *political* he means legislative or deliberative, by *private* court (*dikastikos*) or judicial. Observe, then, that he is here examining every type of discourse.

111. *Are you asking whether we need to?* (258E1)

For since the rational soul has its substantial being after the manner of (*kata*) the intellective part (*to noeron*) within it (for the soul of a human being is reason (*logos*),[22] it is in keeping [with this] (*eikotôs*) that it wishes to produce speeches (*logos*).[23] 'For what else ought we to live', he [*sc*. Phaedrus] asks, 'other than for the invention[24] of this reason (*logos*)?'

He calls those [pleasures that are experienced] through touch or taste 'pleasures that arise from prior pain'. For if one doesn't suffer much (*panu*)[25] prior pain, neither can one experience pleasure in these [areas]. Thus these pleasures are not pure pleasures, but [occur along] with pain, for they also have pain as their cause going along with them and accompanying them. Thus our soul has its substantial being after the manner of the reason (*logos*) and the intellectual activity that are in it.[26]

112. *Certainly not, I suppose,* [for the sake of] *those* [[pleasures] *in advance of which one must feel pain or not feel pleasure at all*] (258E2–3)

He means bodily pleasures that have pain as their origin.

Or not feel pleasure at all: [he says this] because he [*sc*. Phaedrus] is talking about the pleasures associated with sight and hearing but it is the pleasures [experienced] through touch in particular that arise from prior pain.

Pleasures [that] *have been called slavish* (258E5) are those that abstain from some sensations (*pathos*), but are ruled by others. For those who surrender themselves to pleasure are enslaved by pleasure, delivering the whole of their soul there.

113. *We certainly* [have] *time, as it seems* (258E6)

He wants to relate a myth, awakening us through the myth, and not permitting us **(213)** to doze and be lazy in our thinking. But it is necessary to realise that, as we have already said, he is not discoursing on rhetoric alone, but on all writing and all speaking, [explaining] when it is possible to write or to speak appropriately and when not. Therefore he makes his exposition maximally general and maximally scientific. Thus, after first teaching when it is possible to write correctly and when not and [providing] rules for speaking correctly, he next comes to the comparative evaluation of the two speeches – his own and that of Lysias – scrutinising them by way of an example, and in this way moves from the more general to the particular. Since this is what he is about to do, he directs his words (*logos*) up to the deities who are the overseers of speech and its causes, that is to say, the Muses.

[We] *certainly* [have] *time* (*skholê*): [that is, we have the] time for conversation and nothing is distracting us; for it is those who devote themselves (*skholazein*) to [philosophical] contemplation who are most of all said to be scholarly (*skholastikos*).²⁷

In the heat (258E7): the conversation's taking place at midday carries a certain likeness (*eikôn*) to a superior [order of being], for at that time the god Helios illuminates everything as [shining] from the centre [of the sky]. And, moreover, heat is elevating and ascending.

'*If then*', he says, '*the cicadas above our heads* (that is to say, the divine souls or daemons or heroes or gods who are above (*huper*) our heads and superior to (*huper*) us) *were to see* [us] being beguiled²⁸ by pleasure and self-indulgence (*glukuthumia*) and falling asleep, *they would laugh* at us (259A1–4). For if, he says, [even] mortal creatures (*zôion*) such as the cicadas remain awake at midday, it is much more the case that the rational animal (*zôion*) should not nod off and take a midday nap.

To take a midday nap is to nod off at midday and go to sleep.

Being beguiled (259A3): that is, being charmed by the pleasures of the body and self-indulgence and being carried down into [the realm of] generation.²⁹

Through indolence of thought (259A3–4): so that³⁰ it takes on this [earthly] motion that arises from the fluidity (*hugrotês*)³¹ of generation and not the [motion] which awakens our intellection (*noeron*) and our discursive thinking.

114. *Like sheep* (259A5)

That is, falling asleep, having been rendered irrational and [thus] being on a level with dumb animals (*alogos*) or slaves and doing nothing worthy of a person of [any] understanding. It is for this reason that he urges us to dedicate even our nights to wakefulness – at the very least one mustn't **(214)** shorten the days. He taught this very thing, [i.e.] that one should stay awake for part of the night, in the *Republic*.³²

115. *But if they see us in conversation* (259A6–7)

'Just as those', he says, 'who, constrained and beguiled by Sirens, forgot their own homeland, so too do we, if we are beguiled by these appearances and by the cicadas and fall sleep, forget our own homeland[33] and the ascent to the intelligible. But should we awaken our capacity for clear seeing and alertness and not be held back by self-indulgence, then we sail by like Ulysses and disregard (*parerkhesthai*) the life down here and are worthy of our native homeland and the ascent to the intelligible.'

[*They may, out of admiration, grant* us] *the gift they have from the gods* [*to bestow upon men*] (259B1–2): 'Thus when we are able', he says, 'to sail past the Sirens in the perceptible cosmos[34] (as one might call certain daemons who hold souls back in the realm of generation), then the cicadas (that is to say, the divine souls and the gods), seeing that we have risen from the realm of generation and lived in a godlike manner, would give to us the greatest gift for human beings – that is to say, would employ us as attendants. For just as the gods are wakeful with respect to their appropriate activity, so too should we keep ourselves awake to the extent that this is possible, and we are aroused if we awaken the faculty of reason (*logos*) that is within us.'

Those who have interpreted the *Iliad* and the *Odyssey* and the ascent more allegorically (*theôrêtikôteron*) <…>;[35] hence, they say that, because the soul fights its way out of matter, in the *Iliad* [Homer] wrote of (*poiein*) battles and wars,[36] and in the *Odyssey* of <Odysseus>[37] sailing past the Sirens and escaping from Circe, the Cyclopes, Calypso, and all the things standing in the way of the soul's ascent, and, after [all of] this, departing to his native land, that is to say, to the intelligible.[38]

116. *The gift* [*they have*] *from the gods* (259B1)

What gift does he mean? Reporting on our [affairs] to the gods; [for] just as he did with Love[39] in the *Symposium*[40] – he places him midway between gods and humans, calling him a daemon [and saying that] he conveys [reports on] our [affairs] to the gods (in fact the entire daemonic order [is located] midway between **(215)** gods and human beings) – he does in the same way in the case of the cicadas too; for he says that they convey and deliver reports on our [affairs] to the gods. (So it is clear that he intends them to be good daemons.)

They may, out of admiration, grant [*us the gift*] (259B2): [that is, out of admiration] that we have not been borne down by self-indulgence but have lived well. For the souls of humans when, having lived well, they are restored to their starting point (*apokathistanai*), become attendants of gods or daemons or heroes, and each one follows his own god.

Muse-loving (259B5): equivalent to 'philosophical'.

117. *It is said that these* [cicadas] *were once* [*humans, before the Muses came to be*] (259B6–7)

The allegorical interpretation (*theôria*) of the myth is as follows:

Some say that *before* (*prin*) the *Muses* came to be, and *before* music (*mousikê*) came to be, humans were unmusical (*amousos*), *but after* the *Muses came to be* (259B7) they became musical. But how is it not absurd for humans to have come to be before gods [sc. before the Muses]?

The interpretation of the divine Iamblichus will now be stated.[41] He [sc. Plato] is calling 'humans' the souls that have spent time in the intelligible realm, for before they live a mortal life souls are above in the intelligible realm, contemplating the forms themselves in the company of the hypercosmic gods. So in this sense (*houtôs*) humans did exist *before* the *Muses* – that is to say, the spheres[42] and the sensible cosmos – came to be. You should not, of course, take [this to mean] *before* in time, but [as meaning] *before* this[43] procession of the spheres emerged into the visible [realm]; for the genesis of the Muses is this: [their] manifestation (*ekphansis*) in the sensible cosmos, which came about through the agency of the Demiurge. The humans, then, were in the intelligible cosmos, [and] so the Muses, the spheres, the sensible cosmos, and the universal (*holos*) soul of the entire cosmos came to be simultaneously and the individual souls of humans emerged together with them. And inasmuch as the souls were newly initiated (*neotelês*)[44] and had a memory of the things up there, they faced away from the realm of generation and did not want to eat or drink – that is to say, did not want to participate in perceptual opinion because they had had intelligible nourishment, because of which, through starvation (*limos*) of things down here, they died – meaning they were led [back] up.

118. *When the Muses came to be* (259B7)

That is to say, when procession occurred and this sensible cosmos appeared and *song* and harmony *appeared* (259B7–8). (Harmony is in minds and in souls and in the spheres and in all things.)

[*Some were carried away*] *by pleasure* (259B8): that is to say, by divine good cheer (*euphrosunê*).[45]

[Until] *they died without noticing it* (259C1–2): you [can] see that here too the true philosopher, the one who spends his time in the presence of the things that [truly] are, does not even **(216)** see the things that are in front of his nose (*ta empodôn*), as he also said of the leading [philosopher] in the *Theaeteus*.[46] These people, then, despising sensible things, were led [back] up, astounded at the divine harmony.

From whom [*the race*] *of cicadas* [*is born*] (259C2–3):[47] that is to say, these souls became musical and gods of a kind.

[*Having received*] *this gift* [*from the Muses*] (259C3). The story (*logos*) is that the cicadas do not need food, but are content with dew. [Its] allegorical interpretation (*theôria*) is that the person who lives in accordance with intellect, is a lover of the Muses, and a lover of wisdom, and wishes to be led up to the gods, has no need of care of the body and the bodily life but thinks it of no account, wishing to leave it behind; for he is preparing for death,[48] that is to say, for departure from this life, for he knows that the body means trouble for him.

The *gift* is to become an attendant of one's own god. As we have said already,[49] he says in the *Symposium* that the *entire daemonic order* lies *between* gods and humans, *conveying* [reports on] our [behaviour] to the gods. One should be aware that the divine is present to everything in an unmediated manner, but we cannot be connected with the gods in an unmediated manner unless through some intermediary, such as a daemonic one, just as in the case of light we need air to move the light across[50] (*diakinein*) [the intervening space] for us. So what he calls their gift is this: that, he says, the daemons or the souls,[51] coming to the Muses, report on people's good or bad manner of life [and] on who has honoured, or not honoured, one or other of the gods.

119. [*By reporting*] *to Terpsichore* (259C6–7)

They don't report the kind of dance that pantomimic dancers dance, for that is ridiculous. There are divine dances.[52] First that of the gods, then that of divine souls, and then the revolution of the heavenly gods is said to be a dance that the seven gods[53] and the fixed stars dance. And then down here too the initiates perform a certain dance for the gods in the mysteries. And the entire life of the philosopher is a dance. Terpsichore is thus the patron of all dance. So who are those who honour the goddess in dance? Not those who dance beautifully, but rather those who live beautifully throughout the life down here, giving [a beautiful] rhythm to (*rhuthmizein*)[54] their entire way of life and dancing in step with (*sumphônôs*) the universe.

(217) 120. *And to Erato* (259D1)

She was named 'Erato' from the verb 'to love' (*eran*) and from her doing lovely (*erasmios*) things, [that is to say,] the works of Love (*Erôs*); for she is a workmate of Love. Thus 'Terpsichore' (*Terpsikhora*) was named from 'dance' (*khoreia*), 'Erato' from 'love'.

They [*sc.* the cicadas] report, then, *those who have honoured her in erotic matters* (259C7–D2), for those who engage in love in a shameful manner insult her.

*According to the kind (*eidos*) of honour [paid to] each* (259D2–3): that is, in accordance with the distinctive characteristics (*idiôma*) of each goddess.

121. *To the eldest, Calliope, [and to Urania who is next after her (who, among the Muses, are most of all concerned with heaven and with words, both divine and human, and who send forth the most beautiful sound) they make report about those who pass their lives in philosophy and who honour their [*sc.* the Muses'] musical arts]* (259D3–7)

He says 'eldest' because among the Muses too there is an order of first, middle, and last, which are features (*huparkhein*)[55] of philosophy.

She was named Calliope because of her voice.[56] Accordingly, [the cicadas] report [to her] *those who have honoured her* (259C7) in words, whereas to Urania [they report] those who have engaged in astronomy,[57] for it is through these two goddesses that we rescue (*sôizein*) that in us which has gone astray (*planan*): through vision, when contemplating the order of the celestial gods, we set in order the irrational within us – although, we also of course, give rhythm to the disorderly and unrhythmical [element] in us through rhythm and philosophy and [our] hearing. And [so] one must not pursue astronomy for the sake of navigation (*nautikôs*) nor simply to know the motions of the celestial gods, but to order the irrational [element] within us by contemplating the celestial order.

*They send forth the most beautiful sound (*phônê*)* (259D7): and indeed it is said that Pythagoras heard the celestial voice (*phônê*),[58] and some have named the [musical] notes (*khordê*) from the celestial spheres,[59] for example, the 'added' [note] (*proslambanomenê*)[60] is the sphere of Kronos [i.e. Saturn],[61] and they similarly name other notes after other [spheres].

122. *For many reasons, then* (259D7)

For all these stated reasons we must not slumber but [must] awaken [our] intellective aspect, that within us which bears a relationship to the gods; and we awaken [our] intellectual [aspect] by conversing.

Therefore [we ought to examine] what we have just now proposed [to examine] (259E1–2): The philosopher Aristotle seeks some four things in every account (*logos*);[62] two are simple, [namely] 'whether it is' (*ei esti*) and 'what it is' (*ti esti*), and two composite, [namely] 'that it is [the case]' (*hoti esti*) and 'why it is [the case]' (*dia ti esti*). For instance, [one can ask] 'whether there is void' or 'whether there is soul' or 'whether there is a *skindapsos*'.[63] In the cases where it is self-evident, there is no need to enquire 'whether it is', **(218)** but [only] 'what it is'. After all, nobody enquires 'whether there are human beings' because that is self-evident, but [one might ask] what [a human being] is. In the case of things that are not self-evident, however, one must also pose the question 'whether it is' for no one would ask what a *skindapsos* is prior to learning whether there is [such a thing]. In the case of composites on the other hand, in which one thing is predicated of another, one must determine 'that it is' and then 'why [it is]' (*dioti*).[64] For instance, 'that there is an eclipse', for an eclipse is an eclipse of something, so first it is necessary to know that the Moon is eclipsed and [only] then why it is eclipsed.

But there is something else one needs to seek before these four things, [namely,] what the word (*onoma*) itself means. Accordingly, the philosopher Plato too, having first shown – by means of the earlier passage where he says *this is obvious to everyone, that writing speeches is not shameful in itself* (258D1–2) – that one ought to write, then teaches how one should write and *in what manner one writes* and speaks *well or not* [well] (258D7), [thereby] making the question (*problêma*) more general and more scientific, after [first] referring the entire origin of the discussion (*logos*) back to the Muses and the gods.[65] And just as one detects (*krinein*) crookedness by means of the straight edge or what deviates from the square by the set square (*orthê*), in the same way the philosopher resorts to the truth as to a straight edge by which we judge things that are like [it] and things that differ [from it]. In this [same] way the rhetorician ought to have the truth as a straight edge.

123. *Is it not necessary, then, [if the speech is to be delivered well and in the right way (kalôs), for the mind (dianoia) of the speaker to know beforehand the truth of the matters he is going to speak about?*] (259E4–6)

Because, he says, in speaking or writing well it is necessary for there to be truth and knowledge of the matter [in question] beforehand, for the person who does not know the truth of the matter [only] talks about probabilities in connection with it. That it is necessary to have an understanding (*gnôsis*) of the things under discussion and of the facts he has already taught, saying: *Whatever the subject, my boy, there is a single starting point – to know what is being talked about* (logos), *or necessarily get everything wrong* (237B7–8).

Accordingly, it is said that there are three prerequisites for speakers or writers. First, to know the truth. Second, to be able to make the one many[66] – which is [the function] of the method of division – to know, on occasion (*ei tukhoi*), in how many senses the thing in question is said, whether it is homonymous or synonymous, whether it is one in genus or in species, and so on. Therefore one must be skilled in division (*diairetikos*). Third, [to be able] to gather the many together into one, which is [the function] of analysis and definition; for to be able to encompass the many in one formula (*logos*) is the definition of the thing [in question]. Then [there is] also the composition and the propriety of the speech, for it is agreed that one must speak and write things that are appropriate and in accord with [the nature of] the gods.[67]

These things, then, are the **(219)** tools, as it were, of speaking and writing. Above all [one] should know the nature and essence of the matter, that is to say, the truth; for in that way one would know how one should proceed (*hodeuein*), whether it be using the truth or using what seems plausible to one. Indeed the person who doesn't know the truth and [merely] makes suppositions (*doxazein*) (as those who practise (*ekhein*) the popular rhetoric do) often persuades listeners of things that are quite the opposite of what he intends. Thus if he intends to talk about probabilities on this subject[68] <...>[69] on the topic of popular rhetoric, that it is not necessary, he says, to know the truth. Finally, the philosopher sets out how many good things result from the genuine rhetoric and how many bad things from what is falsely [called rhetoric].

124. *The things that are really just* (260A1)

There are three parts of rhetoric, the deliberative, the judicial and the panegyrical. He is referring, then, to the parts through their goals, that is to say, the just belongs to the judicial [part], the good to the deliberative, and the fine (*kalos*) to the panegyrical. And by antithesis, just and unjust belong to the judicial [part], good and bad to the deliberative, fine and base to the panegyrical. And in connection with each of them a certain duality is to be seen: in the case of judicial [rhetoric there is] prosecution and defence, in that of deliberative, exhortation (*protropê*) and dissuasion (*apotropê*), in that of panegyrical, praise and censure. They give speeches in [one or other of] these [three areas] on the basis of (*apo*) what [merely] seems to be just or good or noble.

125. *No [word the wise utter] should be ignored* (260A5–6)

Perhaps, he observes, the *wise* (*sophos*) have a point. But '*wise*' may have been used out of tact, or else because the ancients called those who had anything at all to do with speech *wise*, seeing that Homer says of the carpenter 'well acquainted with [every] skill' (*sophia*).[70]

[*And what was said just now*] *must not be dismissed* (260A6–7): [by this Socrates means:] 'Rather, one must enquire whether one should, as I say, seek the truth about the just, the good, and the noble or, as the rhetoricians say, [merely] the appearance [of these things].'

126. *If I persuaded you* (260B1)

He wants to show him by means of a single example how much difference there is between the **(220)** true rhetoric and the popular rhetoric and to show that the former preserves the person who follows it, while the latter ruins him, involving him in (*emballein*) myriad evils. He takes [as his example] a horse and a donkey and says, '*If*, talking about a donkey as though it were a horse, *I persuaded you* that it is an animal that is very powerful and responsible for victory in wars and for bearing burdens in peacetime, and if neither of us knew [what] a horse [is], and I talked you into (*peithein*) thinking that the [attributes] of a horse [belonged] to the donkey, what do you think the result of this would be?' Surely it is obvious that the nature of things would be turned upside down.

127. [*But I happened to know*] *just this much* [*about you: that Phaedrus thinks that the horse is the domesticated* (*hêmeros*) *animal with the longest ears*] (260B2–4)

For if *we were* entirely *ignorant* (260B2) [about it], then we are not going to be talking about it or persuading someone who knows absolutely nothing [about it].

128. [*That would be*] *ridiculous* (260B5)

The idea (*skemma*), and this [supposed act of] persuasion, [would be] *ridiculous*, he says; it [would be] *utterly ridiculous* (260C2) to think *of a donkey as though it were a horse* (260C7–8).

129. *Well,* [*isn't ridiculous and friendly better than clever and hostile?*] (260C3–4)

He has produced a double means of distinction (*diairetikon*): '*Isn't ridiculous and friendly better*', he says, '*than clever and hostile?*' For the ridiculousness and friendliness [involved in thinking of] a donkey as though it were a horse is preferable to[71] the cleverness and hostility (*ekhthros*) [involved] in [treating] things that are just and good as unjust and bad; for when we think that fine things are bad life is turned upside down, and in the case of the donkey there is no harm when we think the donkey is a horse, but when we consider unjust things just, harm ensues for us through both word and deed.

130. *The donkey's [shadow]* (260C7)

'Donkey's shadow' is proverbial.[72] He has made the knowledge of things that are just or unjust more remote from the rhetoricians than the shadow of a donkey; for he talks of the donkey's shadow not with the intention of praising the shadow of a donkey but [of praising] a horse. But the horse's shadow is far removed from that of a genuine donkey. '*So when*', he says, '*a speaker persuades [people] not about a donkey*, but about unjust and bad things as though [they were] just and good, *what sort of fruit do you expect* [him] *to harvest?*' (260C6–D1)

This too is proverbial: that 'someone who sows evils **(221)** reaps evils'; and indeed, of the speakers who gave public speeches like this, some were ostracised while others became fugitives. 'So what,' he asks, 'do you think the outcome of this [kind of] advice is found to be?'

Certainly not an entirely satisfactory one (260D2): that is to say, a bad one; indeed both the many and those who consult [him][73] attribute failures to him [*sc.* to the speaker].

131. *Well, my good man, [we haven't reviled the art of speeches more boorishly than necessary, have we?]*[74] (260D3–4)

Having said that such orators bring about bad things both for themselves and for the city that takes [their] advice, he says: *we haven't reviled the art of speeches* [too] *boorishly, have we*? He said this wanting to proceed to the intermediate [type of] rhetoric as well,[75] for he has already mentioned the genuine and the popular [kinds]. In general, when the philosopher engages (*strephesthai*) with intelligible being and the contemplation of the intelligibles and of god and has [his] mind's eye directed aloft, he is a metaphysician;[76] but when he has switched (*meterkhesthai*) from [contemplation of] that spectacle (*thea*) to the care of the city and is regulating the city in accordance with [his] vision (*thea*) of those things, he then becomes a political philosopher. And when such a person directs [their] speeches to the state (*koinon*), persuading the people to do what needs [to be done], then he is a genuine orator; for knowing what is true through that [heavenly] vision, he persuades them to do what is true and what is fitting for them. And when, not knowing what is fine or good but, *having hunted opinions* (262C2), he thinks [only] of emotive effect (*pathos*), indulging the emotions (*pathos*) of the many in [his] speeches, then he is a popular orator. And when he delivers his public speeches with their emotive effects in mind but doesn't indulge the emotions of the citizens, but leads [them] in accordance with what seems [the case] to him and what he considers right and through [his] allies and resources brings about, as he thinks, good [outcomes] for the city, then he is an intermediate orator, among whom he [*sc.* Plato] places Themistocles and Pericles, not [thereby] contradicting what was said in the *Gorgias*.[77]

132. *We haven't reviled the art of speeches* [*more boorishly than necessary, have we?*] (260D3–4)

He means the popular rhetoric.

Perhaps it would say (260D4): clearly ['it' means] rhetoric; he is ascribing speeches and public speaking to the genuine rhetoric, making the language (*logos*) more animated by [using] personification. It is not enough, it says, to just have a knowledge of the facts (*pragma*), but one must also possess art, [the] 'artificer of persuasion'.[78] [Being an] 'artificer of persuasion' is not peculiar to rhetoric; craftsmen, carpenters, weavers, and the like also persuade,[79] and a woman persuades **(222)** the many and stirs them to pity by baring her breasts,[80] and weeping children are persuasive. So being persuasive is not [a feature] of rhetoric alone.

To learn (260D6), [i.e. 'to learn'] my art'.

133. *But if a person takes my advice* (260D6–7)

But if a person takes my advice, [only] *after coming into possession of it* (he means of the truth) *does he then take me* (that is to say, the power to persuade)[81] up.[82]

134. *But I do make this large* [*claim*] (260D7–8)

I make this large [claim] for rhetoric, that there is no advantage to a person who has got to know the nature of the circumstances (*pragma*) unless he has a sufficient grasp of my art to persuade [his audience].

135. *Yes, at least if the [arguments advancing upon it testify that it is an art]* (260E2-3)

An art has in view some good, for every art has a good as its goal. One that does not look to some good is not even an art. Thus the popular rhetoric is not an art, for it does not even make the good a goal since it constructs speeches with the aim of [arousing] emotions.

Again, no art corrupts its own standard (*kanôn*), but the popular rhetoric corrupts its standard, that is to say the juror, for he is its standard.[83] Therefore the popular rhetoric is not an art.

Again, as he says in the *Republic*, one wise man has no wish to get the better of another wise man, nor one craftsman, qua craftsman, of another craftsman;[84] but one speaker (*rhêtôr*) does want to get the better of another speaker. The conclusion is obvious.

So since every art has a good as its goal but the popular rhetoric does not, because of this he says *if the arguments advancing upon it testify that it is an art*. For if rhetoric says what it says without looking to the good, it is not an art, but if [it looks] to the good, it is an art.

136. *For [I seem] to hear, as it were, [certain arguments coming forward and attesting that it speaks falsely and is not an art but an artless routine (tribê)]* (260E3-5)

That for rhetoric there is no necessity for truth or for knowledge of the facts, but [only] need of a little practice (*tribê*) to become an orator.

137. *But, the Laconian says, [there is not, and never will be in time to come a genuine art] of speaking [without a grasp of the truth]*[85] (260E5-7)

Without the good **(223)** and the truth, says the Laconian orator, an art is impossible.

138. *As regards these arguments, then (dê),*[86] *Socrates'* (261A1)

[That is,] those [arguments] that attain to the truth and don't just [rely on][87] conjecture, routine (*tribê*) and experience (*empeiria*). Hence one must question them as to just how they stand [on the question as to] whether it is or isn't necessary to pursue the truth. 'Well then', he [*sc.* Socrates] says, 'compare the arguments (since one set says that speakers ought to stick to the truth because it is impossible to know [its] like, that is, what is plausible, without knowing what is true, the other [that they ought to depend on] a routine and experience alone) so that what is being said may become familiar (*gnôrimos*) to us through the comparison. So compare the genuine and the popular rhetoric.'[88]

139. *Come forward, then, worthy* (gennaios) *nurslings . . .* (261A3)

He calls the arguments *nurslings*, for arguments that are substantial, true, and demonstrative are *nurslings* of the soul. Hence he says *worthy*, on account of their achieving great things and their power to talk and their demonstrative ability. So come into our midst, you demonstrative arguments, and persuade Phaedrus that it is impossible for him to become a fine (*kalos*) orator without philosophy and truth.

kallipaida: either because Phaedrus himself is a beautiful child (*kalon paida*) or because he gives birth to beautiful children [in the form of] speeches.[89]

140. [*. . . and persuade Phaedrus*] *that if* [*he does not engage*] *adequately* [*with philosophy neither will he ever be an adequate speaker*] (261A3–5)

Well, haven't orators engaged in philosophy? We maintain that it is not possible for truly good orators to arise without philosophy; and in fact those orators who have acquired the greatest fame did engage in philosophy. Pericles became a pupil of Anaxagoras,[90] and Demosthenes heard Plato,[91] and the rest of the famous orators engaged with philosophy. Or at any rate he says this to encourage Phaedrus [to take up philosophy].

141. *Ask away!* (261A6)

He speaks as though to the 'nurslings'.

Is it not the case?: **(224)** here he explains the purpose of rhetoric: 'isn't this', he says, 'the task of rhetoric, the influencing of the soul by means of words (*logos*)?'

By 'influencing of the soul' he means drawing the soul to itself and bringing about persuasion (*peithô*) in it, not only through (*kata*) the three branches of rhetoric, the judicial, the deliberative, and the panegyrical, but through [everyday] social intercourse. For he says that this [last] too is part of rhetoric and, in a word, he wants speaking well, whether in private or in public, to be characteristic of rhetoric.

[*Not only in courts and other public gatherings but*] *in private* [*ones too*] (261A8–9): he means either *in the courts* or in private conversations.⁹²

142. [*The same when concerned with*] *small matters and with great* (261A9–B1)

What he is saying is this: that the method and the art and the general principles [of rhetoric] have the same power in great matters and small alike, [which is] just what he says in the *Sophist* (227B4–5) [when he says] that the art of hunting retains its specific force not just in the art of generalship but in the art of louse hunting too. And just as we hunt all things by means of the art of hunting, so too do we grasp everything by the method of division. So it has the same power in no greater measure in the case *of great* things (in the case of a city for instance) than in the case *of small* ones, [is] equivalent to 'the same art and method exists in the cases *of great* things and of small and it is not a jot more honourable for it to be concerned with great things than with small'. For it employs the same method and procedure, just as one might call the same thing ethical or economic or political, for one governs a city, a household, and oneself by the same method.

143. *No, by Zeus,* [*not at all like this*] (261B3)

For in ancient time, as now, orators spent their time at the courts and on speeches on state affairs and not at all on privately held meetings.

144. *What,* [*have you only read*] *the* [*arts*] *of Nestor* [*and Odysseus that deal with speeches . . . and not read those of Palamedes?*] (261B6–8)

What is the point of [the reference to] Nestor, Odysseus, and Palamedes? He is likening Gorgias to Nestor because he too was modest⁹³ and long-lived, for he was said to have lived for **(225)** a hundred and eight years. Thrasymachus, as being clever, he likens to Odysseus, and Zeno of Elea to Palamedes⁹⁴ since Palamedes was the discoverer of numbers, of dice, and of many other things. So he compared Zeno to Palamedes as being proficient in his art. What he is saying, then, is this: 'As it seems you have [only] heard long-winded speeches (*logoi*) <and not short ones>', that is to say, dialectical (*dialektikos*) and social (*homilêtikos*) speech (*logoi*).⁹⁵

Perhaps (261C3), then, agrees (*tithesthai*) that 'by Nestor I mean Gorgias'.

145. What do the adversaries in courts do? (261C4–5)

Don't they contradict one another and persuade one another?[96] Is it only possible, then, to contradict [someone] in courts or [is it also possible] in private?[97] *Well then, someone* who engages in *this* contradiction *with art* (*tekhnêi*) is able to make *the same thing seem* (261C10) 'both like and unlike' (261D7–8). And, to put it briefly, by this he means to make truth link up with rhetoric.[98] The sense (*nous*) of what is said next also conveys this. For, he says (261E6 ff.), someone who wants to bring a person from one opposed [position] to the other doesn't do this without intervening steps (*amesôs*), otherwise the person addressed will see [what is happening] and won't make you any concession; but if he does make use of (*lambanein*) small step (*kata brakhu*) similarity, he will, undetected, bring the person addressed to the opposite [position]. But someone who does not know the truth cannot use (*lambanein*) small step similarities; for the person who knows [the truth is the one who] wants to bring [the other party] around to the opposing [position] by means of *small step (kata smikron)*(262A2) similarities. Thus it is necessary to know the truth and the similarity and dissimilarity of the things [under discussion] and for the person who wants to bring someone to the opposite [position] and to make the same thing at one time be seen as just, at another unjust, and the same things [be seen] as similar and dissimilar, to be a philosopher and be skilled in division and definition; because in so far as they share [features] things are similar, so in so far as forms exist, there are also similar things; but, then, they are also dissimilar, for they are different [things]. Aristotle gives the remaining arguments (*sullogismos*) in the *Physics*.[99]

146. So [the art of disputation is found] not only [in courts and public speaking] (261D10)

He has arrived at the present topic (*prokeimenon*) because the *art of disputation* and [the practice of] persuasion are found not only in courts but in everyday conversations too.

[An art] *by means of which a person will be able* [*to liken everything to everything*] (261E2–3): employing which art a person is *able to liken* [any aspect of what is being talked about] *to anything* that has some similarity to what is being talked about.

(226) 147. Does deception [occur more in things that differ greatly or [only] a little]? (261E6–7)

Nature does not lead [things] from opposite [state] to opposite [state] without intervening steps (*amesôs*). Hence *deception occurs in things that differ* [only] *a little*.

It occurs both in [my] perception and in [my] transactions (*epitêdeuma*) when I take quicksilver for silver or bronze for gold or, in the case of living things, a wild pigeon for a tame one,[100] or, in the case of[101] [my] transactions [alone], a sorcerer for a priest. Things that differ greatly, on the other hand, are quite obvious.

148. *Well then, [you will] surely [get to the opposite [position] without being detected more often when switching to it by small steps [rather] than large [ones]]* (262A2–3)

Thus he must know the similarities of things in order to be able to bring the person being addressed around *by small steps* to the opposite [position] without being detected.

Knowing *the similarity and dissimilarity* (262A6) of forms is the role of philosophy. *It is clear*, then, that *this experience* (*pathos*) (262B3) and the deception come about through not understanding its (*autês*)[102] nature.

149. *So is there any way [that someone who does not have a knowledge of each of the facts] will be skilled in the art [of moving a person over by small steps by means of similarities, leading him at every stage away from what is the case to the opposite [position]]?* (262B5–8)

That is to say, if he is skilled in the art, he wants to win [people] over (*paragein*)[103] *by means of similarities*.

'Leading away' (*apagein*) does not mean so as to deceive but so as to persuade *by means of similarities* and what seems like the truth.

[A laughable] *art of discourse, then, my friend* (262C1–2): *so a person who does not know* the nature of things will not possess an art but an unreasoning [empirical] practice.

150. *So would you like [to look at some instances of what I say lacks art and what shows art] in the speech of Lysias [that you are carrying and in those I delivered?]* (262C5–7)

Since what is being said becomes clear in an example, he wants to show through the example[s] of Lysias' speech and of his own, the artlessness of the former and the art (*to entekhnon*) of the latter. So since all the writers on the art of rhetoric say that probabilities and plausibilities are the subject matter of rhetoric and that a juror is persuaded by means of these but do not give the reason why these persuade [him], the philosopher has also given the reason for these [being persuasive], stating that it is because of their similarity to the truth that probabilities are persuasive. Hence truth is the principle of all things and the speaker persuades by knowing what is true. Since, then, he said earlier that someone who knows the similarities and dissimilarities between things can little by little lead whomever he wishes *to the opposite* (262A3) [position], he wants, by means of an example, to demonstrate what he has said, [that is to say,] how a speaker who knows the truth can win [people] over[104] (*paragein*) by means of similarities and how one who is without knowledge of the truth **(227)** is all at sea (*ataktos*).

There being these three in any speech – invention, disposition (*taxis*), and diction – he doesn't criticise Lysias for his invention but [only] for his arrangement (*oikonomia*) and his diction.

151. [*Yes, by all means,*] *because* [till] *now we have been talking rather abstractly* (*psilôs*) [*without providing enough examples*] (262C8-9)

That is to say, when we don't communicate what we are expressing (*legein*) in an example, we are speaking *abstractly* and not envisioning (*noein*) what we are saying. The soul especially takes pleasure in examples[105] and is convinced [by them] because it too is an image of the intellect; so, being an image (*eikôn*) of the intellect, it is, as is reasonable (*eikotôs*), led to [give] credence by means of examples.

152. *And indeed, by* [*some*] *chance,* [*as it seems, two speeches were delivered that provide something of an example of how a person who knows the truth . . . may win over* (*paragein*) *his listeners*] (262C10-D2)

In order that we may know what great advantage accrues from being acquainted with the truth and what great harm from being ignorant [of it].

153. *How a person who knows the truth,* [*while having fun in his speeches, may sway his listeners*] (262D1)

That is, the philosopher treats the speeches of the orators as amusement and what they do in all seriousness – [I mean] winning their listeners over (*paragein*) by means of similarities – he classes as amusement.

154. *I for my part, Phaedrus, hold [the local gods] responsible* (262D2-3)

For Plato refers everything back to the gods, [and] so, in these [matters] of the discovery and determination of the truth, '*I hold the gods responsible*', he says, 'for I have no [skill in the] art (262D5-6)'. For it was Socrates' custom to deny that he had [made] any discovery of his own and to refer everything back to the gods. And for us communion with the gods takes place both without any intermediary when the soul is illuminated from that source and by way of the genera between [them and us].[106] Providence, then, is twofold: either [providence] properly speaking (*idikôs*), that of the gods, or that by way of the superior genera and daemons and local gods. He therefore says, '*I hold the local gods responsible* for such handling and arrangement of the speeches'.

By the 'singers *overhead*' (262D4) he means the higher genera, those that accompany the gods; for one must always call what is superior a daemon,[107] for instance, that which is endowed with reason (*to logikon*) 'daemon of reason', [and] god 'daemon of intellect'.

This gift (262D5) means [the gift of] being able to distinguish between those who speak according to [the rules of] the art and those who don't.

(228) 155. *Come, then, read me [the beginning of Lysias' speech]* (262D8)

He wants to compare two speeches, that of Lysias and his own, and he is critical of (*elenkhein*) that of Lysias from its very beginning.[108] But, being a philosopher, he doesn't go into all of [his] criticisms (*elenkhos*), for finding fault with everything would be the act of a personal enemy.[109] As it is, after indicating a few of the faults of the speech, he moves to his own second speech.

He criticises the beginning of the speech on the ground that the artistry of a speaker reveals itself in the introduction; for the nature (*dunamis*) of the entire speech is [to be seen] in the introduction.

156. *Well, then, isn't [something like this at least] clear to everyone?* (263A2)

That from the beginning Lysias' speech shows itself to be lacking in art and that he approaches its subject matter in an inartistic manner is clear. In the first place, because some things are straightforward, others ambiguous, he should have distinguished [the senses of] the ambiguous word 'love' and stated about what kind of love he says what he says, having [first] enumerated the senses of the thing so that we will have a clear understanding of what is being talked about. One must be aware that the matter in hand itself, that is to say, love here, cannot admit of contrary definitions – for how can the same thing be both good (*kalos*) and not good? – but according to [common] conceptions[110] of it [*sc.* of love] there can be contrary definitions. So he needed to say [just] what the subject is so that we would be able fix our minds on what [his] words relate to, for someone who does not know the truth cannot know the nature of an ambiguous thing. And so an orator who speaks in an orderly manner must have got to know the facts, [observing] whether they are of a simple nature or a complex one, so as to be able to make simple speeches for straightforward [situations] and fitting ones for complex [situations]. For someone who does not have such knowledge, even should he stumble upon the truth, cannot distinguish it from the false. So, love being ambiguous and twofold thanks to the conceptions of the many, one kind being good, the other base, because he has not specified what kind he is talking about, he [*sc.* Lysias] has made his speech unclear; and he has also made it disorderly – since he has begun with things that belong later (*ta hustera*), a charge [Socrates] is going to bring against the speech – and unorganised. So you see that he wants the orator to be skilled in definition and in division and to know the nature of the matters in hand.

157. [*About some of such things*] *we are of one mind,* [*about some at variance*] (263A3–4)

For example, when I say 'stone' or 'log', we are all directed, without argument, to the same items, but about what is just or what beneficial we differ because we don't all agree about them. So in a sense he is showing us the subject matter of rhetoric here, [namely] that it exists in the area of the ambiguous.

(229) 158. [*When someone says the word 'iron' or 'silver'*] *don't* [*we all think of*] *just that*[111] (263A6–7)

For no ambiguity arises as to what [is being referred to].
    In which of the two [[situations] *are we*] *more easily deceived* (263B3) is [equivalent to] this: In what lies the strength of rhetoric? Is it not in ambiguous [situations], so that, by means of plausibilities, [one speaker] may lead [listeners] to one [conclusion], another to another? If, then, the strength of rhetoric lies *in cases where we are uncertain* (263B5), it is clear that someone who doesn't understand the two-sided (*diploê*) nature of a thing or know what arguments he

will use is willing to move the argument (*logos*) in the other direction, and so it is clear that truth is paramount (*proêgeisthai*).

To have divided [these nouns] methodically (hodôi) (263B7): as, for instance, [to see] that the word 'love' indicates [both] the good and, among the many, the bad; and [to be able] to divide the one into many and be able to define each thing.

[To have grasped some] distinctive mark of each kind (263B8): as, for instance, of which kind this love is and of which that, and to define each and to know what kind of speech can win over and persuade the listeners.

159. *At any rate, [Socrates, someone who has grasped that would have understood a] fine [class (eidos)* [of nouns]]*(263C1-2)

That is, to say, a person who is acquainted with the method of division also has the best knowledge of things.

Next, I think [[he must] *not come to each thing unawares but clearly understand to which class (genos) the thing he is going to talk about belongs*] (262C3–5): first it is necessary to know to which *class it belongs*, the straightforward or the ambiguous. Then, if it is ambiguous, one must be clear-sighted and critical about its nature; for if he is talking about genuine (*orthos*) love, he must consider what words are suited to it.

'*Well, then, what do we say love is, is it one of the straightforward things or one of the ambiguous ones*' (263C7–8):[112] He asks this on account of the conception [of love] of the many; for it is not [really] possible for a single thing to have contradictory (*enantios*) definitions and so it is clear that the definitions that relate to different conceptions [of love] are different.

160. *[Certainly to the disputable [terms]. Otherwise do you think I would have allowed you [to say what you just now said about it?]* (263C9–10)

Since, because if they are ambiguous, it is therefore [seemingly] possible to say conflicting things about the same thing, [as in the present case for example,] '*that it is harmful to the beloved*', as Lysias said, [and] then, as my speech said, '*that love is responsible for the greatest of goods*' (263C10-12):[113] and so it is clear that he is not saying conflicting things about the same thing but about two different things; for one lot of statements fits good (*kalos*) love, the other the opposite kind.

For I [do not quite remember] thanks to the divine possession [I mentioned][114] (263D1–2): for someone who is elevated and sojourns among the intelligibles does not know what is under his feet,[115] or [the realm of] perceptible things.

161. *Yes, by Zeus, extraordinarily* [*thoroughly*] (263D4)

That is to say, 'you defined [it] amazingly thoroughly'. Lysias didn't do so at all.

My word, how much [*more artistic*] *you are saying* [*the Nymphs ... and Pan ... are than Lysias ... in* [composing] *speeches!*] (263D5–6): because he [sc. Phaedrus] said 'yes, extraordinarily thoroughly', **(230)** he [sc. Socrates] says '*you are saying that the Nymphs are more artistic than* the art of *Lysias*', for Plato always refers the causes [of things] back to the gods.

162. *Did Lysias too, beginning* [[*his speech*] *about love compel us to understand love as some single thing?*] (263D7)

Because Lysias, having assumed one particular sense of love, even though he didn't define it, said everything [he said] thereafter *in relation to that* (263E1). So far, then, he has shown that Lysias did not define love but composed his speech as though on an agreed subject[116] whereas the philosopher defined [it].

Did [*Lysias*] *compel us to understand* [*love as some particular thing*?]: that is, we have guessed what sense [of 'love'] Lysias is talking about from what was said (*pherein*) [in his speech]; for he didn't speak after [first] defining [it].

163. *Would you like us to read* [*the beginning*] *again?* (263E2)

Someone who engages in criticism with [unbiased] judgement and not out of enmity or for the sake of victory turns the same things up and down, subjecting them to [close] scrutiny, because he is not examining what is said closely out of hostility or ill-will.

[*If you like,*] *but what you are looking for* [*isn't there*] (263E4). For he hasn't defined what kind of love he is discoursing on.

164. *He does indeed seem to fall far short* [*of doing what we are looking for*] (264A4)

He brings another charge against the speech. The first charge [was] that, although the matter in hand is ambiguous, he has not defined [it]. Now he charges that he has begun from the end and has not ordered the topics (*problêma*) chronologically, for he ought to have described the sort of person the lover is during the time when he is in love and [only] then what he is like after the time he has stopped being in love. He has, then, written his speech as though swimming *on his back*

(264A5), behaving arbitrarily, and arranging the speech to suit himself. And so he began contrary to chronology and contrary to what is natural like those who swim upside down.[117] Hence, drawing on Plato, the critics say of Lysias, because of his inventiveness and the disorderliness of his discourse (*logos*), that he was able to generate [material] but not to arrange it [appropriately].

165. *And what about the rest? Don't [the parts of the speech seem to be placed (ballein)] indiscriminately?* (264B3)

He wants to show that Lysias' speech is disconnected and disjointed and anything in it is capable of being a starting point. Hence he compares it to the epitaph [of Midas] (264D3-6) in that its arguments are disconnected and the second could [equally well] be delivered first or third [like the lines of the epitaph].

(231) 166. *For [it seemed to me in my ignorance that,] quite boldly, whatever occurred [to him] [was said by the writer]* (264B5-7)

That is to say, he wrote anything at all that occurred to him.

But I think [you would] at any rate [say] this: [*that every speech must be put together like a living creature*] (264C2-3): he likens the speech to the natural (*phusikos*) make-up of animals (*zôion*) and trees and says that just as a living creature (*zôion*) is continuous with itself and is unified and shows (*ekhein*) an ordering of primary, secondary, and lowermost [parts], so too should a speech constitute a single body.[118] But why must a speech be unified? Because beauty and goodness (*to eu*) is radiated to every thing from the One. Unless it is possessed (*katekhein*) by the One, nothing at all can be good. Thus even beauty is not beautiful unless there is unity of all of its parts. Inasmuch, then, as it does not have unity Lysias' speech has no beauty in it either.

And so be neither without a head nor without feet (264C3-4): that is to say, having a beginning and middle parts and an end and [having] order.

167. *Well, consider [whether your friend's speech is like this or different and you will find that it in no way differs from the epitaph that some say was inscribed for Midas the Phrygian]* (264C7-9)

Because he has neither defined what sort of love he is talking about nor begun from a starting point that observes due order (*tetagmenos*) but it is possible to use [what comes] first second and [the speech] in no way differs from the epitaph that is cited in the text (*rhêta*); for it is possible to place any one of the three [last] lines of the epitaph (*epigramma*) you like first, which is not [a feature] of [proper] sequence and order. Hence some call such epigrams (*epigramma*) triangles because you can begin [them] from anywhere you like.

168. [*You are making fun of*] *our speech,* [*Socrates*] (264E3)

As a friend of Lysias, Phaedrus is rather unhappy with what is being said about Lysias and his speech.

169. *Well then,* [*so you won't be upset, let's leave*] *it* [*be*] (264E4)

Since he was conducting the conversation in the manner of a philosopher, he did not conduct his criticism in an eristic fashion but [only] as far as to indicate certain faults of the speech; for he could have adduced many other [faults], but says: '*so you won't be upset*, I'll hold my tongue'.

170. *Although* [*it does seem to me that it contains*] *many examples,* [*by looking at which a person might profit*] (264E5–6)

He means faults and by [employing the device of] passing over [them] in silence (*parasiôpêsis*) he has hinted at the numberless faults of the speech.

By looking at which a person [*might profit*]: that is to say, a person might profit by looking at these examples and the [other] faults of Lysias' speech and not **(232)** using [them as examples]. And in fact the philosopher [*sc.* Plato] has taught us[119] another sophistic technique, not so that we may use it but so that we may guard against it. Doctors too are acquainted with noxious potions not so they may use them but so that they may guard against them. Lysias' speeches too help us, then, to not make use of them.[120]

171. *And* [*let's go*] *to the other* [*speeches*] (264E7)

One must draw examples from two sources, from faulty speeches, so that one may guard against them [*sc.* the bad examples], and from successful ones, so as to imitate them. So the philosopher, after talking about Lysias' faulty speech and showing that the speech is headless, disorderly, and unclear, wants to move on to his own discourse (*logos*), both the earlier and the later, and show how his own discourse, following the truth as a light, and knowing the nature of the things of which it was going to speak, handled each of the opposed speeches (*logos*), the one against love and the one in defence of love.

To *the other speeches*: he means those with truth.[121]

For there was in them ... something [*worth looking at for those who want to enquire about speeches*] (264E7-8): sc. [their] technique, and [the example they provide of] how one should write.

172. *They were opposed, I suppose* (265A2)

The two speeches were opposed, for the one said that one should not gratify a lover because a lover becomes the cause of great evils, the other the opposite, that one should gratify a lover and that great goods come from love.[122] So how can opposite things be said about the same thing unless one knows the nature of the thing that is being spoken of, as now in the case of love?[123]

173. *I thought you* [*were about to say*] *what is true,* [*that* [*it was*] *madly*] (265A5)

Because both of them said that love is some kind of madness; for Lysias said that one should not *gratify the lover* (235E7) because *the one is mad, the other* [sc. the non-lover] *of sound mind* (244A5), while Plato, used the same starting point, madness, and divided madness in two, calling the one [kind] human, the other divine.

And there are two kinds of madness (265A9), the one worse than human,[124] the other better, which [last] he has further (*kai*) cut up into four.

[*And the* [madness] *that comes about through a divine alteration*] *of customary ways* (265A10-11): for someone who is possessed by a god does not behave normally, for he is no longer his own [master] but is wholly devoted to the gods.

(233) 174. [*And a fourth* [inspiration] *as*] *Aphrodite's and Love's* (265B4-5)

Since Aphrodite is [an aspect] of beauty and Love leads [the way] up to the beautiful, on account of this Love belongs to Aphrodite and follows her, leading [the way] up to [both] sensible and intelligible beauty. We say, then, that love is a

25 divine madness that from a perception of perceptible beauties comes to a recollection of the beautiful-itself.

175. [*We said erotic madness is best*] *and, I don't know how*,[125] [*imaged*] *the erotic* [*passion*] (265B5–6)

When he said *it is like the combined power*, etc. (246A6 ff.), where he gave wings to the horses and the charioteer, imaging (*apeikazein*) erotic passion by way of a myth or fiction (*plasma*), and on account of the elevating power of Love represented (*apeikazein*) him with wings.   245,1

He says *I don't know how* because a person possessed by a god is swept along (*pherein*) as the god wills.

176. *Perhaps touching upon some truth* (265B6–7)

When we have discussed intelligible and divine things.   5

He may have said '*perhaps*' out of modesty; or else he has called [this] '*imaging*' [of his] something that is *perhaps* [the case] on account of all activity in our sphere being an image (*eikôn*) of that activity [there].[126]

177. *But perhaps being led astray in some other direction* (265B7–8)

Because even then [*sc.* in the myth][127] he mentioned the perversions of love.   10

Concocting [*a not entirely implausible story*] (265B8): he reveals the true account by means of this mythical fiction; that is to say, by telling about love and the soul through covert indications[128] (*huponoia*) and delivering the account by means of myths and riddles (*ainigma*), like the theologians when describing the [nature and activities] of the gods by means of myths.[129]

prosepaisamen (265C1) is equivalent to *epaixamen*, and [by it] he means 'we   15 have hymned'.[130]

He calls Love [their] *master* (*despotês*) (265C2) because someone who is possessed surrenders his whole self to the god as to a master.

178. *Guardian of beautiful boys* (265C1–2)

For Love is the guide (*hêgemôn*) of pure and newly initiated souls,[131] and through the *boys* he has indicated the purity of the souls.   20

179. *Well then, [let's take] this [feature] [of it: the way the discourse was able to move from censure to praise]* (265C5–6)

He wants to proceed to the counter-presentation (*antiparathesis*)[132] and to the **(234)** method of definition and division. Moreover, according to Aristotle[133] rhetoric is a counterpart (*antistrophos*) of dialectic, that is, is concerned with the same matters and co-ordinate [with it]: they have the same subject matter, employ proofs (*epikheirêma*) based on common opinion, are called arts (*dunamis*), and argue for (*eis*)[134] opposing [positions]. And the orator employs the method of dialectic and definition according to Plato too. For how can we move from censuring love to praising it without understanding the nature of what is being talked about?[135]

180. *It seems to me that the rest [really was done (paizein) in fun]* (265C8–9)

[He means that] what relates to Love has been adequately (*metriôs*) hymned (*paizein*) and celebrated (*humnein*).[136]

These [two particular types [of procedure]] (265C9): he means those of dialectic and definition.

Having, as it happens, been mentioned (265C9): just as he earlier ascribed his discourse to Pan, the Nymphs, and the Muses,[137] so too does he now refer his statement (*logos*) back to chance.

181. *[It would not be disagreeable if one could] grasp [their power] by means of art* (265D1)

So that one would, following the rules of [the] art (*tekhnikôs*), first divide in two[138] (for this division into two comes first) and say, [for example,] that of living creature one [kind] is rational, another not rational, and not say, [for example,] that one kind [is] a human being, one a dog, and one without feet, or [divide into] species and individuals, or into differentiae and species or the like; rather, one should take what is in front of one (*sunengus*) and employ the method of definition and division appropriately, for that is the way of someone with knowledge [of the art].

182. *[Perceiving all together the things that are scattered in many places to gather them] into one form* (265D3–4)

That is, to define the things that have been divided, for definitions are of species.

How one should gather (*agein*) *the things that are scattered in many places* into 15
one he explained earlier where he says '*proceeding from many perceptions* [*to a
unity*]', etc. (249B7 ff.), [thereby] making it clear to his readers what he is talking
about. And so he is also bringing a charge against Lysias relating to [his mode of]
expression, [namely,] that he has produced a lack of clarity in [his] speech, not
having said what he is talking about.

183. *Just as with the things* [we said] *recently* [about love] (265D5) 20

[That is,] as in the present example *about love*.
  Whether they were well or badly said (265D6): that is, whether we spoke to the
point or ineffectively, 'we did what the art demands and proceeded in accordance
with the art, thanks to which my discourse possessed *clarity and consistency* 25
(*homologoumenon*); for, after stating that **(235)** love is a [kind of] madness,
I divided madness into human and divine [madness] and, by assigning to each
what was appropriate [to it], made my discourse – both that of the counter-
presentation or rebuttal (*antigraphê*) and that of the palinode – clear'.[139]
  More allegorically (*theôrêtikôteron*), *well* applies to [the] right [kind of] love,
badly (265C6) to the licentious [kind]. 30

184. *The reverse,* [*to be able to cut* [things] *up*] *according to* [*their*] *forms* [*at the* 247,1
joints where it is natural [*to divide them*]] (265E1–2)

Having talked of the one type [of procedure], that of definition, because it is
necessary to gather the many into one and produce a definition, he [now] wants
to talk of [another], that of division, [that is,] the need to divide the one into
many, the genus into species, for instance, and to divide further, in accordance
with natural division, first into two, then into three or four, as the account 5
requires, cutting and dividing *at the joints* like a good butcher and not mangling
the parts like an unskilled (*aphuês*) butcher.

185. *The crazed part of the mind* (*dianoia*) (265E3–4)

He means [its] madness, but one person is called crazed in a manner that is
worse than soundness of mind, the one who suffers from (*ekhein*) the human 10
[kind of] madness, another in a manner that is better, the one who is possessed
by a god.

186. *And just as from one body [doubled and homonymous* [parts] *are engendered by nature]* (265E4–5)

Just as nature has divided living creature into two sectors (*diastêma*), creating some things on the right, some on the left, and each of the parts is called by the same names, for example 'eye' and 'eye', 'hand' and 'hand', except that one [is called] 'right', one 'left', in the same way, this derangement or madness being twofold, the one [kind] has inclined to the left, the other to the right. Plato had the support of the Pythagoreans when he understood the columns [of opposites] (*sustoikhia*)[140] in this way here.

The one [speech] *[cut off] the [part] to the left* (266A3–4): the one of rebuttal, the one [composed] after the fashion of Lysias' speech, [Lysias] whom he reviled when using (*legein*) [the terms] 'untrustworthy' (*apistos*) [and] 'unreliable' (*abebaios*), [words] he used of shameful love.[141]

The other [speech], *[having led us] to the parts [of madness] on the right* (266A6): he means the [speech] of recantation (*palinôidia*).

Homonymous [with it] (266A7): since both it and the other are love.

187. *I myself [am very much a lover] of these [divisions and collections, Phaedrus]* (266B3–4)

Having shown that someone who is going to say or write something must know the truth of the matter [and], then, that he must be someone who practises definition and division, none of which Lysias has done, he [now] goes on to sing the praise of dialectic, that is to say, of **(236)** division. He also does this in the *Philebus* (16C5 ff.) and in the *Republic*,[142] saying that division is a gift from the gods given to humans through Prometheus, and in the *Sophist* (235B1) likens it to a tool *that functions as a* [kind of] *net*. For it is not possible to have knowledge of things without division.

188. *[And if I think someone else able to give heed] to things that are one and to things that are many [by nature, I follow him 'from behind in his footsteps like a god's'.... I call those who can do this dialecticians]* (266B5–C1)

That is, 'I follow after a person who is able to understand the nature of things as [though he were] a god'.

He calls *dialecticians* not those who merely know the rational-forming principles (*logos*) [applying] in our sphere (*peri hêmas*),[143] but those who are able to divide the intelligible forms into many and collect them into one – that is, those who [can] distinguish each of the forms.

189. *But for now [tell us what we should call* [it]¹⁴⁴ *if we were to be instructed] by you and [Lysias]* (266C1–2)

Having completed [what he wanted to say] about the true rhetoric, he is about to launch into [an account of] the popular [kind] and what follows is an account (*historia*) of [rhetorical] terms and an enumeration of what are said to be the main aspects of rhetoric. But later (269C6 ff.), after this, he once more turns his attention to (*mimnêskesthai*) the genuine rhetoric, wanting to display the power of the true rhetoric from every point of view. So now he asks '*what should we call* rhetoric? Doesn't the whole art of rhetoric consist in showing [the various types of] introductions, [of] expositions, and [of] everything [else] that is listed?'¹⁴⁵

190. [*Or is this it, the art of* [making] *speeches employing which Thrasymachus and the rest have*] *themselves* [*become*] *clever* (*sophos*) [*at speaking and make others who are willing to bring them gifts as* [though they were] *kings* [clever] *too*] (266C2–5)

He calls them 'clever' either out of tact, or because they deal with speeches and have steered clear of the manual (*banausos*) crafts, or as being skilled in an art.

To bring gifts criticises their love of money, because they do not deliver their demonstration speeches for the benefit of the young or of the truth but for the sake of money.

191. *They are kingly men,* [*but certainly not knowledgeable about the things you are asking about. However you seem to me at least to be naming this kind* [of thing] *correctly in calling it dialectical. But it seems to me that the rhetorical is still escaping us.*] (266C6–9)

[*Kingly*] either because everyone else is all ears to hear the rhetoricians or because they influence and direct the people and the affairs of the city.¹⁴⁶

Certainly [*not*] *knowledgeable about the things you are asking about*: he means about dialectic.

This [*kind* [of thing]]:¹⁴⁷ 'the things mentioned', he is saying -[he means] definition, division, [and] the truth – 'are not characteristic of rhetoric but of dialectic [and] hence we have not said anything about rhetoric'.

249,1 **(237) 192.** [*What are you saying?*] *Could there be anything at all of value*, [*which, while wanting in these things, is nevertheless grasped by art?* [If so,] *it certainly must not be despised by you and me and we must certainly say what* [this] *remaining part of rhetoric is*] (266D1–4)

[That is:] 'And what is there *of value* (*kalos*) that can be grasped *by art while wanting in these things* [of which we] talked – [i.e.] truth, definitions, division?' Or, [more] charitably (*en êthei*): 'As it seems, this [thing], which although *wanting in* the things
5 we talked of is *nevertheless grasped by art*, is *of value*. So, since you say it is of value, it *must not be despised*, but we must test whether what you are saying is true and there can be an art that is achieved without the things [we] mentioned, and *we must say* whether there can be any art at all that is wanting in *these things*.'

193. *And* [*we must certainly say*] *what* [[this] *remaining part of rhetoric*] *is* (266D3–4)

10 Because he [sc. Phaedrus] has stated that what has been said applies to the dialectical and not at all to the rhetorical, he [sc. Socrates] therefore says: 'let us see just *what the remaining part of rhetoric* of which you speak *is*'.
    The sense of everything said in what follows is that introductions, expositions, proofs, and all the [other] rhetorical topics and the hunt for [appropriate] words,
15 are not an art but the preliminaries to art; art is the ordering of these and being able to use them appropriately. The art of rhetoric, then, is not the enumeration of [these] topics but the ability to use the topics well (*kalôs*) for a useful or helpful [purpose].

194. *You've done well to remind me.* [*The introduction* [comes] *first, I suppose, since it must be delivered at the start of the speech*] (266D7–8)

20 In what follows (*loipon*) he lists the aforementioned topics of the art. The *introduction* has the function of rendering the hearer attentive [and] with a completely clear picture of the matter [in hand], which Socrates did. Lysias, on the other hand, said nothing clear in his introductory remarks. Each of them,
25 then, employed (*lambanein*) an introduction, but made different use of it: Socrates used his introduction properly, clarifying the matter in hand, Lysias contrariwise.

195. *You mean, don't you,* [*these refinements* (*kompsa*) *of the art? ... Second* [comes] *an exposition of some kind and testimonies after that ... fourth,* *probabilities; and I believe that most excellent Daedalus of speeches, the man from Byzantium, mentions confirmation and additional confirmation ... But we are not bringing up Evenus of Paros, who first discovered insinuations and indirect praises – and some say he also composed indirect censures in verse for mnemonic purposes – for he was a clever man]* (266D8–267A5)

Socrates politely asks: 'You mean', he asks, '*these* persuasive [tools] (*pithana*) *of the art?*'

And testimonies after that: by testimonies he means[148] those called 'proofs [presented] without [rhetorical] art',[149] such as 'you murdered him, for you were near his freshly-murdered body' and the like. By *probabilities* he means persuasive [arguments]. By *confirmation and additional confirmation* he means to **(238)** add a second proof to a proof.

He says [that Theodorus is] a *Daedalus of speeches* (*logodaidalos*)[150] as being an artificer of speeches and a dialectician and able to do the same things as Zeno and prove that motionless things are in motion,[151] because Daedalus also made statues that virtually (*hôsper*) ran away and moved, for before him statues were closed up and did not have their feet apart but he first separated them.

He gives *indirect praises* so as not to praise directly but to seem to praise [nevertheless]; and likewise with censuring. Evenus was an admirable man (he also praises him elsewhere)[152] who also wrote the following iambic [line]: 'a child is either fear or grief to a father throughout [his] life'.[153] *For mnemonic purposes* because verses are easier to remember than things in prose.

196. *But [shall we let] Tisias [and Gorgias sleep?]* (267A6)

The saying 'from a bad crow (*korax*) a bad egg' is applied to this man and his pupil.[154] For this man, being a sophist, promised to instruct his pupil in such a way that he would win his first case – 'if you give me so many drachmas as a fee', he said. The pupil promised to. The first case he brought to court was on not paying the fees, making the judgement depend on a dilemma so that, winning or losing, he would pay nothing.[155] And the saying was [first] used in relation to this.

Of Gorgias it is said that he urged people to ask for whatever they liked, and when nobody ever asked [for anything], taking a leaf, he would say something to the leaf [and] then to Athena, and make a very long speech.[156]

[On once hearing this from me] Prodicus laughed [and said that he alone had discovered the art of [knowing] *what speeches are needed, and neither long ones nor short ones are required but those of moderate length]* (267B2–5): because

| 25 | Prodicus pioneered (*heuriskein*) precision in the [use of] words, [pointing out] for example the difference between 'delight' (*terpsis*), 'joy' (*khara*), and 'merriment' (*euphrosunê*), calling 'delight' **(239)** pleasure via the ears, 'joy' that of the soul,
| 251,1 | 'merriment' that through the eyes.¹⁵⁷ Accordingly, Prodicus said one should deck out one's discourse using such words and not recycle the same materials in long speeches but strike a due balance (*summetria*).

197. [*And what, again, should we say about Polus'*] *galleries of expressions* (logos) [– *diplasiology, gnomology, and eikonology, for example* – *and*] [the gallery] *of Licymnian words that* [Licymnius] *presented him with for the production of fine language* (euepeia)*?*] (267B10-C3)

| 5 | For this man, they say, pioneered [the use of] evenly balanced (*parisos*) [clauses]; hence he [*sc.* Socrates] has called [Polus' addresses] *galleries of words*¹⁵⁸ because he invariably (*panu*) seemed to ornament his speech with fine diction (*kallilexia*).

Diplasiology is saying the same things twice, 'alas, alas' for example.¹⁵⁹ *Gnomology* [is] as [when] Demosthenes writes 'for someone [who makes and prepares the means] by which I may be captured is at war with me',¹⁶⁰ and
| 10 | elsewhere, 'vice is a terrible thing',¹⁶¹ and the like. *Eikonology* is to present what is being said by means of a likeness or an illustration.¹⁶²

[*Gallery*] *of Licymnian words*: Licymnius taught Polus various ways of dividing words; for example which are proper names, which compound, which cognate, which adjectival – and many other things contributing to good writing (*euepia*).
| 15 | *Yes, a kind of straightforward language* (orthoepeia) (267C6): that is, ordinary diction, for Protagoras approached composition (*logos*) using (*dia*) ordinary words and not comparisons (*parabolê*) and epithets.¹⁶³

198. *Further,* [*the might* (sthenos) *of the Chalcedonian*¹⁶⁴ *seems to me to have mastered by art*] *piteous* [*speeches that are drawn to old age and poverty*] (267C7)

The man from Chalcedon, i.e. Thrasymachus, taught that one should excite pity
| 20 | in the juror and induce compassion <by calling to witness>¹⁶⁵ *old age, poverty, lamenting children, and the like.*¹⁶⁶

He says *might* either referring to the power of his speech or because he wrote in a speech of his something to the effect that the gods do not take heed of
| 252,1 | human affairs; for [otherwise] they would not overlook the greatest good [found] among human beings, justice; for we see that people do not practise this.¹⁶⁷

(240) 199. *As for the final part of speeches* (267D3)

He means the perorations, which *some* (267D4) call a *recapitulation*, others a summary. The purpose of perorations is to remind *the listeners* (267D6) by means of a brief summary *of what was said* in many words and at length.

200. [*Let us look at*] *these things under a* [*stronger*] *light* (268A1–2)

[That is,] 'finally, let us return to what has been said about august rhetoric [and ask] whether they really deserve to be assigned (*tattein*) to the art of speeches.'
  Let us look at [*these things*] *under a* [*stronger*] *light* means 'let us investigate what force they have'.

201. [*But you too* [should] *consider whether it also seems to you as it does to me that*] *there are gaps in their fabric* (268A5–6)

Fabric (*êtrion*)¹⁶⁸ [here] means a well-woven and loose-textured piece of cloth which, [although it] seems well-woven, to someone who looks at it closely has gaps and is loose-textured and not close-woven but soon torn. 'See too then', he says, 'whether these techniques (*theôrêma*) seem to belong to the art but in truth are void of art'. He is transferring the argument from externals to the soul, as though one were to say 'See whether *their* tiny souls (*psukharion*)¹⁶⁹ have *gaps* and have nothing firm or sound about them', so that he is calling [their] little souls a *fabric*.

202. *Tell me then* (268A8)

The¹⁷⁰ philosopher has already explained what the true rhetoric, or rhetoric in itself, is about, teaching that the speaker ought to know the truth of a matter so as to be able to persuade with plausible [arguments]; then [that] he ought to make use of division and definition so as to be able to deliver speeches (*logos*) on opposed [positions] and move from one opposed [position] to the other, understanding their differences and dissimilarities; and [that] he should also know the things they have in common (*koinônia*) so as to be able to define [them].
  After saying this, he asks Phaedrus whether this is rhetoric. He [*sc.* Phaedrus] says that he has not heard that rhetoric is this, but rather [that it is] what the writers on the art say it is, something that has introduction, exposition, and the other things he has listed. Upon hearing this the philosopher says, 'Let us see *whether it also seems to you as it does to me that* [*there are gaps in their fabric*]'

(268A5–6), that is to say, whether they have stated the truth of the matter or only achieved apparent conformity [to it]. Then, by three examples, **(241)** medicine, the art of poetry, and musical theory, he wants to refute what is being said and to show that introductions and summaries and all the [other] things he has listed are knowledge that constitutes a necessary preliminary to the art but are not the art of rhetoric itself.

203. *And to make another man a doctor*[171] (268B3–4)

Since the goal of every art is twofold – the one [sought after] outcome [of the medical art being] to bring about good health, the other to instruct another person and make him a doctor,[172] which [last] is something more valuable than [the practice of] the art, because even a layman can bring about good health, but only the doctor can teach [the art] – on account of this he mentions the twin goals of the art.

204. *What else but to ask [whether he also knew to which people and when he should do each of these things and to what extent?]* (268B6–8)

As though he were to say that it is not just possessing or knowing these things that [is the mark] of a doctor, but the use of medications in such a way that the medication is administered at the right time and is appropriate for the person to whom it is administered – for the same medication harms one person but makes another well – and, in a word, as the divine Hippocrates says, when the doctor carefully considers 'season, place, age, and maladies'[173] and does not dispense his remedies just anyhow but appropriately and to the right people and when and in the quantities required.

That the man is mad (268C2): for it is indeed madness to undertake things of which one has no knowledge.

Understanding nothing of the art (268C4): because the art knows [appropriate] times, [correct] measures, and the nature [of patients and diseases], and the like.

205. *What if [someone were to approach] Sophocles [or Euripides?]* (268C5)

He wants to give his second example [now].

And [that], *when he wanted to,* [he could compose] *piteous* [speeches] *or, on the other hand, fearsome ones* (268C7–8): for tragedies occupy themselves with such emotions.

[*If someone thinks tragedy is something other than*] *an arrangement* [*of these things that puts them together*] *in a manner appropriate to one another and to the whole* (268D3–5): that is, so that the work (*logos*) has a single weave and organisation. He also says something similar in the *Republic*: if someone were to say to the painter that one should apply the most beautiful colour, gold, to the most beautiful part of the body, i.e. the eye, the painter would say to him: 'You don't seem to understand painting. One shouldn't apply the most beautiful colour to the eye but the appropriate one'.[174]

(242) 206. *But they wouldn't,* [*I think, rebuke him*] *boorishly* … (268D6)

That is, they would rebuke (*loidorêseian*) [him] in a civilised manner (*dikaiôs*).[175]

But as a musician would (268D6–7). He is giving the third example, [namely,] that harmony is not tightening and loosening strings, but being able to employ the harmonies fittingly and being able to calm emotions at one time and arouse them at another. For musical practice is this: a theoretical and practical knowledge of the nature of what is harmoniously ordered with the assistance of the cosmos.[176]

207. *What* [*do we think*] *the mellifluous Adrastus* [*or Pericles would say?*] (269A5–6)

Just as he earlier set genuine practitioners of the art against the preliminaries to the arts of medicine, poetry, and harmonics, here too he contrasts (*epistan*) Adrastus and Pericles with those merely called orators (*rhêtôr*). For these were orators [though] not genuine ones of the kind Plato is talking about, but [practitioners] of the intermediate [kind of] rhetoric, who neither indulge (*therapeuein*) the passions of the people nor are of the kind Plato talks of, [the kind] who make speeches that accord with the truth and who make the citizens upright and good.[177]

208. [*One should not be harsh*] *but be understanding* … (269B5)

That is, show them forbearance, for according to Plato their offences are involuntary.[178]

209. … *if some people, having no knowledge of dialectic,* [*proved unable to define just what rhetoric is*] (269B5–7)

He again leads (*pherein*) the orators towards dialectic, for rhetoric is connected to dialectic; for dialectic itself[179] divides both things (*phusis*) and concepts (*logos*).

[*Putting* (*eipein*)] *each of these persuasively* (269C2–3) – i.e. in [the correct] order and in a balanced manner and as required – he leaves to his pupils, as being *no trouble* (269C3) and as though they can deliver them [appropriately] on their own, although they should actually be taught.

Speaking (*eipein*) *persuasively* (269C2–3) is impossible without [speaking] the truth.

210. *Well, Socrates* (269C6)

Because one must not only refute the [ideas] of others but **(243)** establish one's own, for this reason, having shown in what has been said that [merely] delivering introductions, expositions, proofs, and the like is not part of the rhetorical art (for these things are [only] preliminary to the art), but [that it is] using the aforesaid things in [the correct] order and as required [that constitutes the art], and having taken three examples in proof of this, first that of the doctor, when he said that it is not [the proper role] of a doctor to merely purge [patients] by the use of medications if it wasn't done at the right time, in the right quantity, to the right patients, and so on, and having next used the example of poetry and that of harmonics, he now explains just what the nature (*eidos*) of rhetoric is. Hence Phaedrus [now] says: '*It is likely that* the type (*eidos*) of rhetoric [current] among contemporary speakers *is such* as you indicate. So since what you say is *true*, [namely,] that they have taught the techniques (*theôrêma*) that are preliminary to rhetoric but have not taught what the art [itself] is, tell us just what the art *of the orator* is'.[180]

211. *As for being able* [[to acquire the art] *and thus becoming an accomplished performer,*] *Phaedrus,* [*it is likely, and perhaps even necessary, that it is as with other things*] (269D2–3)

Since Phaedrus has said that the art of the orator consists in making speeches, because of this the philosopher advances the view that 'making you *capable* (*dunasthai*) of delivering speeches is [the role] of a gifted nature and not so much of a studious (*epistêmôn*) one', and he takes three things that are linked together in every art and science, [an appropriate] *nature, knowledge, and practice* (269D5). Unless the three coincide, a person cannot excel in the art. Why is there need of [the appropriate] nature? Because if your nature works against you, it's all in vain. But what if someone should have the [necessary] nature but not the *knowledge*? Is it not clear that, lacking knowledge, he would employ his natural abilities (*phusis*) haphazardly, falling into error and not knowing what he was composing or saying? And even should these last [two] come together, there will be need of practice so he won't lose what he has learned through negligence and laziness.

Perhaps even necessary: by adding *necessary* he has corrected *likely*. 30

As with other things: that is, just as with every [other] art and science there is need of these three things for the outcome to be first rate, so too is it in the case of rhetoric.

212. *But as regards as much of it as is art*, [*it seems to me that the way* (methodos) 256,1 *appears not to be the one Lysias and Thrasymachus follow*] (269D6–8)

'It is [now] my task to teach what is the art of the orator and what its nature ought to be and how one can make speeches in accordance with the art [and] not as Lysias or Thrasymachus do.'

Well which way [*then*]? (269D9): [That is, which way should] this enquiry [lead]?

(244) 213. [*It is fair to say that Pericles was*] *most accomplished of all* [*in the art of* 5 *rhetoric*] (269E1–2)

He means among the other popular orators (*dêmagôgos*).

All great sciences (269E4): because, he says, Pericles took up philosophy, he became high-minded, having joined with Anaxagoras,[181] who had set mind over the entire cosmos while everyone else called airs and suchlike the causes of the 10 creation of the cosmos (*kosmopoiia*).

'Subtle thinkers' (*adoleskhês*) [is what] the ancients used to call those who occupied themselves (*diatribein*) with astronomical and atmospheric phenomena (*ta meteôra*).[182] See how he elevates rhetoric, as being a great (*megalos*) art, to the level of the gods; for a speaker should speak (*rhêtoreuein*) as befits the situation and so ought both to know the truth and to study the splendour (*megaleion*) of the cosmos; for he considers the whole world as nothing.[183] He also said 15 something similar in the *Alcibiades* when he said:[184] 'rule [over] all of Greece or [over] the non-Greek (*barbaros*) peoples of Europe seems as nothing to you' and the like.

214. [*All great sciences have need of subtlety (adoleskhia) and lofty speculation (meteôrologia) about nature;] for [that] high-mindedness [and general effectiveness seems to come from some such source]*(269E4–270A3)

Despising things here [on earth] and considering speeches of great moment go hand in hand (*artan*) with this subtlety.

[*And having arrived at* [an understanding] *of the nature] of mind and lack of mind* (270A5–6):[185] for he ascribed everything that is well-crafted (*dêmiourgein*) to mind, and those crafted otherwise to matter, [and] so[186] is describing matter and what has been brought about by necessity as 'lack of mind'.[187] [Or] rather he [*sc.* Plato] means this: '*having arrived at* the investigation of intelligible and material things'.

215. *The same goes, I suppose, [for the art of medicine as for* [the art] *of rhetoric]* (270B1–2)

He compares rhetoric with medicine and says that the former deals with the body,[188] the latter with the soul, and just as the doctor must consider the bodies [that are framed] from the whole elements, [determining] whether the body is simple or composite and from which [elements] and how much [of each it consists] – in the *Timaeus* the philosopher says[189] that the young gods, borrowing from the All, framed our components (*morion*), taking a portion (*meros*) from the whole of fire and of air and of the other [elements], and so someone who considers body in the best way must go back to the wholes and the first principles; for knowledge comes from first principles – so too must one consider in the case of soul first whether it is simple (*monoeidês*) or tripartite, and if it is tripartite, divide the parts of the soul, and then, dividing the parts of speeches, fit[190] them to each [of the parts of the soul]. For one must also know the distinctive characteristics of souls; for the characteristics of Thracians are of one kind, those of Laconians of another, those of Athenians of [yet] another,[191] and one must adapt one's speeches to each.

(245) 216. [*Do you think it is possible to understand] the nature of the soul [in a worthwhile fashion without* [understanding] *the nature of the whole?*] (270C1–2)

He says that it is impossible to know parts (*merika*) without having studied and gained full knowledge (*kataginôskein*) of the wholes. Accordingly Socrates' discourse mounts up to the wholes.

217. *Certainly if [one is to give any credence] to Hippocrates the Asclepiad, nor [is it possible to understand] about the body without [following] this procedure]* (270C3–5)

Observe how he praises Hippocrates for saying that it is not only impossible to study [particular] aspects of soul without studying soul as a whole, but [similarly impossible to study particular] aspects of body [by themselves].[192]

218. *Yes, he does well to say it, my friend* (270C6)

That is,] that it is impossible to study the parts proficiently without having studied the wholes.

  But in addition to Hippocrates, we must [examine [his] account and see whether it is in accord [with the facts]] (270C6–7):[193] that is, one must not be satisfied with the generally accepted belief, but advance a convincing argument, not just stating that Hippocrates said [this], but adding his reasons (*dia ti*) for talking in this way.

219. *Well then, on the subject of nature* [*consider just what Hippocrates and the true argument say*] (270C9–10)

He[194] brings together the aphorism of Hippocrates and the true account, or [the rule] that if you want to study anything, it is necessary to employ the method of division; for instance [you might ask] whether the body is simple or complex, and say that if it is simple, this or that is applicable (*harmozein*) to it and it is its nature to be acted on (*pathein*) by some things and to act on others (for which reason Hippocrates, wanting to show that it is not simple, said 'if body were a unity (*hen*), it would not suffer pain'),[195] while if it is complex, [say] of how many things it is composed and of what kind – [i.e.] that it is [composed] of four elements: hot, cold, dry, and moist.

  And '*having enumerated these*' (270D5–6):[196] *as*[197] he says a thing does or has done [to it] by [other] things *in the case of a single thing* (*hen*), thus does each of these [sc. the parts of a complex thing] also, one supposes, *of its nature do* (270D6–7) *and have done to it by something* [else].

220. *But, assuredly, [the person who approaches anything with art] should not be likened [to a blind or deaf person]* (270E1–2)

But the person who approaches things *with art* and knowledge *should not be likened to a blind person* but to an enlightened (*phôteinos*) and intellective (*noeros*) man.[198]

76   Hermias: On Plato Phaedrus 257C-279C

221. *Rather, it is clear that should someone [impart* [the skill of making] *speeches] to someone else [with art, he will precisely indicate the essence of the nature of the thing to which* [that person] *will be applying the speeches. And this will I assume be the soul]* (270E2–5)

It is clear that the case of the soul is analogous: just as the person who administers medications to the body understands the nature of the body, so too must someone who is going to deliver speeches to the soul as medications investigate
10   the nature of the soul, [asking] whether it is **(246)** simple or complex, and if it is complex, of what kind and how many parts it is composed, [namely,] that it is [composed] of three [parts], the rational, the spirited, and the appetitive, and [discover] by what kinds of speeches the rational [part] is gladdened, [namely,] by thoughtful (*theôrêtikos*)[199] ones – and the appetitive [part] by those such as [itself] – and so on.
   With art (*tekhnêi*): [is equivalent to] through art (*dia tekhnês*).

222. *And this will I assume be the soul* (270E4–5)

15   As the body to which [the doctor] administered (*prospherein*) medications was in the case of medicine there [in that earlier passage], even so is the soul to which [the speaker] *will be applying* (*prospherein*) *speeches* (270E4) in rhetoric. Therefore his whole *effort* is aimed at planting *belief* (271A1–2) in the soul, as [it was at engendering] health in the body there; so, just as [a doctor] does not engender health without administering every [medication] appropriately,
20   neither does [a speaker] engender belief without having employed speeches fittingly.

223. *It is clear, then, that* [*Thrasymachus, and anyone else who imparts the art of rhetoric in a serious manner ... will make* [his pupils] *see whether the soul is by nature one and uniform or, like the shape of the body, multiform*] (271A4–7)

It is *clear, then, that* someone who has taught the *art of rhetoric* examines the nature (*eidos*) of the soul, [asking] *whether* it is simple or complex and *multiform*
25   like the nature of the body. For to know *whether* [it] is simple or complex or the like, this is to know the nature of the thing being investigated.
   Imparts (*didonai*) stands for teaches (*paradidonai*).

224. *And, second,* [[he will make them see] *by virtue of which* [of its forms] *it naturally does what or suffers what at the hands of what*] (271A10-11)

Just as he considered in the case of the body what things it is affected by and what it acts on, so too is it necessary to consider in the case of soul by which things it is affected and by which it isn't.

225. *And, third,* [*having classified the* [various] *kinds of speeches and of souls and the ways the latter are affected, he goes through all the causes* [of this], *joining each* [kind of speech] *to each* [kind of soul]] (271B1–3)

[That is to say,] after classifying and distinguishing the parts of soul and its [various] types, [showing] that it has, for instance, an imaginative part, a spirited one, an appetitive one, and so on, and the types of speeches likewise, [showing] that some are demonstrative, some judicial, some panegyrical, and so on, to then join like to like. For instance, the ruler who is guided (*hepesthai*) by valid argument (*logos*) is guided by demonstrative speeches and takes pleasure [in that], while the person who lives [a life] governed by appetite takes pleasure in sycophantic and panegyrical speeches.

226. *Indeed, my friend, in no* [*other way will anything,* [whether] *it is being* [written] *for display* (*endeiknunai*) *or delivered orally, ever be spoken or written with art, neither anything else nor this*] (271B7–C1)

[That is,] displayed in no other way is it art;[200] [and] therefore, [to be] in accordance with art, one must proceed in this way **(247)**.

And knowing [*perfectly well*] *about the soul hide* [*their knowledge*] (271C2–3): he is putting this – i.e, 'knowing nothing about the soul, they say nothing' – politely.[201]

To give the actual words [*is not easy*] (271C6): because it is the role of the philosopher to provide the frameworks (*tupos*), not to go into the details. He says something similar in the *Republic*,[202] [namely that] the citizens should acquire [musical] modes (*harmonia*) for the sake of [their] virtue is for the philosopher to state and to know; [just] which modes and the musical detail – that [it should be] Phrygian, say, or Lydian, and so on – is for the musician to know. So he is saying here: 'It is not our [task] to give the details; providing frameworks and recounting the varieties (*eidos*) of soul and of speeches is our [task]'.

227. [*To give the actual words is*] *is not easy* (271C6)

That is, 'I can't give [them] offhand'; for he did not say it was impossible.

... *but* [*I want to say*] *how one must write* (271C6–8): that is, we shall teach the principles (*theôrêma*) of the art, but not the details; for instance, *it is not easy* for us *to say* how many types of speeches there are, and that one kind is plain, another grand, and so on.

228. *Since the power of speech is* [*a leading of the soul*] (271C10)

He wants, one might say, to impart what he has to say by means of (*epi*) an example, for having [earlier] drawn an analogy between medicine and rhetoric and said that just as the former is concerned with bodies, the latter is concerned with soul, and the rest of what he said [there], he now talks about (*hupo*) one [of them], calling the ability to lead and persuade the soul '*a leading of the soul*' (*psukhagôgia*).[203]

As regards *the soul,* [*someone who is going to be a skilled speaker must*] *at least then* (*goun*)[204] [*know*] *how many forms it has* (271D1–2): it is incumbent on [him] to know the nature of the soul and the parts of the soul – that it is tripartite, and that, if one divides it into [its] large parts, they are these: rational, spirited, and appetitive.

229. *Hence some* [*people*] *are of such and such a kind,* [*others of such and such*] (271D3)

Because those who are guided (*akolouthein*) by reason (*logos*) take pleasure in demonstrative speeches, those who are guided by their spirited part in macho speeches and in winning, those in the grasp of [their] appetitive part in pleasantness and in soothing speeches.

230. *The number of* [*kinds*] *of speeches is in turn such and such,* [*each* [*form*] *being of such and such a kind*] (271D4–5)

Because among speeches some are demonstrative, some sophistic, or (*êgoun*) some grand, some plain, and so on.

And *for this reason* (271D6): so that there should not be just trial and error (*peira*) but art as well. For trial and error [comes] first, then experience, then, when one is also able to understand the reason, **(248)** art emerges.[205]

[*Easy to persuade*] into [acts][206] *of this or that kind* (271D6): that is to say, actions (*pragmata*).

231. *He must,* [*after having adequately apprehended*] *these things* … (271D7)

What things does he mean? The things he is referring to are about seven in number. First is to know what is true and what false. Then comes division. After that definition. Then the foundation (*hupokeimenon*) (that is, to understand the nature of soul, [namely] whether it is simple or complex). After that to understand the [various] kinds of speeches. Then to know which kinds of speeches suit which parts and which dispositions (*êthos*) of soul. And, finally, to know the right time [to apply this knowledge].

Hence *he must, after having adequately apprehended these things* and having distinguished [them] on his own, or, rather, with his teacher, recognise them in his work and in practice.

[*Be able to*] *swiftly* [*follow up (epakolouthein)*] *his perception* (271E1): [that is, see] that it was this or that we were writing speeches about[207] in [our] books.

Or [it must be the case that he has] *as yet* [come] *to know nothing more* (271E1–2) [than what he got from his teacher]: that is, since he has not put [them] to the test, these things [only extend] as far as words with him, and he will have heard them in vain if he does not employ them appropriately in practice (*pragma*).

Being with (271E2): 'his teacher' is omitted.

Swiftly [*follow up*] *his perception*: he means (*boulesthai*) to report in a somehow discursive manner from perception as from a messenger.[208]

232. *Whoever is present* (271E3)

[That is,] in court or the popular assembly (*dêmos*). Thus, acquainted with each of the [seven topics] listed [earlier] and with the nature of the soul of the listeners and of speeches, he then, at the appropriate time, employs the topics, on one occasion speaking piteously, on another using indignation, and [and on others] all the other [types of speech, delivering them] at the required time, to the required people, and in the required quantity.[209]

233. *The person who is not persuaded wins* [the argument] (*kratein*) (272B2)

[That is,] the person who, like me, *is not persuaded* that [rhetoric] is an art by those who, contrary to what has been said (*ta eirêmena*) [by us], claim that rhetoric is an art *wins* [the argument]; for unless it has all the features described above (*ta eirêmena*), it is not an art but an inartistic routine (*tribê*).

234. *For this reason [we must, turning all the arguments upside down, consider whether an easier and shorter road to this art comes to light anywhere]* (272B7-C1)

Since he has seemed to have talked at some length when explaining the things he said earlier, for this reason he says that if someone can get across what he said in fewer words and more concisely it would be a good thing; but if it cannot be done in any other way, one should take, and not depart from, the longer road.

For this reason: that is, for the sake of truth and accuracy it is necessary to turn all the arguments about and investigate whether it is possible to reach the same goal through shorter and fewer arguments; for concision is a virtue of discourse.[210]

(249) 235. *As for trying, [I might]* (272C5)

He[211] wants to come to the plausible and to that popular rhetoric that proceeds by trial and error and experiment without [any] art – at any rate, he says *So do you want me to tell* [you about] *a statement (logos)* [*I heard from some of those concerned with such matters*]? (272C7-8) – for one must not only develop one's own theories but investigate those of others, in order that one may come to know the truth through a comparison of opposed [positions]; for [it is one and] the same science [that] is able to understand [each of a pair of] opposites. So, having set out the features of the true rhetoric, [telling us] how many there are and what their nature is, he also wants to describe the popular rhetoric, or the opposite of the genuine rhetoric, [the rhetoric] which one should call a mere routine, which states that one need not know the truth but [only] what is plausible, not what appears to be the truth (which is what the philosopher states) but what seems to be the case to the many, which is often the very opposite of the truth.

236. [*Well, it is said, Phaedrus, that it is right*] *to also give the wolf's* [side of the story] (272C10-11)

There is a proverb that says that a wolf that has seen shepherds, or perhaps [their] dogs, eating a sheep, says 'If I had been doing this, what a great uproar there would have been'.²¹² So, since he has spoken about the true rhetoric at some length, for this reason he has brought up the proverb, because the champions of the popular rhetoric would have criticised the amount that has been said [on the subject]. 'If we had spoken at such length', [they would have said], 'what an uproar there would have been among the philosophers'.

237. *Well, they say there is no* [*need to take these things so seriously*] (272D2)

Here he gives an account of the plausible, not of what appears to be the truth, but of what seems to be the case to the masses, the account that Polus and Gorgias and the other rhetoricians would give.

[*They say*] *there is* [*no*] *need to take these things* [*so*] *seriously*: for nobody took rhetoric as seriously and exalted it as highly as Plato himself did,²¹³ saying that it must know the truth and the natures of souls [and] of speeches and the other things he spoke of.

238. *Taking the long way round* (272D3)

[i.e.] going round in a circle.

[*Or for that matter about men*] *who are* [just and good] *by nature or by nurture* (272D5-6): because *someone who* **(250)** *sets out* (*mellein*) *to be an orator* (272D6-7) need not be educated in scientific reasoning (*logoi*) or be truthful by nature.

[*In the courts nobody*] *has* [*any*] *concern for the truth* [*of these matters but only for plausibility*] (272D7-E1): in saying this he is scoffing at such rhetoric, if they really do not concern themselves²¹⁴ (*periergazesthai*) with the truth but [only] with what seems to be the case to the many.

The probable (272E1): [that is,] what seems to be the case to the many, or what is generally accepted (*endoxos*), as Aristotle puts it.²¹⁵

239. *And, moreover,* [*sometimes one should*] *not* [*say*] *what* [actually] *happened* (272E2)

That is, one must *sometimes* hide the truth of what was done, *if it is not probable* (*eikotôs*)²¹⁶ *that it was done* (272E3) and would not seem to be the case to the many, and not speak the truth.

And in any circumstance in which one speaks [*the probable must, of course, be pursued*] (272E4-5): that is, at every turn saying what seems to be the case to the many.

263,1 **240. *The probable must, of course, be pursued* (272E4)**

And so, even if [something] is false, but seems to be the case to the many, admit nothing and have no concern for the truth.

For if this [is in evidence] *throughout the entire* [speech, *it furnishes the whole of the art*] (272E5–273A1): that is, what is inferred from probabilities (*eikos*), not
5 what is true, furnishes and provides us with the art; for he has recalled that he has already spoken briefly about the probable (*eikos*)[217] and the plausible (*pithanos*). But he does not mean that kind of probability – the kind that seems to be the case to the many – but the kind that seems like (*eoikôs*) the truth. [For them,] of [all] the aspects of popular rhetoric, *probability* is the most important part of the art, as they say themselves.

241. *Well,* [*you've trampled all over*] *Tisias himself at least* (273A6)

10 That is, you have shown that Tisias is of no account.[218]

242. *So let* [*Tisias*] *tell* [*us this too: whether he says that the probable is anything other than what seems to the many to be the case.*] (273A7–B1)

He wants to show [what] *the probable*, or the plausible, [is] for (*para*) the many.

Having, as it seems, [*found*] *this of all things* (*dê*) [both *wise and part of the art*] (273B3):[219] he wants to take an example of [what] the probable [is] among the
15 rhetoricians, showing by this itself just what sort of thing the plausible is in practice for them; and Tisias takes two men, one of them weak and manly, the other *strong and cowardly* (273B4–5), considering each one [both] from the point of view of his body and from the point of view of his spirit (*psukhê*); for he took one as weak in body but courageous and bold in spirit, the other, conversely,
20 as *strong* (273B4) of body but cowardly of spirit. And he says that if the *weak* (273B4) and bold man had taken **(251)** the *cloak* (273B5) of the strong and cowardly one and was brought *before the court* (273B5–6), neither the man brought [to court] nor the man bringing him, i.e. neither of them, will tell the *truth* (273B6), but both will lie, the latter saying that he was robbed of his garment after being beaten up by a number of men, [thereby] concealing the cowardice of
25 his spirit, and the former, not displaying the audaciousness of his spirit but saying: 'Being weak, I would not have been able to get the better of him'. And so each of them hides the truth.

243. [*Tisias,*] *or whoever else* [*it might have been*] (273C8)

He perhaps said this on account of Korax, since Korax was said to be a pupil of Tisias.[220]

244. *But, my friend,* [*should we or shouldn't we say to him* ...] (273C9)   264,1

He says this: 'We earlier said that the probable is that which is like the truth, not just that which seems to be the case to the many'.
    That, Tisias (273D2): he repeats what he said about the true rhetoric, [saying] that it was earlier stated just what sort of thing *the probable* (*eikos*) (273D3) ought   5 to be, that it [should be] what resembles and is very like the truth and not what seems to be the case to the many. And he briefly summarises the rest of what he said about the true rhetoric, [namely,] that this *probability* (*eikos*),[221] by being like (*eoikenai*) the truth, convinces souls and the many thanks to its similarity to the truth,[222] so that someone who knows the truth knows *the probability*.   10

245. *That unless one* [*makes a count of the natures of those who will be hearing one's speech*] (273D8–E1)

If he does not speak in agreement with what *we outlined* earlier but in opposition to those observations, *we* shall not *give credence* to him.[223]
    Without much diligent study (273E4–5): for the gods bring about good things for us through [our own] efforts, and one cannot acquire virtue other than   15 through [those] efforts. So the gods prescribe (*hupotithesthai*) for us the struggles that are involved in being able to acquire good things, and Hesiod says, 'but [the immortals] have placed sweat on the path to[224] virtue'.

246. [*Which task a sensible man should not undertake for the sake of*] *speaking and acting* [*in the human sphere*] (273E5–6)

He has done well to add '*acting*' (*prattein*) so that it will not appear that rhetoric   20 consists in words (*logos*) alone but in action too; for one must not only please listeners but make them noble and good [as well]. Therefore, having already taught [us] the art of [producing] speeches in what has gone before, he now teaches [us] their end. And what is their end? *To speak* and to write *things that are pleasing to the gods* (273E7) [that is,] hymns, dances (*enorkhêma*),[225] and the   25 like.

(252) He says *not for the sake of speaking* because rhetoricians practise rhetoric for the sake of the spoken word and saying or doing (*prattein*) things that are pleasing and pleasurable and worthy of praise in the eyes of men. But one should be aware that someone who is doing things that are pleasing to human beings is not performing acts that are pleasing to the gods, but, conversely, someone who is doing things that are pleasing to the gods is also doing them for human beings; for the worse [element] follows one who hymns the divine, or [,that is,] the better [element].[226]

Men wiser than us [*say*] (273E9): for example, the Pythagoreans. For Polus in the *Gorgias* openly says that there is no need for the orator to know the truth.[227] Socrates adequately rebuts him [there], and so what seems the case to Socrates [also] seems so to the wise, but the opposite [seems to be the case] to those in the camp of Polus.

247. [*A sensible man*] *should* [*not think about gratifying his*] *fellow slaves* ... (273E9–274A1)

Because the gods are masters of us all, he says that one should not be gratifying men.

... *except* (*hoti mê*) *as a secondary activity* (274A1) is equivalent to 'unless (*ei mê*) *as a secondary activity*',[228] (i.e. incidentally); for the priority is to gratify the gods, and it is incidental that those who say things that have gratified the gods also say things that have gratified human beings.

248. *And so, if the way around is long* (274A2)

[That is,] the road of the true rhetoric.

[*For one must travel around it*] *for the sake of great things* (274A3): you see that he has elevated the end of rhetoric to [the level of] the gods, 'for one must', he has said, 'do *things that are gratifying to the gods* (273E7) and not say or *do* (273E8) just anything and not gratify human beings, unless as a secondary activity.

249. *Through those things* (274A5)

That is, through the gods;[229] for when the enjoyment of what is said and done is on the part of the gods, then all goes smoothly[230] with us.

250. *But surely in the case of someone who attempts* [*fine things it is even a fine thing to suffer anything he may happen to suffer*] (274A8–B1)

That is, to attempt all that is fine (*kalos*), and to bear with whatever god may assign [to us] in a noble manner. The attempt, then, at fine actions is to be praised, even if a person is doomed to fail or suffer something, whatever it may be, on account of that very [attempt].

(253) 251. *So,* [*let that be enough on the subject*] *of art* [*or the want of art in speech-writing*] (274B3–4)

266,1

The method he has taught us is 'an art'; the one promulgated by (*kata*) Lysias and the other rhetoricians is a 'want of art'.

252. [*What is left is*] *the matter of propriety* [*and impropriety in writing*] (274B6–7)

From this point he discourses on the propriety or impropriety of writing and when one should write. Thus he says: 'When one speaks with knowledge, knowing the truth and the facts (*pragmata*), and in addition to this for the sake of teaching another, and, further, in order to use the writing as a pastime and not as something very desirable [for its own sake], [only] then is writing a good thing.'

5

253. *So do you know how you will most* [*please god in the matter of discourse, whether acting* (prattein) *or speaking?*] (274B9)

10

For writing[231] with propriety is this: saying things that are pleasing to the gods;[232] for since they have gifted us with speech (*logos*) itself, one should raise propriety of speech to [the level of] the gods and use this instrument for the contemplation of them.

254. *I can recount a tradition* [*of our forefathers*] (274C1)

15

When Socrates asked Phaedrus '*Do you know* how *to speak* to achieve [results that are] gratifying to the gods?' (274B9–10), he says '*Not at all. If you* know, tell *me*' (274B11). Then the philosopher said '*I can recount a tradition* [*of our forefathers*]' (274C1). For it was, very prudently (*eugnômonôs*),[233] Socrates' custom to ascribe (*anapherein*) things originating with himself to the gods or to men who were attendants of the gods, and in fact he did not think it inappropriate to call holy (*theios*) men 'gods' in the *Sophist*.[234] And indeed wise and holy men

20

are gods as compared to [the run of] men. It is his custom, then, to frequently attribute his writings to holy men,[235] in the †*Phaedrus* to Pythagoras†,[236] in the *Charmides* to a certain wise man [named] Zamolxis; and in the *Timaeus* he attributes the account (*logos*) of Atlantis to the Egyptians.[237] Here too, then, he attributes invention relating to languages (*logos*) to Lord Hermes, not in this case to wise men but to gods, and says that Lord Hermes, along with many other [innovations], introduced the art of writing (*grammata*).

267,1 **(254) 255. But if we could discover this by ourselves, [would the notions of human beings any longer be of any concern to us?]** (274C2–3)

If we must write things that are pleasing to the gods, in what way will human beings be any longer of concern to us? For someone who pleases the gods and has been elevated [to that level] disdains the whole of human nature. He said this because most writers do this [*sc.* write] in order to be marvelled at or praised, or in order to please people (*tines*), writing things that give pleasure, in order to leave behind a reminder of themselves, not out of a desire to please the gods.

256. Well, I heard that in the region of Naucratis [in Egypt there was one of the old gods of that [country]] (274C5–6)

The myth is clear, but we shall comment on the matters investigated from the viewpoint of the literal meanings[238] (*rhêton*) and part by part.

He says *I heard* either because it is his custom to attribute his own words (*logos*) to others or indicating by it the ancient and everlasting [nature of the story].

One of the old gods: that is, one of the first gods, [one] of the highest, and more senior (*hêgemonikos*), and higher ranking; for among the gods and daemons and heroes too there are ranks of the primary, the secondary, the tertiary, and the lowest.

He attributes the invention of languages, then, to Lord Hermes,[239] and to the Egyptians; for he everywhere, including in the *Timaeus*,[240] reveres the Egyptians as ancient on account of Egypt never having been decimated by flood or fire while all other states were so decimated. Because of this, inventions among the Egyptians are undying, and the things the Greeks attribute to Palamedes or Prometheus, the philosopher attributes to Egypt and to Hermes, the presiding god of languages.

257. [*To whom* [belongs]] *the sacred bird* [*they call the Ibis*] (274C6–7)

Since it has kinship (*oikeiotês*) to its related (*oikeios*) god, for the gods convey their own specific (*oikeios*) activities down to [their] lowest forms;[241] for[242] it has a heart-like shape, and the heart is a principle of the living creature.[243] [And] then the tips of its wings are black, its other parts white, [this] description (*logos*) indicating that from within the truth is clear but from without concealed; for thoughts (*logos*) are hidden through outside factors, but, from within, unfolded, they reveal divine images,[244] as Alcibiades used to say of Socrates in the *Symposium*.[245] [And] then too its steps from foot to foot are symmetrical.[246] And, most important, it delivers its egg through its mouth,[247] and the uttered (*prophorikos*) word, which is our offspring, is brought forth (*propherein*) through the mouth.

(255) 258. *The name of the daemon himself* [*is Theuth*] (274C7)

You should know that there are angels and daemons and heroes and humans akin (*oikeioun*) to each god. So since it was necessary for the invention of the god Hermes to come to humans through some intermediary (for divinities do not approach humans without an intermediary (*amesôs*)), and the daemonic nature is what is in between, because of this he has alluded to the daemon Theuth carrying out the distribution of the inventions [of the god Theuth] to us lower [ranking beings]; for every distribution [of benefits] to us is made via the daemonic [order], for Theuth [is what] he calls Hermes.[248]

259. *Now this* [god] *was the first* [*to discover*] *number* [*and calculation, and geometry and astronomy, and draughts and dice too, and above all writing* (*grammata*)] (274C8–D2)

What is being said is this: that Hermes himself, the god of calculation (*logikos*), invented every art and every invention involving calculation (*logikos*).[249]

Number is first, since the arithmetical entity is an incorporeal thing which ranges over the intelligible and the sensibles and through all things. Then, after number, he has added calculation, which is observed in a relationship between numbers, for number is as simple as [anything] could be, but calculation displays a relationship of number to number while still being an incorporeal thing itself. Then, after these, he mentions *geometry and astronomy*, which are located (*tattein*) in extension and continuity, and remaining and standing still, and, finally, in bodies. Next, finally really coming down to the [sphere of] sensible things, he has listed *draughts and dice*, which are given as a joke, although they too are useful and able to divert us from other desires, by involving (*tattein*) the non-rational [side of us] in rational education. This education[250] is twofold, one [kind] imparted for the sake of dice, the other for the sake of draughts. And in them there is also need of luck, while the earlier ones (*ekeinos*) possess the stability and fixedness of sciences (*mathêma*). He has mentioned *writing* last because images are the final [forms] of the soul's thoughts.

(256) 260. *Now [at that time Thamus was] king [of the whole of Egypt ... and [the Greeks call] Thamus Ammon]* (274D2-4)

The myth for its part (*to men*) is clear, but (*de*)[251] he wants to elevate Lord Hermes to a higher and more kingly power, for there is rank among the gods too, and inferior things are perfected by being elevated to higher powers. What Zeus is among the Greeks, [namely,] 'creator of the entire perceptible cosmos', this[252] is what Ammon is called among the Egyptians, bringing [as he does] all things from obscurity to visibility.[253]

261. [*Coming to him* [sc. to Thamus]] *he revealed* [his] *arts* (274D5)

By this he both shows the freedom from envy[254] and the unstinting giving of divine activity and teaches that the invention of letters[255] (*logoi*) ought not to rest with the inventor but [one] should, without envy, share it with everyone.

262. *And he asked what* [*benefit each would provide*] (274D6-7)

He teaches that one should not precipitously accept or reject a thing before learning the benefit [to be gained] from it and [its] usefulness.

263. [*As he* [sc. Theuth] *went through them, he* [sc. Thamus] *criticised or praised*] *whatever* [*he seemed to be getting*] *right or wrong* (274D7-E1)

As being a discerning (*kritikos*) god, he finds fault with some things and praises others, for invention is [the task] of one person, judgement of another. For judgement is superior to invention, since invention is a matter of merely natural intuition, whereas judgement involves a certain rational and intellectual activity.

For example, the shipbuilder makes the rudder, but the steersman judges it, and the bridle maker makes the bridle, but the horseman judges it.[256] In this way the [activities] of (*ta para*) the lower ranking and particular gods are referred (*anapherein*), in unitary mode, to the higher gods. Accordingly [both] the invention and the judgement are referred to Lord Ammon in unitary mode, while, in divided mode, the judgement is referred to Thamus, as being of a higher rank [than Hermes], and the invention to Hermes.[257]

264. *But this [knowledge], King, [said Theuth, will make the Egyptians wiser and improve their memories]* (274E4–6)

He delivers an encomium of writing.
 One person is able to beget [the [constituents] *of an art]* (274E7–8): that is, to beget is one thing, to judge another, for the ability to judge (*to kritikon*) is of a higher order.

265. *And now you, being the father [of writing]* (274E9–275A1)

Because fathers normally love their own children even if they are bad, **(257)** on account of this he says: 'And you, as *being the father of writing* (*gramma*), are praising your own compositions (*sungramma*). It's actually the opposite of what you say, for they make both writers and readers less wise and apt to forget [things]: the writer because, thinking that he has stowed his thoughts (*logos*)[258] away as though in a [hoard of] treasure, looks down on thoughts and no longer instigates them in himself, while they fill the reader with [a specious] belief in his own wisdom and other people's notions got from reading thanks to his having no teacher; for a teacher deposits thoughts in the soul of the pupil, but someone who learns from books takes away only that,[259] [and] often, erroneously, [something] other than the writer intended; and it is obvious that the book is neither questioned nor answers a question.

266. *[In that, because of their trust in writing, they are reminded* [of things]] *from without by means of marks made by others* (*allotrios*), *[not reminding themselves on their own from within]* (275A3–5)

That is, receiving other people's [thoughts] by report (*akoê*) alone; for [it is] discussion (*logos*) by way of question and response [that] stimulates thought (*logos*) in us.

267. [*Therefore you have not found a potion for memory*] *but one for reminding* (275A5–6)

For the person who composes the writings they are aide-mémoires (*hupomnêma*) for old age, and if they are aide-mémoires, it is clear that they are the real cause of [merely] apparent wisdom in learners [and] not of true [wisdom].[260]

[*They will seem to be*] *very knowledgeable* (275A7–B1): that is, they will seem to know many things, in reality knowing nothing.

Usually (275B1): [that is,] for the most part.

268. *And hard to be with* (275B2)

That is, in interactions [with others], in that, being full of supposed wisdom,[261] they believe they are [really] wise and want to outshine the [truly] wise.

269. *Socrates,* [how] *easily* . . . [*you fabricate stories!*] (275B3–4)

When Phaedrus saw that the tale had been made up he said as much, and the modesty of Socrates is to be marvelled at in that, although he makes up stories (*logos*) himself, he attributes them to the gods who preside over speech (*logos*).

270. *I know, my friend*[262] (275B5)

What he is saying is this: 'People of earlier times used not to worry about who was speaking, [about whether it was] an oak, a rock, or anything else, but would closely scrutinise what was said [to determine] whether it was true or false. You, on the other hand, want to learn *who is speaking and where they are from* (275C1) and the like, not concentrating on the truth of the matter.'

(258) 271. *So someone who thinks* [*he has left behind him*] *an art* [*in writing* . . . *would be quite simple-minded and be truly ignorant of Ammon's prophecy*] (275C5–8)

Just as, on the point of launching into [a discussion of] the art that is concerned with speech (*logos*), he referred the issue (*problêma*) to the gods and the Muses[263] and *the* [question] *of the propriety or impropriety of writing* (274B6) to the gods Hermes and Ammon,[264] stating that propriety in composition is (to put it briefly) saying things that are pleasing to the gods, distinguishing what is true and fine (*kalos*) to the advantage of the speakers, and impropriety seeking for the [rewards] of glory and human ambition, in the same way he also does this now.

One should understand that Plato is not abolishing writing. Many venerable and much honoured men, such as Orpheus and Hermes, wrote – although Pythagoras and Socrates didn't write. Accordingly, Socrates here teaches [that there are] the following limitations (*horos*) on writing: [one must] have knowledge of the subject matter, and, having knowledge of the truth, [one may write] for the purpose of reminding [us of things so as to counter] the forgetfulness in old age[265] or for the benefit of learners,[266] not [ever] taking [writing] seriously, but using it as a pastime. [Only] then does one write rightly and appropriately. He says that those who lack knowledge and come to it [*sc.* writing] as though to a matter of moment and a desirable thing or for the sake of glory are writing inappropriately.

There is a story in circulation about how one should not stow one's thoughts away in writings which goes something like this. A certain pupil of Plato, having recorded in writing everything said by him, sailed away, and suffering shipwreck, lost everything, and returned to his teacher, having proved by experience [the truth of the principle] that one should not stow one's thoughts away in books but in the mind (*psukhê*).[267]

272. [*So anyone who thinks he has left behind him an art in writing, and moreover anyone who receives it as though something clear and reliable will come from writing*], *would be quite simple-minded* [*and be truly ignorant of Ammon's prophecy*] (275C5–8)

Because the one thinks to bequeath an art [that is embodied] in soulless letters, the other to learn from soulless things.

And be truly ignorant of Ammon's [*prophecy*]: [*sc.*] that these letters give birth to forgetfulness and the conceit of wisdom.

273. *Supposing*[268] [*written words*] *to be more* [*than refreshing the memory of a person who is familiar with whatever it is the writing is about*] (275C8–D2)

Observe [how] it is shown here in what connection writing (*to graphein*) is a good thing, [namely,] that writing (*grammata*) is a reminder for those with knowledge [of the subject matter]. It doesn't generate knowledge in [uninformed] readers, so books should be written for those with knowledge [of the subject].

272,1   274. *For surely, Phaedrus, [writing has this* [about it] *that is] strange [and truly like painting]* (275D4–5)

Next he makes a comparison of inanimate and animate words. By an 'inanimate' [word], I mean the one which he also calls a 'bastard' (*nothos*)[269] [word], the one in writing, and by the *legitimate* and 'animate' *brother* (276A1) of the internal
5   word [I mean] the [word] that is **(259)** placed in the soul of the learner when someone has been able to make [another person his] pupil, as Socrates did Plato, Plato did Xenocrates, Xenocrates did Polemon, [and so on,] following the [Platonic] succession.[270]

Why does he say here that a word (*logos*) written in inanimate letters is like a *painting* (275D5)? Because just as in a picture you see a figure (*zôion*) that neither
10   utters a sound nor answers questions nor is able to move itself at all, so too in writing do you see nothing that resembles a living person but only the appearance [of one]. Hence the reader is misled. Thus the written word has this oddity: it doesn't activate speech (*logos*) in us but is like [any] inanimate thing, giving no answer beyond the ones it has, and speaking in the same way in the presence of the intelligent or the foolish. [And] then, even when reviled by its readers, it is
15   unable to defend itself.

275 [*And if you ask anything about what is being said*], *they are quite majestically silent*. [*And the words are the same*] (275D6–7)

He says *majestically* because majestic people habitually maintain silence.
Words: [i.e.] written words.
And if you ask anything about what is being said: as for instance that the soul is immortal, [or] that the soul is a self-moving substance, it will say nothing
20   [further] but always [just] the same thing.

276. *And when once it is written*, [*every composition is tossed around all over the place in the same way*] (275D9–E1)

He adds another peculiarity. For he says that it has the property of not making a sound but resembling something inanimate and dead and not something living and self-moving. And then [he adds] this [further] peculiarity, that it is circulated
25   equally among the wise and among the foolish. It was the custom among wise men such as the Pythagoreans not to tell everything to everyone but [only] to those who needed [to know];[271] from others they would hide their doctrines, and

Socrates would similarly introduce different pupils to different [doctrines][272], matching them according to the suitability[273] (*epitêdeiotês*) of each. The written word, on the other hand, presents itself to everyone *in the same way*.

Is tossed around: that is, it is not its own master but is carried [around by others]. 30

277. *And when it is ill-treated [and unjustly reviled, it always needs the help of its father]* (275E3–4) 273,1

The written [word] also has the peculiarity that it cannot help itself [when ill-treated].

278. *What[274] other [type of] discourse do we see [[that is] a legitimate brother of this?]* (276A1–2)

He wants to move on to the other word, the one in the soul, the one stowed away 5
in the thought[275] of the pupil.

He says *legitimate* because he calls the uttered word the *legitimate brother* of the word [that is] in the soul or internal, and the other, the written one, 'bastard' and 'inanimate' and 'other-moved'.

(260) 279. *You mean the [living and ensouled] speech of a person with knowledge* 10
[of which the written [word] would be justly called a kind of image] (276A8–9)

Not only because it is brought forth from a living soul, but because the word itself is self-moved in its own right, being able both to answer (*anthistanai*) objections and to give birth to offspring of its own, as Socrates' word begot [offspring] in Plato and Plato's in Xenocrates.

An image: in the way we also call letters symbols for the content of thought. 15

280. *Exactly. Now [tell] me this* (276B1)

Having[276] taught the nature (*ousia*) of each [kind of] word he wants to talk about their use and their power (*energeia*), comparing the true word and the written one by means of an example from horticulture (*geôrgia*). There is a horticultural 20
amusement (*paidia*), which we too indulge in as children, when we put soil in pots and plant corn, or grow something else, which after germinating and

shooting up in eight days, withers after a few [more] days. Written words – which he calls gardens of Adonis because Lord Adonis is set over things that grow and die in the soil, and all coming into and passing out of existence among us resembles [these] gardens – he compares to this amusement, and the true word to genuine agriculture, the kind that involves serious engagement and much hard work. So you [can] see that he opposes seriousness to play [and] the perfect to the imperfect (for the former produce is imperfect, the latter perfect), the one time to the other time, the one being of eight days duration, the other of eight months.

281. [*Or would he do*] *these things for the sake of amusement* [*and for the festival*]? (276B5)

What the entire cosmos' being their plaything in the mundane creation means in the case of the gods – as the poet says, 'unquenchable laughter broke out among the blessed gods as they saw Hephaestus'[277] (that is, when they saw [his] creations, they rejoiced and laughed) – what, then, the cosmos [was] to the gods, is what activity in relation to external matters is to the serious man; for it is like play, whereas [activity] within the soul [is like] serious work.

282. [*And shall we say that*] *a person* [*with knowledge of*] *the things that are just* [*and beautiful and good pays less attention to his own seeds than the farmer* [*does to his*]]? (276C3–5)

(261) The argument is from the lesser [to the greater]: 'Do fine and just things seem to you worthy of less serious attention than corn and the like?'

283. *He won't then* [*write them*] *with serious intent* [*in black water through a reed* [*pen*]]. (276C7–8)

Just as the person who sows [seeds] in pots does it *for the sake of play* (276D2), so too does the person who writes *with black water through a reed* [pen] write in play, not with serious intent.

But that[278] *in writing* (276D1): he will talk about the usefulness of writing, [namely,] that it stores *for him*, and for knowledgeable people like him (it isn't for the ignorant), a treasure of *reminders against old age* (276D3), because of the loss of memory [that brings].

Watching them (276D5): that is, comparing this amusement with other amusements, those in games of dice or drunkenness or the like.

284. *He will take pleasure [in watching their tender growth]* (276D4–5)

He also says this in the *Timaeus*: '*when, putting aside thoughts about things with [true] being*, one reaps *a pleasure that is not to be regretted* from the sciences'.[279]
 Tender (*hapalos*): equivalent to 'delicate' (*eupathês*).
 Moistening (276D6): that is, renewing and †moistening† *what is flowing from (to aporreon) the soul*.[280]

285. *You are talking [, Socrates,] about entirely beautiful play in contrast to [the] paltry [kind], [that of someone able to play with words (en logois) while telling stories about justice and the other things you mention]* (276E1–3)

[That is,] telling stories (*muthologein*)[281] about justice and the rest of virtue, [stories] that are remote from [more] paltry amusement.
 Telling stories: observe how, since the entire phenomenal creation as compared to the true one is a story (*muthos*), he has again called things in writing 'story' as compared to the truth of the [words] of the soul.

286. *But I think [this seriousness becomes] much [finer when someone, employing the art of dialectic [and] taking an appropriate soul, plants and sows, along with knowledge, arguments (logos) that are capable of defending themselves and the person who has sown them and are not fruitless but bear seed]* (276E4–277A1)

[That is,] 'but I think that seriousness is much finer when someone stows away his teaching in his pupils, who can both help themselves and produce similarly good [men]; for everything that is mature (*teleios*) generates its like'.
 An appropriate soul: that is, a suitable one.

287. *Capable of passing [this [seed]] on [forever] immortal* (277A2–3)

For you can see that, thanks to Aristotle and thanks to Plotinus, Plato is tantamount to immortal.

15 **(262) 288.** [*This agreed*], *Phaedrus,* [*we can*] *now* [*decide about*] *those* [*other matters*] (277A6-7)

From this point he wants to give an overview of all that has been said about the art of rhetoric and propriety of discourse and [accordingly] gives an extremely brief summary [of it]: 'Since, then,' [he says], 'we have reached a conclusion as to the kind of art and propriety a person who writes correctly should employ, we
20 can now look closely at the censure of Lysias in [regard to] his speech-writing; for it is clear that if the [activity of] speech-writing takes place in the way we have described, it is no reproach but fine and good, but when otherwise, [it is] shameful.'

289. *The ones that* [*we wanted to look into* [*and so*] *reached this point,* [*that is,*] *how we should look at the reproach of Lysias with regard to* [*his*] *writing speeches, and actual speeches, which may be written with or without art*] (277A9-B2)

25 In reality the discourse on rhetoric began at the point where Socrates told Phaedrus to advise Lysias to sing a palinode and Phaedrus said that he probably wouldn't do that because certain people had reproached him for being a professional speech-writer.²⁸²

276,1 290. *So,* [*it seems to me that*] *what belongs to the art* [*and what does not has been made reasonably clear*] (277B2-3)

He summarises the requirements of the art here, saying that one must have knowledge of the facts (*pragma*), know the truth, [have a knowledge of] definition, division, the nature of the soul, and the types of speech, and of all the things he has already mentioned.

5 291 [*It did indeed seem so, but*] *remind me* [*again*] *how* [*it went*] (277B4)

That is, summarise and give [me] the main points of the argument.
Until one [*knows the truth of each thing one speaks or writes about*] (277B5-6): he says that the writer must have knowledge of the issues and now briefly summarises all the things he has mentioned.
[*Addressing*] *complex* (*poikilos*) [*speeches*] *to a complex* [*soul*] (277C2-3): a
10 complex soul is one that takes pleasure in examples, stories, and, above all, in

different styles of composition (*logos*). Observe that Socrates has done this, for he varied his mode of discourse (*logos*) in different ways.

292. *Not before* [[that]] *will he be*] *able* [*to handle the class of speeches with art*] (277C3–5)

Rhetorical speech too, which persuades by means of plausible [arguments], would have no other way of persuading if it did not know the truth. Persuasion is twofold, the didactic and the kind that creates belief.[283] So one can [successfully] use neither the didactic kind nor the kind that creates belief unless one goes through these arts and learns [about] both the matter in hand and the different types of speeches and everything else he has talked of.

(263) 293. *And what about* [the question as to] *whether it is fine or shameful* [*to deliver or write speeches?*] (277D1–2)

Having reviewed the aspects of discourse that fall under the art and those that don't – it's clear that what runs counter to what has been said by him is foreign to the art – he now turns to a review of propriety and impropriety of discourse, showing that writing is in a way good, in a way not but even a matter for reproach. And he said [before], and says [again] now, that much blame attaches to it, condemning those who enthuse about writing as though it were a great thing, [claiming] that they are deserving of reprimand, even though they are praised by most people, because, unaware of what is true and what false and of the nature of things (*ta onta*) – he compares waking vision with [a perception of] the truth of things and epistemic knowledge and a dream with a conception of the imagination; for a dream contains images of the truth – and bragging about it as though it were a great thing, they put their faith in writing.

A waking vision and a dream (277D10) that is, what is really true and what is apparently true but isn't the case.[284] Certainly, to be ignorant of what the truth is, of what is just and what is not, and the like, is a matter for reproach.

294. [*Thinking there is*] *some great* [*certainty and clarity*] *in it* (277D8–9)

He means in the speech.

But someone who [*thinks that there is necessarily much playfulness about everything*] *in the written speech* (277E5–6): Writing as though about serious matters is inappropriate, but to classify [it] as play, knowing what is true, and above all with the object of engraving the words in the soul of the learner[285] and not in the written word, is appropriate. He gives an overview of what is appropriate to someone who writes in the right fashion, [requirements] he has already mentioned earlier.

10   *Sons* (278A6) are what he has called the words in oneself, 'brothers' (278B1) those in the souls of others ([that is, others] with understanding), 'progeny' (278A7) those in one's pupils.

295. *So let's take it that we have now played* [*enough on the theme of discourse*] (278B7)

[That is,] let it be taken that what has been said on the subject of discourse was played with and talked about by us as in a kind of game. For in relation to
15   Socrates' inner activity, what has been said and external things [in general] are play, even though they are worthy of great seriousness. So, just as the creative activity of the gods in the case of the cosmos is a game when compared to that at a higher (*anô*), divine, and intelligible level, so too is external and spoken discourse play when compared to internal discourse.

296. *Go and tell Lysias* ... (278B8)

20   Just as he offered the beginning of this discourse to the gods, so too does he dedicate its end to the gods,[286] and [moreover] **(264)** dedicate the conclusion of the whole of [his] discourse to the gods. *The Nymphs* (278B9) are divine souls, superior to those of humans, who oversee the whole of generation. Thus these divinities too are contributors to the gift of the god of language (*logios*), Lord
25   Hermes, to the whole cosmos. So you see that language (*logos*), since it permeates all things, permeates all of the middle genera.[287]

He has mentioned Lysias, Homer, and Solon, [or], as you might say, political, poetic, and legislative discourse.

[*And anyone else who*] *has written compositions* [*in political speeches calling them laws*] (278C3–4): he is laying down quite explicitly how one should write and in what connection it is good to write and [adding] that someone who writes in this manner
30   should not be called a politician[288] or a rhapsode[289] or a lawgiver but a philosopher.
278,1   For *to call him wise* (278D3) oversteps human limitations (*meson*). While before Pythagoras everyone who was knowledgeable about anything was called

wise (*sophos*), when Pythagoras came along, he called only divinity wise, assigning the word to god as being special, and called those who strove for wisdom philosophers (*philosophos*).²⁹⁰ In this way Socrates called Love 'wise' and not 'a philosopher' in the *Symposium*,²⁹¹ for '*none of the gods*', he says [there], 'is a philosopher'. Who, then, are the philosophers? Those who strive after wisdom.

297. *On the other hand, the man who does not have anything of greater value [than the things he has composed or written … you will, I suppose, rightly call a poet or a speech-writer or a drafter of laws?]* (278D8–E2)

The man who does not have anything of greater value [to offer] than the things he has written, stitching together texts with words, you would appropriately call a professional speech-writer; for this fellow writes in a shameful manner.

298. *For [we should] not [neglect] your friend either* (278E5–6)

Isocrates was said to have become such a great friend of Socrates that he wore black for a year after his death. And it is said that he took some [youths] who wanted to learn philosophy to Anytus and Meletus, saying: '*You* educate [these] young men'.²⁹² He did this because he reproached them for the death of Socrates.

The philosopher doesn't praise Isocrates for the artistry (*tekhnê*) of [his] speeches – he was a young man and Lysias' inferior in that respect – but because of his nature and character.

(265) 299. *What shall we say he is?* (278E9)

That is to say, shall we call him a philosopher, a professional speech-writer, or what?

Isocrates is still young, Phaedrus (278E10): for Socrates knew the lion by his claw and what kind of person Isocrates was by nature.

300. *[In his natural endowments] he seems to me better [than [what is shown] in the speeches associated with Lysias and to be endowed* (*kerannunai*) *with a nobler character]* (279A3–4)

Observe how he does not praise him as being better at writing than Lysias but because of his nature.²⁹³ In time, he says, he will in all likelihood be much superior to Lysias.

279,1 **301.** [*Also* [it would not be surprising]] *should these things not be enough* [*for him*] (279A7–8)

That is, speech-writing; 'but may he, by some good fortune, be turned to philosophy' [, says Socrates].
    And you [proclaim] *the other things* [*to Lysias*] *as being your* [darling] (279B2–3): because Phaedrus was a lover of Lysias and of his speech.

5 **302.** *Isn't* [*it fitting to go* [only]] *after praying* [*to the* [gods] *here?*] (279B6)

He both began with the gods when commencing the speech and now closes the present discourse by finishing with a prayer, because the gods embrace beginnings and endings and everything [else]. He addresses the prayer to the gods of the locality.

303. *Dear Pan and . . .* (279B8)

10 Pan is the god who governs the universe (*to pan*).
    But why, he asks (*phêsi*), do they make his upper parts human in form, his lower parts those of a goat and shaggy? Indicating [he answers] by the upper parts the rational and animal (*zôôdês*),[294] by the lower the bestial (*thêriôdês*) and irrational, and because it is necessary to master irrationality.[295]

304. *Grant that I become good* [*within*] (279B8–9)

15 Why [does he say this]? Was he bad? [Clearly not.] We say, then, that he prays so as to remain good within.

(266) 305. *And that such external* [goods] *as I have* [*be in harmony* (*philios*) *with my inner* [qualities]] (279B9–C1)

He wants all externals, both bodies and possessions, to be fittingly coordinated with [his] soul and to be commensurate with [his] internal [qualities], in order
20 that they not be excessive, and he be preoccupied with externals, and he not perish because they are lacking.

306. [*May I consider the wise man*] *rich* (279C1)

A rich man is someone of independent means, the wise man someone who is satisfied with what he has – and is on that account rich.

307. [*And may*] *the quantity of gold* [*I have be as much as none but the moderate man could carry or take away*] (279C1–3)

For excessive wealth makes [people] arrogant and distracts them from contemplation [of higher things].

308. *For the things of friends are* [held] *in common* (279C6–7)

This saying refers not just to external things but to the prayer as well, for we pray for the same things for our friends as we would pray for ourselves.

Notes

1. Hermias marks this turning point in Plato's text with a brief summary of the topics highlighted in his commentary in volumes 1 and 2 of this translation.
2. cf. *Phaedrus* 257B1–5. At 218,6 in volume 2 of our translation, Hermias notes that Polemarchus, from Book 1 of *Republic*, was the brother of Lysias.
3. *ouk oimai ei* is odd (although *TLG* shows a few occurrences) and Lucarini suggests the possibility of emending *ei* to *hoti*, which is what we have translated.
4. See Lampe s.v. B 1 for this rendering of *apoteleisthai*.
5. cf. *Phaedrus* 264C2–5.
6. Or perhaps of speeches in general, but the singular and the addition of 'composition' suggests that the reference is to Lysias' speech.
7. At this point the sentence becomes somewhat anacoluthic.
8. We translate *rhêtôr* 'rhetorician' when it is used of a teacher of rhetoric and 'orator' or 'speaker' as seems best elsewhere.
9. cf. Aristotle, *Rhetoric* 1413b3–29. Aristotle certainly regards speech-writing as a different form of rhetoric from oral delivery since each involves different stylistic elements. But he does not observe any strict linguistic distinction between the speech-writer and the orator.
10. In effect, Phaedrus' remark about Lysias reinforces Hermias' assignment of Lysias and his speech to the realm of appearance. That, after all, is where good repute and the esteem of one's fellow humans dwells.
11. Socrates' reply, in effect, seeks to advance Lysias up the ladder of beauties in the *Symposium* so that he is not concerned, as Phaedrus supposes, with matters of appearance like repute and esteem among men.
12. *psophodeeia* ('fear of noises') isn't normally particularly associated with the sound of insects and the idea here may be that those who suffer from it are *even* frightened by the buzzing of a fly. This comports well with its use in Andronicus, *On the Passions* (*SVF* III 409) where it is described as an empty fear. Phonophobia, actually a modern medical term, means the fear of loud noises, so 'phonophobic' does well enough here. Hermias obviously felt that Plato's use of *psophodeês* needed glossing and gives its literal sense, but he can hardly have failed to see that Plato isn't using it literally.
13. Hermias too is arguing from common opinion. Below at 232,9–14 he will distinguish such great rhetoricians from both the true rhetorician, who truly has *tekhnê* and thus great power, and the demagogue, who truly has neither. In truth,

Pericles and Themistocles are 'intermediate' rhetoricians and thus not as great as common opinion supposes.

14 *sc.* include their names and references to the Athenian people and/or council in the record of a decree.

15 Socrates is equating inscribed Attic decrees with speeches by the proposers of the measures recorded in them and taking the inclusion in these decrees of a formula stating that the measure has been approved by the council or the people as recording their admiration of these 'speeches'. For more see Yunis' note on *Phaedrus* 358A4-5.

16 Hermias is actually offering an explanation of the force of the article *ton* in Plato's phrase *ton heauton dê legôn ... ho sungrapheus*, but this doesn't really come across easily into English and we have taken a certain liberty with the translation.

17 *basileis nomothêtas* is a little awkward and perhaps Hermias actually wrote *basileis ê nomothêtas* ('kings or lawgivers').

18 Couvreur plausibly assumes a lacuna after *tropos* in line 23 and Bernard and Lucarini and Moreschini follow him. Couvreur offers *bouletai nun eipein ou monon tis ho tropos* as a possible supplement. This assumes that *to peri tês rhetorikês ... peri tou legein* (221,23-4) comments on *tis oun ho tropos*, but it looks more like a comment on *deometha ti ... hôs idiôtês* (258D8-11), in which case the lacuna would be more extensive.

19 *to dialegesthai* appears to be an articular infinitive, but it is hard to know how to translate it after the lacuna.

20 cf. Aristotle, *Prior Analytics* 67a21 ff.

21 cf. Aristotle, *de Interpretatione* 16a3 with Ammonius' commentary ad loc. While Aristotle here discusses only the dependence of vocal sounds on thoughts and written signs, in turn, upon vocal sounds, Ammonius includes facts (*pragmata*) as prior to thoughts. Blank, in his translation of Ammonius, *On Aristotle On Interpretation 1-8*, notes that Ammonius seemingly drew on his joint reading of Aristotle's text with Hermias' classmate, Proclus. Blank also supposes that Ammonius drew on Syrianus' commentary. cf. Blank 1996, 4.

22 cf. Proclus, *in Tim.* 1,246,22-3, where Proclus says that 'our entire essential nature is *logos*' (tr. Runia and Share 2008).

23 The play on different senses of *logos* can't be rendered in English.

24 Our rendering assumes that this means something like 'the exercise of invention on the part of this reason of ours'. 'Invention' is, of course, one of the standard branches of rhetoric.

25 Or perhaps 'doesn't suffer prior pain at all', for which cf. some of the passages in LSJ under *panu* A.3.

26 The argument in this section is very compressed and, as a result, not very clear. We surmise that Hermias takes Phaedrus' remark to evoke a commitment to hedonism

not unlike that of Protarchus in the *Philebus*: any plausible commitment to living for pleasure is a commitment to living for the best pleasures and these must be the *pure* ones that presuppose no antecedent pains (cf. 160,7–8 supra). The claim that the rational soul has its substantial being after the manner of (*kata*) the intellective part (*to noeron*) in it seems to be invoked in the first paragraph as a premise. When Hermias adds that the human soul is a *logos*, this seems to involve a double sense: it is both a *logos* in the sense of an image or projection of the intellective part in it and also reason in some rather unspecified sense. Since it is a *logos* in one or both of these senses, it is in keeping with this that it should seek to give birth to further *logoi* – perhaps by generating something similar or in keeping with (*eikotôs*) itself.

Now, we might expect the second paragraph (which we introduce to correspond to *de* in line 19) to provide an additional line of argument for this conclusion and in some ways it does. If we can assume as an unstated premise that what the human soul has to live for can't be mixed pleasures, then perhaps this too shows that its goal is the discovery of *logoi*. But we have no argument that the enjoyment we take in discovery of *logoi* is not itself a mixed pleasure. (And anyone who has written a book might find such an unstated premise highly implausible!) But rather than showing that the pleasures involved in the discovery of *logoi* are pure, Hermias now restates the opening premise about the substantiality of the human soul being in accordance with reason and the intellectual activity in it *as if it were the conclusion of the previous reasoning* (cf. *oun* in line 23). An argument for the claim that the pursuit of *logoi* is a pure pleasure might be found in Hermias' next remark in §112. If reading or listening to discourses involves the senses of sight and hearing rather than touch and taste, they have a claim to be pure. But this still does not explain how what seems to be invoked as a premise at 222,16 is then framed as a conclusion at 222,23–4.

27 For *skholê* LSJ suggests A. leisure, rest, ease; B. that in which leisure is employed … especially learned discussion, disputation, lecture, and the adjective *skholastikos* and the verb *skholazein* have similar ranges of application. Socrates is clearly using *skholê* in the first sense, while Hermias wants to read it in the second.

28 Hermias has the compound verb *katakêlein* in place of Plato's *kêlein* and this heightens the sense that one is carried downward in being beguiled by such things.

29 Bernard compares Plato, *Laws* 635C where the thought is similar and the word *glukuthumia* ('self-indulgence') is also used.

30 Perhaps an instance of *hina* introducing a result clause, for which see Lampe s.v. 2.

31 See vol. 1, n. 450 and vol. 2, n. 448 for other references to the fluidity or moisture of generation. The contrast to these earthly motions – the one that awakens our intellection – is probably the celestial motion; cf. *Timaeus* 90D.

32 Probably a reference to *Republic* 404A9 ff.

33 *sc.* the intelligible realm, as opposed to the earthly realm of appearance.

34 At *in Crat.* (§158) 88.15-26 Proclus attributes three types of Sirens to Plato, the heavenly, the generative, and the purificatory. The 'generative Sirens' are associated with Poseidon and the realm of becoming, which is symbolised by the sea. Through these Sirens, human souls are 'lured astray by generation'. See also *in Remp.* 2,68, 9-14, 'In any case, the Sirens preside over this harmony – a harmony which someone who is led upward and is redeeming himself will 'sail past', pursuing the harmony that is better and truly musical; but the ordinary person will delight in being bound by the Sirens and will remain in the realm of nature and nature's sweet pleasures, bewitched by them' (trans. Baltzly, Finamore, and Miles 2022).

35 Couvreur indicates a lacuna here and suggests that something like *tês psukhês eipon apeikasai* has dropped out, giving: 'Those who have interpreted the *Iliad* and the *Odyssey* more allegorically have also said that Homer represented the ascent of the soul'. Lucarini and Moreschini indicate a lacuna at the same spot but suggest that it is also possible that it belongs before *kai tên anodon*. (Bernard, and possibly Lucarini and Moreschini, assume that *anodos* means 'return' here, but it doesn't seem to be attested elsewhere in that sense.)

36 For such an allegorical reading, see Hermias himself at 82,16-83,12, translated in volume 1.

37 Couvreur, again followed by Lucarini and Moreschini, also indicates a lacuna here. In his apparatus he suggests *ton Odussea* as a possible filler and we have translated that. (Bernard rejects the idea of a lacuna and translates the transmitted text.)

38 For a simpler moral allegory for the Odyssey, see Heraclitus, *Homeric Problems* §70. Here Circe and the Cyclops are interpreted as passions such as pleasure and anger that can ensnare us. The interpretation of Odysseus as the soul or its rational powers and the poem in terms of a specifically Platonic ascent that Hermias offers here is similar to remarks in Proclus, *in Euc.* 1,55,16-23 and *in Parm.* 1025,29-37.

39 As in the earlier volumes of our translation, we use 'Love' rather than 'Eros' for the name of the god.

40 202E3-4.

41 225,22-226,4 = Iamblichus, *in Phaedr.* fr. 7 (Dillon).

42 For these spheres, the spheres of the visible universe, cf. 141,26-7. Proclus also associates the Muses with them at *in Tim.* 2,234,20-24.

43 Perhaps referring back to lines 25-6, or perhaps meaning 'the procession of the spheres in this visible universe'.

44 Hermias conspicuously connects these human souls with Plato's earlier mention of newly initiated souls at 250E1-251A3. See 188,16-189,21 above (translated in vol. 2).

45 Previously Hermias has identified this divine good cheer with the vision of the intelligibles (at 226,9) and, through the quotation of Solon fr. 26 West, with the Muses (at 41,16).

46 173C6 ff.
47 The Greek is *ex hôn de tôn tettigôn dêlon*. *dêlon* is difficult. It isn't clear whether it is meant to be part of the quotation from the *Phaedrus* (as Lucarini and Moreschini punctuate it) or of Hermias' comment (as Couvreur punctuates and Bernard translates). In the former case it would be unattested elsewhere in the tradition and an awkward addition, in the latter the addition of *dêlon* to *toutesti* would be unique in Hermias and it would be hard to see what could have motivated it. Couvreur clearly sees the problem and in his apparatus suggests the possibility of emending *dêlon* to *genos* ('race'), the next word in the text of the *Phaedrus*. This would solve the problem, but it's hard to see how *genos* could become *dêlon*. Lucarini and Moreschini, perhaps wisely, are content to obelise *de tôn tettigôn dêlon*. (*de* doesn't occur in the manuscripts of the *Phaedrus* either.) In the translation we have simply omitted *dêlon*.
48 Bernard compares Plato, *Phaedo* 67D and Hermias' interpretation of the myth of Boreas and Orithyia at 29,22 ff.
49 225,5–7. The reference to the *Symposium* is to 202E3–4.
50 But *diakinein* doesn't seem to be attested in this sense, so perhaps something like 'set the light in motion' (for which cf. the revised entry for *diakineô* I.1 in the supplement to LSJ) would be better.
51 In Plato's text, the cicadas carry these messages but the cicadas are now equated with souls or daemons.
52 Pantomime dancing differs from choral dancing. In choral dancing, which dates back to the Archaic period, a group of dancers both dance together and sing. Pantomime dancing emerged in the Hellenistic period and was a popular form in late antiquity. The pantomime dancer performs solo and acts out a story, taking various parts as the narrative unfolds. The pantomime dancer indicates by gestures which character in the story is now being imitated in dance. Choral dance figures as an image in Platonic dialogues, e.g. at *Phaedrus* 257A7 and *Timaeus* 40C3–D3, but Neoplatonist authors also make mention of pantomime dance. In *Enneads* 4.4.33,1–44, Plotinus compares the performance of the pantomime dancer to the activity of the cosmos as a living organism; cf. Sheppard 2020, 105–8. Other Neoplatonists stress the conventional character of the movements through which a dancer signifies that he is now imitating, say, Achilles rather than some other character, comparing the conventional aspects of movements with their natural aspects; cf. Sheppard 2017. It seems likely that Hermias' dismissive attitude towards pantomime dancing in this passage reflects its status as popular entertainment at his time rather than any of these deeper issues about the conventional and natural aspects to language. His remarks seem to contrast the few and true devotees of Terpsichore whose life-involving 'performance' is more than mere physical movement in front of the crowd.

53 cf. Plato, *Timaeus* 38C5, with Proclus, *in Tim.* 3,53–70, and *Timaeus* 40C3. The seven gods are the sun, the moon, and the five planets known to the Greeks, each of which was named for a god, as it still is.

54 The noun *rhuthmos* can be used of any regular recurring motion and, as well as occurring in musical and poetic contexts, the verb *rhuthmizein* can simply mean to order or arrange in various ways. Where one's way of life is concerned, it would normally simply mean ordering it in an appropriate manner, but here the context gives that a musical colouring.

55 For *huparkhein* with the genitive in this kind of sense see Lampe s.v. 5. The Muses are sometimes listed in the order of their birth, which is perhaps behind this statement. Syrianus also talks of first, middle, and last kinds of philosophy at *in Metaph.* 61,27–8.

56 LSJ glosses *Kalliopê* 'beautiful-voiced'.

57 Plato does not say anything about astronomy specifically. Hermias draws this connection because the heaven (*ouranos*) is naturally associated with Urania (*Ourania*) and, of course, because he sees this passage in light of *Timaeus* 90D.

58 Lucarini and Moreschini compare Iamblichus, *Vita Pyth.* (Deubner) 36–7 and apparatus fontium.

59 Lucarini and Moreschini compare Nicomachus of Gerasa, *Harmonicum enchiridion* (Jan) 241–2, while Bernard compares Aristides Quintilianus, *de Musica* 123,5 ff.

60 'It was for purposes of nomenclature only that theorists, during the fourth century BC, worked out an extended note-system. The "Perfect System" was compiled of two pairs of conjunct tetrachords separated by a tone of disjunction (*diazeuxis*) – the double octave being completed by a bottom note, whose name *proslambanomenos* (implying the masculine noun *tonos*) indicates an 'addition' from theory, not from music.' (Wellesz 1957, 345). The occurrence of the feminine form *proslambanomenê* rather than the normal *proslambanomenos* in Hermias presumably implies the feminine noun *khordê*, here more or less synonymous with *tonos*.

61 Earth (Plutarch, *De An. Proc.* 1028F6–7) or the four elements (attributed to Ptolemy at Jan 1895, 419, line 7) were also associated with the *proslambanomenos*.

62 *Posterior Analytics* 89B,23 ff. Aristotle has *to hoti, to dioti, ei esti, ti esti*, in that order, which Barnes 1975 renders 'the fact, the reason why, if it is, what it is' in his translation.

63 In a context like this *skindapsos* serves as a nonsense word and is probably best left untranslated. The point is that the question 'whether it is' (i.e. whether there is such a thing) can be asked of anything at all.

64 Notice that Hermias writes *dia ti esti* in line 9 above but reverts to Aristotle's *dioti* here.

65 The reference is to the myth of the cicadas (*Phaedrus* 259B5 ff.), which Socrates uses as an (additional) incentive to continue his discussion with Phaedrus despite the

noonday heat. (With 228,23–5 cf. 223,12–14 in a similar summary of Socrates' procedure.)

66 It seems unlikely that anything deeply metaphysical is meant here – such as the impossibility of making the One many. The *to hen* in this context is simply any single term. Couvreur would athetise *to*, perhaps on the basis that it would involve such a metaphysical reading, but Lucarini and Moreschini and Bernard rightly retain it.
67 cf. *Phaedrus* 273E4 ff.
68 It isn't clear what *peri toutou* ('on this subject') refers to.
69 At this point the editors assume a lacuna.
70 *Iliad* 15.412.
71 Emending *to de* to *tou* and removing the full stop at 231,4.
72 The proverb was used of something not worth bothering about. A *TLG* search shows that it was quite common.
73 Or perhaps 'those advised [by him]', but *sumbouleuesthai* doesn't seem to be attested in this sense.
74 In Plato this question is introduced by *ara ou*, which means that Socrates expects Phaedrus to agree that he has perhaps been rather too hard on rhetoric, but 231,25 shows that Hermias wants to read *ara mê* rather than *ara ou*, which should mean that Socrates was asking Phaedrus to agree that he has *not* been too hard on it.
75 The introduction of an intermediate form of rhetoric between the true rhetoric of the *Phaedrus* and the artless rhetoric that is a mere routine or *tribê* is common to Olympiodorus' *Gorgias* commentary as well. It is tailored to accommodate people like Pericles, who are not demagogues, but whose success – such as it is – is not due to art. See Bohle 2021, who is reacting, in part, to Jackson, Lycos, and Tarrant 1998, 37–41.
76 'Metaphysician' translates *prôtos philosophos*, which is literally 'first philosopher'. (Perhaps the definite article *ho* at 232,1 should be deleted.)
77 *Gorgias* 455E.
78 cf. *Gorgias* 453A2.
79 Gorgias too agrees that experts can persuade through their teaching, so that it is not merely the rhetorician who is the artificer of persuasion; cf. 453D7–11.
80 cf. Ps.-Plutarch, *Decem oratorum vitae, Hypereides* (Plutarch, *Moralia* 849E).
81 In Plato it is the study, or practice, of rhetoric that is in question.
82 The text of the quotation is largely that of manuscript T of the *Phaedrus*, which differs from that of other manuscripts and that of the OCT edition.
83 There seems to be a shift in the meaning of *kanôn* from 'rule' or 'standard' to something like 'judge' or 'umpire'.
84 *Republic* 349E ff.

85 Quoted, without acknowledgement, by Plutarch in the *Apophthegmata Laconica* (= *Moralia* 233B9–11).
86 *dê* is the reading of manuscripts B and D of Plato. The manuscripts T and W and the OCT text of the *Phaedrus* have *dei*. *dê* is difficult and it's unclear what Hermias may have made of it.
87 It isn't actually clear what verb should be supplied here and Ast, followed by Couvreur, believes, perhaps correctly, that something has been lost after *empeiriâi* ('experience').
88 This could be read as a kind of summary of the argument from here to 274B, or of most of what remains of the dialogue.
89 *kallipaida*, from *kallipais*, (which, for obvious reasons we have not translated) can indeed mean either 'beautiful child' or 'with beautiful children'. Modern scholars have favoured Hermias' second suggested interpretation here because of 242A8–B5, where Socrates claims that Phaedrus has been responsible for many speeches.
90 cf. *Phaedrus* 270A3 and 256,7 below.
91 In *Brutus* 121 Cicero claims that Demosthenes attended the lectures of Plato and at *Orator* 15 he tells us that the relationship between the men was evident from Demosthenes' letters. These letters are now regarded as spurious, but the proposition that Demosthenes studied with Plato was common among writers on rhetoric. For an argument against the consensus among contemporary scholars that this ancient view was wrong, see Altman 2022.
92 At 235,1–2 Couvreur emends to *en tois idiois dikastêriois* and Lucarinini and Moreschini obelise *dikastêriois*. Like Bernard, we have assumed that Hermias is primarily concerned to give an explanation of *idiois*. This would have been clearer if he hadn't chosen to paraphrase the whole of 261A8–9.
93 At Aristotle, *Nicomachean Ethics* 1108a32 the modest man is said to plot a course between bashfulness and shamelessness and this would fit the character of Gorgias in Plato's *Gorgias* well enough.
94 This identification will have been inspired by *Phaedrus* 261D6–7.
95 Adding *tôn de brakheôn ou* after *akêkoas* at 236,4, as suggested by a reader. *ho legei . . . homilêtikôn logôn* (236,2–3) is clearly meant to clarify *all' ê tas Nestoros . . . anêkoos gegonas;*' (261B6–8) and so should contain references to both public and private rhetoric, but as things stand it only refers to one kind, private rhetoric being the best fit. Adding *tôn de brakheôn ou* produces the expected twofold reference. *kata apotadên* ('long-winded', 'prolix' or the like when adjectival as here) is at first sight puzzling since it could on occasion apply equally well to either public or private speech or to neither. Perhaps the explanation is that Nestor, whom Socrates has associated with public oratory, is rather loquacious in the *Iliad*. It is possible too that Hermias chose to use dialectic as one example of private rhetoric because Socrates has associated Zeno with private rhetoric and there was a tradition that he

was the inventor of dialectic (according to Diogenes Laertius 8.57 and 9.25 and Sextus Empiricus, *Adversus Mathematicos* 7.7; Aristotle so described him in his lost dialogue *The Sophist*). Finally, it seems possible that something more radical has gone wrong with the text since Socrates' question is really about Phaedrus' view of the scope of rhetoric rather than whether he is familiar with private rhetoric in its various forms.

96 It seems unlikely that Hermias would have thought that litigants spent time trying to persuade each other of anything in court. Perhaps Hermias actually wrote 'persuade others' (*peithousin allous*) rather than 'persuade one another'.

97 The expectation is clearly that the answer will be that it extends to private arguments and the continuation assumes such an answer.

98 The sense seems clear enough. Hermias is saying that Plato now wants to establish a link between truth and rhetoric. However, the Greek is difficult. As things stand the genitive *tês rhetorikês* is naturally taken with *tên alêtheian* giving 'the truth of rhetoric', which would make the infinitive *sunapsai* intransitive and give something like ' . . . this means to make the truth of rhetoric be adjacent', which is hardly the intended sense. To get something like the required sense we have changed the genitive *tês rhetorikês* to the dative *têi rhetorikêi* and also changed *touto* to *toutôi*, as suggested by a reader. (Bernard translates ' . . . dies soll heissen, dass die Wahrheit sich mit der Rhetorik verknüpft', without any note.)

99 Bernard suggests that 261b15–26, where Aristotle points out that something may have more than one contrary, may be relevant, but it can hardly be all that Hermias had in mind. Aristotle actually discusses *homoios* and *anomoios* at *Metaphysics* 1018a15–19 and 1054b3–14 and Hermias was conceivably thinking of these passages, although it could hardly be said that Aristotle 'gives the remaining arguments' there. (If the material Hermias has in mind is really in the *Metaphysics*, '*Physics*' could be a mistake, whether authorial or scribal, for *Metaphysics*.)

100 cf. Plato, *Theaetetus* 199B5

101 Adding *epi* before *epideumatôn* at 237,6, as Lucarini suggests in the apparatus.

102 As Bernard says, the reference of *autês* is unclear. Cases could be made for 'the truth', for 'deception', and for 'likeness'.

103 'Mislead' is what first comes to mind but Hermias' next comment rules that out.

104 See the note at 237,15 for this translation of *paragein*.

105 cf. 276,9–10 below.

106 cf. the reference to the role of daemons at 42,13 (in vol. 1) and note ad loc.

107 For a similar 'relational' account of things that may be said to enjoy the status of a daemon, see Proclus' report of Syrianus' explanation for why *Timaeus* 40D6–7 refers to the sublunary gods as daemons at *in Tim*. 3,154,24–32.

108 Or perhaps 'from the very outset'.

109 A theme that Hermias rehearses again below at 241,24–7.

110 We supply 'common' here in view of Hermias' further use of *tas tôn pollôn hupolêpseis* at 239,20 and 240,30. cf. 21,20 where Lysias is said to be an image of the *hupolêpsis* that fails to hit the mark, while Socrates is an image of the opinion that hits the mark.

111 Plato has 'the same thing' (*to auto*) rather than 'just that' (*touto auto*).

112 Largely paraphrase rather than quotation.

113 Again, more paraphrase than quotation. It is *seemingly* possible to say opposite things because, in truth, there is no *one thing* here. There are different kinds of love, as Hermias explains. See below 244,7–20.

114 For this see 241E3-4 and 262D2-5.

115 For the phrase cf. Plato, *Theaetetus* 175B6.

116 *sc.* as though they had agreed beforehand what kind of love he was to write about.

117 The image of swimming on one's back at 264A5 is one that seems to stick in Hermias' mind. It is part of his summary of the dialogue at the beginning (2,16). Perhaps not coincidentally, the *huptios* or relaxed style is one that Hermogenes contrasts with the vigorous or rapid style (*gorgotês*) in his work *On Styles* at 2,1,5–6. This vigorous style is one that Proclus claims that Plato uses in his *Parmenides*; cf. *in Parm.* 665,33.

118 On the Neoplatonic interpretation of this requirement of unity, see Heath 1989, 14–19 and Gardiner and Baltzly 2020, 71–3 in reply.

119 Bernard sees a probable reference to the *Euthydemus* and also compares *Republic* 453B2–454D1.

120 Presumably this means that they serve as an example of how not to write.

121 i.e. those that tell the truth about love.

122 cf. *Phaedrus* 244A3–8.

123 cf. *Phaedrus* 259E4–6; *Gorgias* 460A5–7; 245,27–9 below.

124 It isn't clear what noun should be supplied with *anthrôpinôn*. Perhaps 'madnesses' or perhaps something more general like 'norms'. Plato actually has 'the one coming about through human illnesses'.

125 In Plato something like 'somehow or other' would be appropriate, but Hermias' comment on the phrase suggests that he understands it as we translate it.

126 Translating *êgoun dia touto apeikazontes ho isôs eipen*, the reading of manuscript A, at 245,6–7. (Lucarini and Moreschini and Bernard follow Couvreur in adding *to* before *apeikazontes* and emending *ho* to *to* at 245,6–7.)

127 Presumably at 253E5 ff.

128 For *huponoia* in this sense, see LSJ s.v. II. Bernard, not unreasonably, translates 'mit Hilfe von Allegorien'.

129 In support of his claim that Plato takes such mythic communication to take place through *huponoia* and riddles, Proclus cites *Republic* 378D and *Alcibiades 2*, 147B; cf. *in Remp.* 1,186,4–22.

130 *epaixamen* is from *paizein*, *prosepaisamen* from *prospaizein*. Both forms are first person plural aorists, in the case of *prosepaisamen* in its Attic form, in that of *epaixamen* in a later form. The basic meaning of both verbs is to play or play with, but both can mean to sing. The second meaning is clearly uppermost here, but modern commentators often suggest that the first is also present. (We haven't translated the two verbs in the text because Hermias' point is that they have the same meaning here.)

131 Bernard suggests that these are recently embodied souls fresh from contemplation of the noetic realm, but it seems to us that they could equally well be those of new converts to philosophy.

132 *sc.* to his own speech, which is also referred to as an *antiparathesis* at 9,16.

133 *Rhetoric* 1354a1.

134 cf. Diogenes Laertius 4.28, where Arcesilaus is said to have been the first to argue *eis ekateron* ('on both sides of a question').

135 cf. 244,10–11.

136 Not, of course, what Socrates means. (See the note on the ambiguity of *paizein* at 245,15.)

137 *Phaedrus* 238C5–D3; 263D5–6 and cf. 245A1–8 and 228,23–5 above with note there.

138 Hermias here appears to endorse an account of division in which *dichotomous* division by a term and its complement is *in some sense* primary. Among the dialogues in which Plato's characters engage in divisions, the *Sophist* illustrates dichotomous division, while the *Statesman* and the *Philebus* seem to allow or even encourage non-dichotomous divisions (cf. *Statesman* 287C). While Aristotle adopted some aspects of the method of division (*Posterior Analytics* 96b15–20) he was critical of the utility of strictly and exclusively dichotomous divisions (*Parts of Animals* 642b5–7). Hermias' casual remark about the priority (in some sense) of dichotomous division is common to the tradition of commentary on Porphyry's *Isagoge*; cf. Barnes 2003, 132–3.

139 Not actually a quotation, but Hermias puts these words into Socrates' mouth and we have kept Lucarini and Moreschini's quotation marks.

140 For the Pythagorean *sustoikhiai*, or columns of opposites, which are also mentioned at 134,8 ff. (in vol. 2), see Aristotle, *Metaphysics* 986a22 ff. According to Aristotle, items in the left column were bad, those in the right, good. Hermias takes it that Plato has these columns in mind when making his division of madness.

141 *apistos* and *abebaios* are used together of the lover who has ceased to love at 1,20 in Hermias' summary of Lysias' speech and at 4,14–15 in his summary of Socrates' first speech. Plato describes him as *apistos* at 240E9 and 241C2 but doesn't use *abebaios*. The argument seems to be that by reviling base love Socrates is reviling Lysias, who Hermias believes wrote his speech in an attempt to persuade Phaedrus to become his lover (for this see Hermias 1,14 ff.).

142 Couvreur emends *Politeiâi* to *Politikôi* on the ground that Prometheus isn't mentioned in the *Republic*. However, although the *Statesman* passage he cites (274C) does mention Prometheus, it isn't really a good fit, and Bernard is probably right to think that the reference to Prometheus only applies to the *Philebus*. The *Republic* will then only be cited as a dialogue where, along with the *Philebus*, Plato praises dialectic (perhaps, as Bernard suggests, at 533A ff.) and the (admittedly awkwardly placed) reference to the gods and Prometheus only apply to the *Philebus*.

143 The contrast case for the dialectician who can divide the *intelligible* forms is not exactly clear. The 'rational-forming principles' are likely to be images in the human soul of the intelligible forms and simultaneously rational-forming principles in Nature or the World Soul that shape matter. On this dual role for *logoi* in Plotinus, see Helmig 2013, 186–95, and on the inheritance of this general idea in Syrianus and Proclus 268–72.

144 Plato actually seems to be referring to the people he is currently calling dialecticians, so the appropriate supplement would be 'them', but 248,14–15 suggests that Hermias takes it that he is referring to rhetoric. (266C1–2 is actually rather difficult and different explanations of the syntax have been offered.) Bernard suggests a way in which Hermias could have read the lines that would have legitimised his reference to rhetoric at 248,14–15. It involves treating *ta nun* at 266C1 as the direct object of *kalein* in the next line – Bernard doesn't suggest a translation for *ta nun*, but it would presumably have to mean something like 'the [procedures] now [under discussion]' – rather than as equivalent to the adverb 'now' (for this see LSJ s v. A 1) as translators normally take it. We don't find Bernard's suggestion very convincing. Apart from anything else, Hermias begins what amounts to a loose paraphrase of 266C1 ff. at 248,14 ff. with the adverb *nun*, which strongly suggests that he read Plato's *ta nun* as adverbial.

145 The phrasing suggests that in formulating this second question Hermias is looking forward to 266D7–267D8 rather than to 266C2–5 as one would expect.

146 'Turn their ears' would be more literal for 'is all ears' and 'lead and carry' for 'influence and direct'.

147 What follows is actually a comment on 266C7–9.

148 Following Bernard in rejecting a lacuna at 249,30.

149 The Greek is *atekhnoi pisteis*. Aristotle uses the phrase in the same sense at *Rhetoric* 1355b35 and 1375a22.

150 As an adjective *daidalos* means 'cunningly or curiously wrought', and as a proper noun is the name of the, mythical, first sculptor. In Plato *logodaidalos* is probably best translated along the lines of Yunis' 'cunning speech-maker' or, Hackforth's 'master of rhetorical artifice', but Hermias appears to see a reference to Daedalus.

151 There seems to be an implication that Zeno aimed to prove that apparently motionless things are actually in motion whereas the opposite was notoriously the

case. Perhaps it's just that what Theodorus can prove is just as improbable and difficult of proof as what Zeno aimed to prove.
152 Socrates praises Evenus' poetry at *Phaedo* 60D8 ff. He is also mentioned, though not praised, at *Apology* 20B8 ff.
153 West, Evenus fr. 6.
154 Hermias makes Tisias the master, but the master is more often named Corax (*Korax*) and Tisias the pupil, as the saying would suggest. A version of the anecdote is also found in Sextus Empiricus *Adv. Math.* 2.96–9 and Sextus claims that the story is well-known. (In Sextus' version, the name of Tisias is absent and Corax is the teacher.) A very similar story is related of Protagoras at Diogenes Laertius 9.56, so perhaps this sort of anecdote was applied generally to convey populist contempt for teachers of rhetoric. Wolfsdorf 2011 lists other parallels and pursues the question of Hermias' or Syrianus' source for what he says here about Tisias, Gorgias, and Prodicus. In reality little is known about Corax and Tisias and it has even been suggested (Cole 1991) that they are one and the same person, Corax being a nickname.
155 The dilemma being that if the pupil lost the master hadn't delivered on his promise, if he won he wouldn't have to pay anyway. Elsewhere the story is that Corax put the opposite case and the jurors made the punning observation as they threw the pair out of court.
156 The anecdote about Gorgias is unparalleled in any surviving Greek literature. cf. Wolfsdorf 2011, 135.
157 DK, Prodicus test. 13. cf. *Protagoras* 337A1–C4, where Prodicus makes such a verbal distinction, and 358A6–B2 where, with a laugh, he accedes to Socrates' request that he refrain from doing so. In both cases, as here, the vocabulary of pleasure features.
158 Some scholars believe that *mouseia logôn* ('gallery of speeches') was the title of a work by Polus, but Hermias doesn't seem to.
159 Hermias clearly believes that this means repeating the same word. Some modern scholars would agree, but others (see Kennedy 1994, 31) think it refers to the use of compound words based on two different roots.
160 *Third Philippic*, 17,10–11. (Bracketed words supplied from Demosthenes.)
161 *Against Aristogeiton I*, 24,6, where Demosthenes has *itamos* ('bold', 'reckless') rather than *deinos* ('terrible').
162 *Diplasiologia, gnômologia*, and *eikonologia* are probably coinages of Polus or of Plato and only *gnômologia* seems to have caught on. We follow Kennedy 1994, 31 in rendering them as we do in the belief that this best suits the obvious irony in Plato. Possible English translations would be 'repetition of words' (or 'use of compound words'); 'use of maxims'; 'use of simile' if they describe characteristics of Polus' style; or 'Collection of Compound Words', etc. if they are titles of works of his.

163 i.e. using plain language without ornament; on this see Classen 1986, 219–23. It is sometimes suggested (e.g. by Hackforth) that *Orthoepeia* was the title of a work by Protagoras. As Classen says (p. 222), this doesn't seem to be the view of Hermias.
164 An ironic imitation of such Homeric periphrases for a proper name as *sthenos Idomenêos* (*Iliad* 13.248).
165 Adding *katomosanta* after *homoia* at 251,20, as suggested by Lucarini in the apparatus.
166 DK, Thrasymachus fr. 6.
167 DK, Thrasymachus fr. 8.
168 The basic meaning of *êtrion* is 'warp' (as in weaving), but LSJ does list one other passage where, in the plural, it refers to 'a thin, fine cloth'.
169 *psukharion* is rare in Plato and the Platonic tradition. We suspect that Hermias' use of it here is meant to evoke *Republic* 519A1–4 ('Have you never observed in those who are popularly spoken of as bad, but smart men, how keen is the vision of the little soul, how quick it is to discern the things that interest it, a proof that it is not a poor vision which it has, but one forcibly enlisted in the service of evil' trans. Shorey (LCL). This passage was also included in Iamblichus' *Protrepticus* 83,7–12 (Pistelli).
170 What follows is a brief summary of 259E–269C.
171 'Doctor' isn't present in Plato, although it is to be supplied from the context.
172 cf. *Gorgias* 449B1 where the ability to teach is part and parcel of possessing a *tekhnê*. Olympiodorus (*in Gorg.* 3.10) connects this doctrine with *Alcibiades 1*, presumably 118C.
173 Hippocrates, *Aphorisms* 1,2.
174 *Republic* 420C–D.
175 Punctuating as Bernard does. Lucarini and Moreschini, following Couvreur, punctuate: 'That is, in a civilised manner. *But they would rebuke him as a musician would*.'
176 As Bernard comments, this definition is a little obscure. Perhaps the idea is that there is a relationship, or at least a similarity, between cosmic harmony and musical harmony, which is perhaps also implied at 226,7–8, where Hermias says: 'Harmony is in minds and in souls and in the spheres and in all things'. Compare Proclus, *in Remp.* 2,4,16 where Apollo, leader of the Muses, fills the whole cosmos qua single entity with a divine harmony. The Muses then seem to pluralise this cosmic harmony. At this point, the text of the *Republic* commentary has a gap, but the fact that the Muses narrate the loss of harmony among the rulers of the ideal city and its subsequent degeneration suggests that political and psychic unity are achieved through assimilation to some sort of cosmic harmony.
177 Couvreur assumed a lacuna at 254,20 because no verb follows *agatha kai kalous tous politas* and Lucarini and Moreschini follow him in this regard. Bernard does

not, since she supposes that *poioumenoi* from the previous line could be understood here as well. But the reasons to posit a lacuna may not be wholly grammatical. Given the parallel text in Olympiodorus' *Gorgias* commentary (34.3) on the way in which the intermediate kind of rhetoric contrasts with both the true rhetoric and the popular rhetoric, one might have assumed that this sentence would continue to describe the contrast between the latter two, having given the way in which the intermediate rhetoric differs from the true one. Yet we do not find such a contrast and, in fact, we appear to be missing a verb, as Couvreur noted. These considerations, even taken together, are hardly decisive and we think that Bernard is right to be conservative. Nothing *forces* us to posit a gap in the text at this point, though the reader is left wondering about how the intermediate rhetoric differs from the popular one.

178 Lucarini and Moreschini cite *Apology* 26A, *Sophist* 230A, *Protagoras* 345D, *Laws* 861C, and *Timaeus* 87B.
179 Although the construction points to 'itself' as the appropriate rendering of *autê* (254,26), something like 'the selfsame dialectic' would make better sense than 'dialectic itself'.
180 The material under this lemma is a rather loose paraphrase of 269C6–D1.
181 Yunis regards Socrates' claim about Pericles' connection to Anaxagoras as Platonic irony, p. 209, with references to other studies of Pericles. Hermias, however, sees no irony here, nor did his classmate Proclus. Compare *in Alc. 1* 147,9–16.
182 'Prattlers' for *adoleskhas* and 'waste time' for *diatribontas* would be more in line with the evident irony in Plato, which Hermias, as often, seems to miss.
183 Assuming that *ou* in line 14 is pleonastic, as the context seems to demand.
184 *Alcibiades I* 105A–C, where Socrates suggests that Alcibiades' ambition is such that if it was put to him that he would rule the whole of Europe but not Asia too, he would rather die than accept such a limitation.
185 Or 'of wisdom and folly' as Hackforth translates; but we have preferred Yunis' 'mind and lack of mind' because it makes the reference to the importance of mind in Anaxagoras' cosmology clear and fits Hermias' interpretation of the passage better.
186 For *hina* introducing a result clause, see Lampe s.v. 2.
187 For the roles of mind and necessity in creation, see Plato, *Timaeus* 42E–43A.
188 The comparison is, of course, common to the *Gorgias* 446A–466A as well. Olympiodorus' remarks about the parallel between the physical *tekhnai* for the body (medicine and gymnastics) and the psychic *tekhnai* for the soul (law and judicial proceedings) takes a similar cosmic tone. While both medicine and gymnastics are genuine *tekhnai* that aim at what is good (rather than at what is pleasant, like cosmetics and cookery), there is no single genus for them. This is because they have to do with bodies and are thus less unified than their corresponding *tekhnai* for the soul: law and the judicial proceedings fall under the

common genus of the political and this is because the soul, as incorporeal, is more unified than bodies. cf. Olympiodorus, *in Gorg.* 13.2.
189 Plato, *Timaeus* 42E–43A.
190 *prosarmonisai* (here translated 'fit') is an emendation of Couvreur's. The verb isn't in the dictionaries or, apart from this passage, in *TLG*. Perhaps *prosarmosai*, from *prosarmozein*, would be a more plausible emendation, although it is not as close to the transmitted text.
191 cf. Proclus, *in Remp.* 1,221,20–6 where he discusses the psychic character of different ethnicities. In Thracians, Proclus asserts, the spirited part of the soul predominates. In grasping Phoenicians, of course, it is the appetitive part.
192 As Lucarini and Moreschini remark, there does not seem to be a reference to any particular passage in Hippocrates.
193 We've tried for a translation that reflects what seems to be Hermias' reading of the passage, but we aren't entirely clear what that is!
194 What follows is a paraphrase of 270C9–D7.
195 Hippocrates, *De natura hominis*, 2. The passage is also quoted by Proclus at *in Tim.* 2,28,24–7 and by Olympiodorus at *in Alc. 1* 124,17–18. The connection between pain and the multiplicity of the body was a theme for those in the Platonic tradition; cf. Slaveva-Griffin 2022.
196 Hermias has *katarithmêsamenon*, Plato *arithmêsamenon* for 'enumerated'.
197 Both the *Phaedrus* and the manuscripts of Hermias have *hoper* at 258,1 but the syntax (*houtôs* in particular) suggests that Hermias either wrote *hôsper* or treated *hoper* as equivalent to it and we have translated accordingly.
198 Bernard says ad loc. that the terms *phôteinos* and *noeros* here can't be adequately translated into German and it is hard to know what to do with them. (Perhaps 'in the dark' for *tuphlos* and 'clear-sighted' for *phôteinos*, though far from literal, might work.) *noeros* perhaps suggests that Hermias is claiming that someone who masters an art or body of knowledge adequately is exercising intellection (and thus on the way to escaping from the attraction of the sphere of generation).
199 Or perhaps even 'philosophical'. Presumably he has in mind speeches like Socrates' second speech.
200 At 259,10 (1) *endeiknumenon* is Couvreur's emendation inspired by the text of the *Phaedrus*; the manuscripts of Hermias have *endeiknumenên* (and, according to Couvreur, in one case *endeiknumenê*). (2) According to Couvreur, *tekhnê* is the reading of the manuscripts of Hermias with the exception of A, where a late reader has written *tekhnên* where the original text was illegible. Couvreur himself emends to *tekhnêi* (here too inspired by the text of the *Phaedrus*) and Lucarini and Moreschini print *tekhnên*, obelising *houtôs tekhnên*. Obviously it is not at all clear what Hermias wrote – or was aiming to say. (To make things worse, it isn't at all clear how the *Phaedrus* passage in the lemma should be translated. No two

translations of those we have consulted translate it in quite the same way.) In translating, we have rejected Lucarini and Moreschini's obelising, accepted Couvreur's emendation *endeiknumenon*, and retained *tekhnê*, the reading of most, or all but one, of the manuscripts. (*houtôs* will introduce an apodosis after a protasis (for examples of this see LSJ s.v. A. I. 7). In such cases it is often difficult to give it one of its usual translations.)

201 Hermias hasn't missed the obvious irony here.
202 For *tupoi* versus the filling in of detail, cf. 379A and 414A, for the example of the musical modes, cf. 398C1–400E4. The question of why Socrates delegates the detailed work on the politically appropriate modes to the musician and what, specifically, is delegated seems to have been a live question for the members of the Athenian school. It is the subject of the fourth of the ten questions about Plato's view of poetry in Essay 5 of Proclus' *Republic* commentary.
203 Since the rhetoric under discussion is likened to medicine, one might reasonably suppose that it is the true rhetoric that is at issue here – not the popular one. But in the summary at the beginning of the commentary (at 7,4–9) Hermias identifies the popular rhetoric and not the true one with *psukhagôgia*. This apparent tension is perhaps resolved in the thought that, when the true rhetorician functions as or serves the true statesman (who is, in turn, the philosopher when he shifts from contemplation to cooperation in the administration of divine providence), he will lead the souls of the citizens towards the good. So both the true rhetoric and the popular one are exercises in soul-leading.
204 *goun* isn't in Plato.
205 The progression is very similar to the famous opening of Aristotle's *Metaphysics* (980b27 ff.) where art results from initial *memories* that are solidified as experience and subsequently become art when knowledge of the cause is added. One might characterise memories as arising from trial and error (*peira*) which, over time, become *empeiria* or experience. Curiously, Aristotle quotes the rhetorician Polus from Plato's *Gorgias* in his account of the linkage between experience and art.
206 Probably not what Plato had in mind but suggested by Hermias' *pragmata*. Yunis, for example, suggests 'easy to persuade into [holding] positions of *such and such* a kind'.
207 The Greek is *epoioumetha tous logous*. We have followed Bernard in assuming that the *logoi* are practice speeches embodying the principles the pupil is being taught.
208 We are not sure what Hermias is getting at here. For purposes of translation we have assumed that Plato (or Socrates) is the subject of *bouletai* and that the successful student must be able to report back on his observations to his teacher, but we can see other possibilities.
209 On these three requirements, cf. 255,7 ff. (especially 10–11).
210 cf. Hermogenes, *On Types of Style* 2.1 on *gorgotês* ('rapidity' or 'vehemence'). Being concise is the best method for the achievement of this style.

211 Although the lemma is taken from Phaedrus' statement at 272C5–6, Hermias' comments relate to Socrates' response to it.
212 cf. Plutarch, *The Dinner of the Seven Wise Men* 156A6–9 = Perry, no. 453. There is no parallel for Hermias' introduction of the dogs.
213 cf. Bohle 2021, who takes this claim as her starting point. She takes it that most modern interpreters would regard Hermias' claim that nobody took rhetoric as seriously as Plato nor exalted it as highly as outrageous. After all, isn't Plato the earliest and most famous *opponent* of rhetoric? This claim, she argues, looks less surprising once one distinguishes the popular from the true rhetoric, as both Olympiodorus and Hermias do in their commentaries on Plato's *Gorgias* and *Phaedrus* respectively.
214 See Lampe for this rendering of *periergazesthai*.
215 *Topics* 100b21–2.
216 *eikotôs*, which echoes Plato, is rather awkward here and the translation isn't literal. *eikota* would be easier.
217 At 267A6 ff.
218 At *Phaedrus* 273A6 the verb *patein* ('tread on', 'trample' when transitive as there) is obviously used metaphorically. Hermias evidently takes the metaphorical meaning as something like 'demean', 'belittle', whereas modern translators, more plausibly, opt for renderings such as 'study', 'explore', 'thumb through'.
219 The editors treat *touto dê hôs eoike* ('this of all things as it seems') as part of Hermias' comment rather than as lemma.
220 Elsewhere Tisias is said to have been a pupil of Corax. See above n. 154.
221 Probability as the true rhetoric understands it.
222 Readers might reasonably wonder why understanding those things that have a likeness to the truth should *also* be the most effective means towards persuading most people. After all, Socrates has just rejected the view of Tisias that all the orator needs to know is what seems to be the case *to the multitude*. 'The probable', with which the true rhetoric concerns itself, is the likeness to the truth. One reply is that the true orator will also know the nature of the people he is addressing and can lead them towards the right course of action through his superior knowledge of both the truth and the things that resemble it to a greater or lesser degree. This is the point of the next lemma. But you might still wonder whether the grasp of the psychology of various audiences is what is effective – not the understanding of the truth about the matter being discussed. Whatever may be Plato's view, Hermias' comments make clear that knowledge of the truth is essential to the practice of the true rhetoric because the goal of the true rhetoric is to say and do what is *pleasing to the gods* (264,25–265,1). If it pleases the audience and if this pleasure is mobilised towards the end of making them better or persuading them to do the right thing, that is simply a bonus. If we please the gods, all will go well for us (265,19–20) – at least in

the true sense of 'going well' – so that what non-philosophers might take to be failures or reverses for the true rhetorician are not really so (265,23–4).
223 This comment relates to 273D6–8 (*hôst' ei men allo ti . . . peisometha*) rather than to the lemma.
224 Literally 'in front of'. The Hesiod line is *Works and Days* 289.
225 *enorkhêma* doesn't appear in LSJ but *orkhêma* (a dance) and *enorkheisthai* (to dance) both do.
226 This is obviously an explanation of how it is that what is pleasing to the gods is also pleasing to humans. It is however awkwardly expressed and Lucarini and Moreschini may be right to obelise *kai tôi beltioni to kheiron*.
227 Presumably at *Gorgias* 461B3–C4, although it isn't quite an explicit statement that the rhetorician doesn't need to know the truth.
228 *hoti mê* and *ei mê* are more or less synonymous in contexts like this. Hermias presumably thought that *hoti mê* needed glossing.
229 In Plato 'those things' refers back to the 'great things' of 274A3, which in turn refers to the gratifying of the gods; Socrates is claiming that the kind of rhetoric he advocates will also, if incidentally, deliver the benefits that the practitioners of popular rhetoric hope to achieve.
230 *Kat' orthon hêmin*; cf. *katorthôma* or 'successful outcome' at 213,11. The term *kathorthôma* has a technical sense in Stoic moral philosophy and means an action that springs from a virtuous character. Regardless of the outcome, the virtuous person lives in accordance with right reason and this is pleasing to the gods; cf. the response of the oracle to the man who accidentally killed his comrade while trying to fight off bandits on the way to the shrine in Simplicius' commentary on Epictetus' *Enchiridion* 111,30–40.
231 'Writing' (*graphein*) suggests that Hermias may take *prattein* in the lemma to refer to the composition of speeches.
232 The manner in which Socrates asks Phaedrus if he knows how to use words 'so as to please god' (274B9) opens the door for Hermias to provide a theologically-anchored theory of good writing to match the theologically-anchored account of the true rhetoric. Socrates' comment at 274C2–3 that if we could discover how to please the gods, we would care little for human opinions confirms him in this idea. Just as addressing an audience is an act of piety for the true rhetorician, so writing is an instrument (*organon*) for contemplation of the divine for those who understand when, how, and why to write.
233 Or perhaps 'in a right-minded fashion', 'properly'.
234 *Sophist* 216A5–B6.
235 Bernard points out that Socrates wrote nothing and draws the conclusion that the subject is now Plato, but it may well be the case that Hermias is just not distinguishing between the two.

236 The obeli are Lucarini and Moreschini's; although it is generally agreed that Plato was influenced by Pythagorean thought, he doesn't credit the *Phaedrus*, or any other work of his, to Pythagoras or even acknowledge his influence.
237 *Charmides* 156D3 ff.; *Timaeus* 21C ff. De Campos 2022 looks at Hermias' other references to Pythagoras in the commentary and draws some generalisations about Hermias' views on unwritten philosophies. While he acknowledges that Lucarini and Moreschini, as well as Couvreur, obelise this passage, he fits it into his account of Hermias' attempt to reconcile the superiority of oral philosophy with written philosophy.
238 As opposed to its allegorical interpretation. (For this sense of *rhêton* cf. LSJ *rhêtos*, A.IV and Lampe *rhêtos* 3.d.)
239 Hermias evidently identifies Theuth (or Thoth) and Hermes, although, as Yunis says ad loc., there is no evidence that Plato does.
240 *Timaeus* 22A-B.
241 No single term in English seems adequate. The principle that Hermias relies on here seems to be one and the same with what is called 'vertical causation' in Proclus. The lower products or effects in such chains of vertical causation resemble their higher causes but differ in their essence. So Theuth is not an ibis, but the ibis is in some sense an image of this god and its markings reveal some of the activities of Theuth. On vertical causation, see Martijn 2017, 52-4.
242 It isn't clear what the point of *gar* ('for') is here.
243 Aelian (*On the Nature of Animals* 9,29) says that the ibis can take on a heart-like shape when it buries its head in its breast feathers. It might also be relevant that in Egyptian texts one of Theuth's titles was Heart of Ra (Budge 1969, 400, 407) and one of his functions was to record the results of the weighing of the hearts of the deceased in the judgement of the dead. And, perhaps most relevantly, Horapollo says, with some justification, although the truth is more complicated, that the hieroglyph for the heart was a drawing of an ibis (ibid., 402).
244 Theuth, or the ibis, don't seem to have a direct relationship to truth, but his spouse Ma'at does -in fact 'truth' is one possible meaning of the word *ma'at* (Budge 1969, 417) - and according to Budge Theuth and Ma'at often seem to merge and assume each other's characteristics (ibid., 420).
245 *Symposium* 215A where Alcibiades likens Socrates to the Silenus figures sold in shops. Externally, these have the appearance of crude, unrestrained satyrs, but when the hinged statue is opened, they reveal images of gods inside.
246 This rather mysterious statement may be a reference to Theuth's role as the god of equilibrium, which he assumes when, in the guise of a dog-headed ape, he sits on the beam of the scales that weigh the heart of the deceased against the feather of Ma'at and reports the result of the weighing to Theuth in the guise of the ibis-headed scribe of the gods (ibid., 403, 407 for details).

247 For the claim that the ibis lays its eggs and/or mates by way of its beak, see Aristotle, *On the Generation of Animals* 756b13 ff. (Aristotle attributes the latter view to Anaxagoras and takes the trouble to refute it), Pliny, *Natural History* 10.15.33, Aelian, *On the Nature of Animals* 9.29, Solinus *Polyhistor* 32.33.

248 It seems that there are two manifestations of Theuth, one as a god and one as a daemon, each aligning with different aspects of Hermes.

249 It's hard to find an appropriate rendering for *logikos* here. 'Involving calculation' does well enough for most items in Plato's list of Theuth's inventions, but 'involving words' would be more appropriate in the case of writing, the last item in the list, and we have opted for 'rational' in line 22 below.

250 Preferring *paideia*, the reading of some manuscripts, to *paidia*, as printed by Lucarini and Moreschini, in line 23. Reading *paideia*, *hautê* ('this') will look back to *paideiâi* earlier in the line, whereas with *paidia* it is hard to see what it could look back to.

251 We are taking it that there is a contrast between the surface meaning of the myth and its deeper meaning as there is by implication at 267,9–10.

252 We have assumed that *houtos* looks back to *hoper* in line 1 but has been attracted to the gender of *dêmiourgos* in the previous line.

253 Bernard suggests that an Egyptian etymology of the name Ammon lies behind this last comment and a passage in Plutarch's *On Isis and Osiris* may seem to support this. The passage reads: 'While the majority still believe that Amûn (which we modify into Ammon), is the proper name of Zeus among the Egyptians, Manetho the Sebbenyte thinks that it means "what is concealed" and that concealment is signified by this word, whereas Hecataeus the Abderite says that the Egyptians also use this expression whenever they greet someone, the word being one of address. Hence they name the supreme god, whom they believe to be one with the universe, Amûn, since they address him as one invisible and concealed, and exhort him to become manifest and clear to them.' (354C–D, tr. Griffiths 1970, 131. Griffiths, ibid., 285, believes that Manetho's explanation of the name is probably correct). However, although a knowledge of the Plutarch passage, or a similar one, may have influenced Hermias' terminology, the phrase 'bringing all things from obscurity to visibility' is clearly intended to explain his claim to the title 'creator of the entire *perceptible* cosmos'. (There may also be a reference to the role he has as a sun god thanks to his identification with Ra.)

254 A familiar allusion to *Tim.* 29E1–2. See Hermias 150,12; 196,31 and 218,2 (in vol. 2) for other instances.

255 For this see LSJ *logos* VI.3.e, but perhaps something like 'speeches' or 'discourse' is intended.

256 cf. Plato, *Republic* 601C6–602A2.

257 Hermias finds three gods in Socrates' story and the text of the manuscripts can be read that way, but most modern interpreters see only two. Many accept Postgate's

emendation of *theon* to *Thamoun* at 274D4, which identifies Thamus and Ammon, and the manuscript text itself can be read as making the same identification if one translates *kai ton theon Ammôna* at 274D4 'and [they call] the god Ammon' and assume that 'the god' refers back to *Thamou* in the previous line. (Incidentally, either of these last readings makes Thamus a god and not just a king, something that wouldn't necessarily be the case otherwise.)

258 Or perhaps, both here and later, 'words'.
259 *sc.* only what he reads.
260 Presumably Hermias' thought is that if the writings can *only* serve to remind the one who knows of what he *already* knows, then they are incapable of producing knowledge in the first instance.
261 *Doxosophia* or the conceit of wisdom was a concern for the members of the Athenian school. Hermias' classmate, Proclus, prays to the gods that he may not fall into it in his exegesis of the *Parmenides* (*in Parm.* 617,9). In this context, he prays that he may instead, in the image from *Phaedrus* 246E–251B, remain connected to those realities 'from which the eye of the soul is refreshed and nourished'. Proclus also connects *doxosophia* with dialectic and the form of sophistry discussed at *Sophist* 231A; cf. *in Parm.* 654,7–655,6. The philosopher, using dialectic, really refutes the person who has the conceit of wisdom and purges him of 'double ignorance'. The sophist, by contrast, merely appears to purge the person, but cannot really purify him since he is himself unpurified or purged of such a conceit of wisdom.
262 Hermias has *oid' egô phile* here, the reading of manuscripts B and D of the *Phaedrus*. Modern scholars normally follow manuscript T, which has *hoi de g' ô phile*, which is probably what Plato wrote. (Hermias' commentary is a paraphrase of 275B5–C2.)
263 As Bernard says, it isn't immediately clear which passage Hermias has in mind here, but comparison with 223,4–14 and 228,18–25 above makes it clear that it is the myth of the cicadas at 259B5 ff.
264 Here the reference is to the myth of the invention of writing by the Egyptian god Theuth at 274C ff. which introduces a discussion of the appropriate and inappropriate uses of writing.
265 Hermias here omits the concern he earlier raised about the manner in which such written reminders can lead to overconfidence in our retention of our knowledge. In addition to the written aide-mémoire, we may require practice or exercise of our knowledge to retain it (8,15 in vol. 1).
266 A puzzling concession in light of 270,14–16 above and 271,30–1 below. Perhaps Hermias means only that students may rehearse or refresh what they have learnt *viva voce* through the use of writings.
267 This seems to be the only surviving mention of this anecdote. Lucarini and Moreschini suggest that Hermodorus may have been the pupil.

268 Hermias has *pleon gar* in place of Plato's *pleon ti*. The *gar* doesn't make sense in the Platonic context and we have not translated it.
269 Plato doesn't actually use the word *nothos*, but the illegitimate status of the written word is implied by *toutou adelphon gnêsion* ('the legitimate brother of this') at 276A1.
270 Buckley 2006 argues that part of the significance of the Platonic succession to the Neoplatonists and the importance of learning true Platonism from true Platonists stems from the centrality of the image of initiation and the guided tour of the gods in the *Phaedrus*' palinode. One might add to this consideration the insufficiency of the written word for the transmission of true Platonism.
271 Or perhaps 'to those they needed [to share them with]'.
272 Assuming that *allois* (line 27) looks back to *dogmata* earlier in the line.
273 Or perhaps 'aptitude'. For similar remarks about how Socrates tailors the manner of his conversation (whether through dialectic methods, midwifery, or erotic methods) to the aptitude or level of development of his interlocutor, see Proclus, *in Alc. 1* 27,14–29,6.
274 Following Lucarini's punctuation *ti de allon*. In the OCT edition of the *Phaedrus* Burnet, probably correctly, punctuates *ti d'; allon*, giving 'Well then, do we see another [type of] discourse ...'.
275 Compare the way in which here the *logos* is 'stowed away' in the soul with the manner in which it was 'stowed away in books' by Plato's shipwrecked student at 271,18–23.
276 What follows comments on 276B1–8 and explains its position in Socrates' argument.
277 Homer, *Iliad* 1,599–600. See Proclus' more extensive allegory of this episode at *in Remp.* 1.126,5–128,23. Because Hephaestus is the demiurge of the sensible cosmos (cf. *in Tim.* 2,27,16), the gods' laughter at him is a symbolic representation of the fact that their providential co-creation of the sensible with Hephaestus is a game and that they exercise this providence 'with the ease that is appropriate to them and without departing from the comfort (*eupatheia*) which belongs to them' (*in Remp.* 1,127,18–20, trans. Baltzly, Finamore, and Miles 2018). Hermias' point, then, is that a person who writes in the proper way should emulate the gods in this regard.
278 Plato has *alla tous men en grammasi kêpous* ('but [he will sow] the gardens in writing'), Hermias simply *alla to men en grammasi*.
279 *Timaeus* 59C7–D1. The last few words are Hermias' paraphrase.
280 Couvreur believes that *ardontes* is corrupt and Lucarini and Moreschini obelise it. If *ardontes* is indeed corrupt, it has presumably replaced another participle. Our not very convincing rendering of Hermias' comment (which is similar to Bernard's, who translates 'das heisst, das aus der Seele Abfliessende zurückgewinnend und benetzend') is one of several possibilities that occur to us, none of them any more convincing.

281 *muthologein* could be translated 'relating myths' and *muthos* 'myth'.

282 At 257B–C.

283 The division of the persuasive art (*hê peithô*) into the *didaskalikê* and the *pisteutikê* is introduced only at the point at which Hermias is explaining Socrates' summation, but cf. *Gorgias* 454E3–455A2. 'Didactic' is certainly clear enough for one branch, since the person who teaches persuades the student by explaining the grounds for the truth of what is believed and this means the audience has an *informed* belief. 'The kind that creates belief' might equally be rendered 'the kind where it is taken on trust': the persuasion occurs and the audience holds the belief because the speaker has persuaded them to take it on his authority. That, of course, is not teaching and the result is not 'informed belief' on the part of the audience.

It is presumably uncontroversial that the person who doesn't understand a matter cannot create informed belief in his audience through teaching. You can't *teach* what you yourself don't understand. But it is far more doubtful that a person who doesn't understand a matter cannot get others to take what they say on trust or to believe it, albeit in an uninformed way. This is exactly the situation described by Gorgias at *Gorgias* 454B–D. He says that, although he is no doctor, he has persuaded patients to undergo treatments that his brother, who is a doctor, has been unable to persuade them to take. Hermias insists that this cannot happen since Gorgias has not learned 'about the matter at hand' as well as about 'the different types of speeches' (276,18). We submit that this is wildly implausible. We take Hermias' real view of the shortcomings of popular rhetoric to be that the person who does not know the truth cannot speak in a way that is pleasing to the gods. As 277,1–2 makes clear, the ground for reproaching someone in Gorgias' position is not their *ineffectiveness* in persuading equally ignorant human beings, but rather the simple fact of their *ignorance* – and in particular their ignorance of the kinds of things that orators normally persuade other people about: matters of justice and injustice.

284 Bernard compares Plato, *Republic* 476C2–8 and 520A6–D5.

285 At 272,12 Hermias said that the written word cannot *activate* (*kinein*) the *logos* in the soul and so it seems that one cannot learn simply from books. Here, however, writing engraves (*enkharattein*) the *logoi* upon the soul of the learner. We suppose this means that the written word can serve as an adjunct to personal teaching in *some* way. However, the contrast between engraving *logoi* in the soul through writing rather than engraving them in written characters is puzzling. If you are giving students written works as an adjunct to personal instruction, then you are engraving the words in the student's soul by means of first engraving the words in written characters. The idea that a writer might write for the sake of the words on the page rather than for the sake of his readers is bizarre.

286 cf. the similar passages at 215,11–12; 279,6–7. The *Phaedrus* reference is to 237A7–B1.

287 The 'middle genera' are presumably nymphs, daemons, heroes, and the like, who are midway between gods and human beings.
288 See 231,28–232,4 above. When the philosopher turns his attention to public matters and persuades the citizens towards what he knows to be right by virtue of his command of dialectic, then the philosopher is the true statesman and the true orator. Olympiodorus seems to distinguish the persons of the statesman and the true orator, but nothing in his position seems to preclude both roles being occupied by one and the same person. cf. Bohle 2021, 150.
289 For an argument that Plato, in fact, envisioned a 'true rhapsody' that was analogous in many ways to the true rhetoric, cf. Baltzly 1992. The author – a PhD student at the time – could not have imagined that he was, in fact, vindicating Hermias' claim.
290 A *philosophos* is, of course, a 'lover of wisdom' but not necessarily its possessor. Diogenes Laertius claims that it was Pythagoras who first used *philosophos* to describe himself and what he did (Diogenes Laertius 1.12). It seems probable that this is an idea Diogenes derived from Heraclides Ponticus. It is possible that the fragments of Heraclitus support this claim. In 22 B35 DK, Heraclitus says: 'Men who are lovers of wisdom must indeed be inquirers into many things.' This fragment is unlikely to describe Heraclitus himself; it probably belongs together with B40 which was a pointed reference to Pythagoras' polymathy. This might lend some support to the notion of Pythagoras' self-attribution of the term. cf. too Nicomachus of Gerasa, *Introduction to Arithmetic* I 1.1.
291 Plato, *Symposium* 203E4-204A1.
292 Anytus and Meletus were the joint prosecutors of Socrates. The point, of course, is that by charging Socrates with impiety and corrupting the youth, they had deprived them of Athens' best teacher. The story is repeated by Olympiodorus in his *Gorgias* commentary (§41.5). As Jackson, Lycos, and Tarrant note, the same anecdote is found in Diogenes Laertius, but with reference to Antisthenes rather than Isocrates. For Isocrates' wearing of black cf. Ps.-Plutarch, *Lives of the Ten Orators* 838F4-6.
293 This is quite consistent with Hermias', and perhaps Plato's, revisionary understanding of what makes someone a good writer: their knowledge and the motives for which they undertake writing.
294 'Animal' here includes human beings. In fact *to zôôdês* is at first rather puzzling. Perhaps the explanation for it can be found at Simplicius, *in Cat.* 55,8–9 where Simplicius writes: 'for "rational" is not simply a quality, but it is an animal-like quality' (trans. Chase 2014 – 'rational' translates *to logikon* and 'animal-like' *zôôdês*). As Chase says in a note, by describing rationality as a quality Simplicius 'seems to mean a quality which pertains essentially to the genus "animal"'. However, whereas *thêriôdês* describes the beings of which irrationality can be predicated reasonably well, *zôôdês* doesn't do so for rationality. Its range is too wide. On the one hand, rationality can't be predicated of all living beings (wild animals themselves are

'animals', for instance), on the other it could equally be used of the entities of which irrationality can be predicated.

295 Punctuating with a question mark after *tetrikhômena*. Couvreur and Lucarini and Moreschini place the question mark after *emphainotes*, Bernard after *phêsi*, removing the commas before and after it. For purposes of translation, we have assumed that Syrianus is the subject of *phêsi* and that he is answering his own question. However, this leaves the answer to the question without a finite verb and the text may well be defective. (In fact Couvreur's apparatus shows considerable disagreement between the manuscripts throughout this scholium, although Lucarini and Moreschini strangely fail to record this.)

Bibliography

Altman, William H. F. (2022), *Plato and Demosthenes: Recovering the Old Academy*, Lanham, MD: Rowman & Littlefield.

Ast, Friedrich (1810) (ed.), *Platonis* Phaedrus *recensuit Hermiae scholiis e Cod. Monac. XI. suisque commentariis illustravit*, Leipzig: Schwickert. (cited as Ast)

Baltzly, Dirk (1992), 'Plato and the New Rhapsody', *Ancient Philosophy* 12(1), 29–52.

Baltzly, Dirk (2023), 'Proclus on Plato's Dialectic: Argument by Performance', in M. Mouzala (ed.), *Ancient Greek Dialectic and Its Reception*, Berlin and Boston: Walter de Gruyter, 413–25.

Baltzly, Dirk, John Finamore, and Graeme Miles (2018) (tr.), *Proclus' Commentary on Plato's* Republic, vol. 1*, Essays 1–6*, Cambridge: Cambridge University Press.

Baltzly, Dirk, John Finamore, and Graeme Miles (2022) (tr.), *Proclus' Commentary on Plato's* Republic*, vol. 2, Essays 7–15*, Cambridge: Cambridge University Press.

Baltzly, Dirk and Michael Share (2018) (tr.), *Hermias on Plato*, Phaedrus *227A–245E*, London: Bloomsbury Academic.

Baltzly, Dirk and Michael Share (2023) (tr.), *Hermias on Plato*, Phaedrus *245E–257C*, London: Bloomsbury Academic.

Barnes, Jonathan (1975), *Aristotle's Posterior Analytics*, Clarendon Aristotle series, Oxford: Clarendon Press.

Barnes, Jonathan (2003), *Porphyry: Introduction*, Oxford: Clarendon Press.

Bernard, Hildegund (1997) (tr.), *Hermeias von Alexandrien, Kommentar zu Platons* Phaidros, Tübingen: Mohr Siebeck. (cited as Bernard)

Blank, David (1996) (tr.), *Ammonius on Aristotle* On Interpretation*, 1–8*, London: Duckworth.

Bohle, Bettina (2021), 'The Neoplatonists Hermias and Olympiodorus on Plato's Theory of Rhetoric', in Albert Joose (ed.), *Olympiodorus of Alexandria: Exegete, Teacher, Platonic Philosopher*, Leiden: Brill, 141–60.

Buckley, Tim (2006), 'A historical cycle of hermeneutics in Proclus' *Platonic Theology*', in Harold Tarrant and Dirk Baltzly (eds), *Reading Plato in Antiquity*, London: Duckworth, 125–34.

Budge, E. A. W. (1969), *The gods of the Egyptians: Vol. 1*, New York: Dover.

Caluori, Damian (2014), 'Rhetoric and Platonism in Fifth Century Athens', in R. Fowler (ed.), *Plato in the Third Sophistic*, Berlin: De Gruyter, 57–72.

Chase, Michael (2014) (tr.), *Simplicius on Aristotle*, Categories *1–4*, London: Bloomsbury.

Classen, Carl Joachim (1986), *Ansätze: Beiträge zum Verständnis der frühgriechischen Philosophie*, Amsterdam: Rodopi.

Cole, Thomas (1991), 'Who was Corax?', *Illinois Classical Studies* 16, 65–84
Couvreur, P. (1901) (ed.), *Hermiae Alexandrini in Platonis* Phaedrum *scholia*, Paris: Librairie E. Bouillon. (cited as Couvreur)
De Campos, Rogério G. (2022), 'The Unwritten Doctrine of Pythagoras in Hermias of Alexandria', *Peitho: Examina Antiqua* 13(1), 185–98.
Deubner, Ludwig and Ulrich Klein (1975) (eds), *Iamblichi de vita Pythagorica liber*, Stuttgart: Teubner.
d'Hoine, Pieter and Marije Martijn (2017), *All from One: A Guide to Proclus*, Oxford: Oxford University Press.
Diels, H. (1951–2), *Die Fragmente der Vorsokratiker, Griechisch und Deutsch*, 6th edn, ed. W. Kranz, 3 vols, Berlin: Weidmann. (cited as DK)
Dillon, John (1973) (ed.), *Iamblichi Chalcidensis in Platonis dialogos commentariorum fragmenta*, Leiden: Brill. (cited as Dillon)
Gabor, Gary (2020), 'Hermias on Dialectic, the Techne of Rhetoric, and the True Methods of Collection and Division', in J. Finamore, C.-P. Manolea, and S. K. Wear (eds), *Studies in Hermias' Commentary on Plato's Phaedrus*, Leiden: Brill, 50–67.
Gardiner, Quinton and Dirk Baltzly (2020), 'Hermias on the Unity of the *Phaedrus*', in J. Finamore, C.-P. Manolea, and S. K. Wear (eds), *Studies in Hermias' Commentary on Plato's* Phaedrus, Leiden: Brill, 68–83.
Griffiths, J. Gwyn (1970) (ed. and tr.), *Plutarch's* De Iside et Osiride, Cardiff: University of Wales Press.
Hackforth, R. (1952) (tr.), *Plato's* Phaedrus, Cambridge: Cambridge University Press. (cited as Hackforth)
Heath, Malcolm (1989), *Unity in Greek Poetics*, Oxford: Clarendon Press.
Helmig, Christoph (2013), *Forms and Concepts: Concept Formation in the Platonic Tradition*, Berlin: De Gruyter.
Jackson, Robin, Kimon Lycos, and Harold Tarrant (1998) (tr.), *Olympiodorus, Commentary on Plato's Gorgias*, Leiden: Brill.
Jan, Karl von (1895), *Musici scriptores graeci*, Leipzig: Teubner.
Kennedy, George A. (1983), *Greek Rhetoric Under Christian Emperors*, Princeton: Princeton University Press.
Kennedy, George A. (1994), *A New History of Classical Rhetoric*, Princeton: Princeton University Press.
Kennedy, George A. (2003), 'Some recent controversies in the study of later Greek rhetoric', *American Journal of Philology* 124(2), 295–301.
Krämer, H. J. (1996), 'Platon's Ungeschriebene Lehre', in T. Kobusch and B. Mojsisch (eds), *Platon: Seine Dialoge in der Sicht neuer Forschungen*, Darmstadt: Wissenschaftliche Buchgesellschaft, 249–75.
Krämer, H. J. (2012), 'Plato's Unwritten Doctrines', in D. V. Nikulin (ed.), *The Other Plato: The Tübingen Interpretation of Plato's Inner-Academic Teachings*, Buffalo: SUNY Press, 65–82.

Lampe, G. W. H. (1961) (ed.), *A Patristic Greek Lexicon*, Oxford: Clarendon Press. (cited as Lampe)

Liddell, H. G. and R. Scott (1996) (comps), *A Greek-English Lexicon*, rev. H. Jones, with a New Supplement, 9th edn, Oxford: Clarendon Press. (cited as LSJ)

Lucarini, C. M. and C. Moreschini (2012) (eds), *Hermias Alexandrinus: in Platonis Phaedrum scholia*, Berlin and Boston: De Gruyter. (cited as Lucarini and Moreschini)

Martijn, Marije and Lloyd Gerson (2017), 'Proclus' System', in M. Martijn and P. d'Hoine (eds), *All From One: A Guide to Proclus*, Oxford and New York: Oxford University Press, 45–72.

Miles, Graeme and Han Baltussen (2023), *Philostratus: Lives of the Sophists; Eunapius: Lives of Philosophers and Sophists,* Loeb Classical Library vol. 134, Cambridge Mass.: Harvard University Press.

Perry, Ben Edwin (1980) (comp.), *Aesopica*, New York: Arno Press. (cited as Perry)

Pistelli, H. (1888), *Iamblichi protrepticus ad fidem codicis Florentini*, Leipzig: Teubner.

Rabe, Hugo (1931), *Prolegomenon Sylloge*, Leipzig: Teubner.

Runia, David and Michael Share (2008) (tr.), *Proclus, Commentary on Plato's* Timaeus, *Volume II, Book 2: Proclus on the Causes of the Cosmos and its Creation*, Cambridge: Cambridge University Press.

Saffrey, H. D. and L. G. Westerink (1968–97), *Proclus: Théologie platonicienne*, 6 vols, Paris: Les Belles Lettres.

Sheppard, Anne (2017), 'Neoplatonists and Pantomime Dancers', in R. L. Cardullo and F. Coniglione (eds), *Reason and No-reason from Ancient Philosophy to Neurosciences*, Sankt Augustine: Academia Verlag, 65–78.

Sheppard, Anne (2020), 'Plotinus on Choral Dancing', *Classics Ireland* 27, 98–109.

Slaveva-Griffin, Svetla (2022), 'Reconsidering the Body: From Tomb to Sign of the Soul', in Svetla Slaveva-Griffin and Illaria L. E. Ramelli (eds), *Lovers of the Body, Lovers of the Soul: Philosophical and Religious Perspectives in Late Antiquity*, Washington DC: Center for Hellenic Studies, 111–32.

Strauss, Leo (1964), *The City and Man*, Chicago: Rand McNally & Co.

Tarrant, Harold (2007) (tr.), *Proclus, Commentary on Plato's* Timaeus, *Volume I, Book 1: Proclus on the Socratic State and Atlantis*, Cambridge: Cambridge University Press.

Tarrant, Harold (2017) (tr.), *Proclus, Commentary on Plato's* Timaeus, *Volume VI, Book 5: Proclus on the Gods of Generation and the Creation of Humans*, Cambridge: Cambridge University Press.

Tarrant, Harold and Dirk Baltzly (2018), 'Hermias: On Plato's *Phaedrus*', in H. Tarrant, D. Layne, D. Baltzly, and F. Renaud (eds), *Brill's Companion to the Reception of Plato in Antiquity*, Leiden: Brill, 486–97.

Tresnie, C. (2020), 'Rôles et place des méthodes de division dans les commentaires de Proclus', in S. Delcomminette and R. Van Daele (eds), *La méthode de division de Platon à Jean Scot Érigène*, Paris: Vrin, 133–52.

Watts, E. (2006), *City and School in Late Antique Athens and Alexandria*, Berkeley: University of California Press.

Wellesz, Egon (1957), *Ancient and Oriental Music, New Oxford History of Music*, vol. 1, London: Oxford University Press.

West, M. L. (1992) (comp.), *Iambi et elegi Graeci ante Alexandrinum cantati: Vol. 2*, 2nd edn, Oxford: Oxford University Press. (cited as West)

Wolfsdorf, David (2011), 'Prodicus on the Correctness of Names', *Journal of Hellenic Studies* 131, 131–45.

Yunis, Harvey (2011), *Plato*: Phaedrus, Cambridge: Cambridge University Press. (cited as Yunis)

English–Greek Glossary

account: *logos*
activity: *energeia*
address: *prosdialegein*
aide-mémoire: *hupomnêma*
allegorical interpretation: *theôria*
allegorically: *theôrêtikôs*
amusement: *paidia*
ancient: *palaios*
animal: *zôion*
animate: *empsukhos*
apparent: *phainomenos*
appetitive: *epithumêtikos*
art: *tekhnê*
art, skilled in: *tekhnikos*
artificer: *tekhnitês*
ascent: *anagôgê, anodos*

bad (adj.): *kakos*
beautiful: *kalos*
beautiful-itself: *autokalon*
beauty: *kallos, to kalon*
begin: *arkhein*
beginning: *arkhê*
beguile: *kêlein*
beloved (n.): *ho erômenos*
body: *sôma*
body, of the: *sômatikos*

case: *dikê*
cause: *aitia, aition*
celestial: *ouranios*
city: *polis*
compare: *paraballein*
composition: *sungramma*
conception: *ennoia, hupolêpsis, huponoia*
consider: *skopein*
contemplation: *theôria*
cosmos: *kosmos*
creation: *dêmiourgia, dêmiourgêma*
creator: *dêmiourgos*
criticism: *elenkhos*

daemon: *daimôn*
daemonic: *daimonios*
dance (n.): *khoreia*
dance (v.): *khoreuein*
death: *thanatos*
define: *horizein*
definition: *horismos, hê horistikê, to horistikon*
definition, of: *horistikos*
dialectic: *dialektikê*
dialectical: *dialektikos*
dialectician: *ho dialektikos*
difference: *diaphora*
different: *diaphoros*
differentia: *diaphora*
discourse: *logos*
discursive thinking: *dianoia*
disorderly: *ataktos*
dissimilar: *anomoios*
dissimilarity: *anomoiotês*
distinctive characteristic: *idiôma*
distinguish: *diairein*
divide: *diairein*
divine possession: *to enthousiastikon*
division: *diairesis*
division, of: *diairetikos*
doctor: *iatros*
dream: *onar*

elevate: *anagein*
elevating: *anagôgos*
end: *telos*
erotic: *erôtikos*
evil: *to kakon*
example: *hupodeigma, paradeigma*

failure: *hamartêma*
false: *pseudês, pseudos*
fault: *hamartêma*
fine: *kalos*
first principle: *arkhê*
follow: *hepesthai*

form: *eidos, idea, indalma*
framework: *tupos*

general: *katholikos*
generation: *genesis*
genus: *genos*
goal: *telos*
god: *theos*
good: *agathos, kalos*
grand: *hadros*
gratify: *kharizesthai*

harmony: *harmonia*
health: *hugeia*
hero: *hêrôs*
human: *anthrôpos, anthrôpinos*
human being: *anthrôpos*
hymn (n.): *humnos*
hymn (v.): *humnein*
hypercosmic: *huperkosmios*

image: *eidôlon, eikôn*
immortal: *athanatos*
inanimate: *apsukhos*
incorporeal: *asômatos*
indulge: *therapeuein*
intellect: *nous*
intellectual: *noeros*
intelligible: *noêtos*
introduction: *prooimion*
investigate: *zêtein*
irrational: *alogos*
irrationality: *alogia*

judge (v.): *krinein*
judgement: *krisis*
judicial: *dikanikos*
juror: *dikastês*
just: *dikaios*
justice: *dikaiosunê*

kind: *eidos*
knack: *tribê*
knowledge: *epistêmê, gnôsis, mathêma*
knowledgeable: *epistêmôn*

language: *logos*
law: *nomos*
lawgiver: *nomothetês*

lead up: *anagein*
learn: *manthanein*
legislative: *nomothetikos*
lie: *pseudesthai*
life: *bios, zôê*
likeness: *eikôn*
live: *zên*
living being: *zôion*
Lord: *despotês*
love (n.): *erôs*
love (v.): *eran*
love, be in: *eran*
lover: *erastês, ho erôn*

madness: *mania*
many, the: *plêthos*
matter: *hulê*
medication: *pharmakon*
medicine: *iatrikê*
method: *methodos*
mind: *dianoia, nous*
mode (musical): *harmonia*
mortal: *thnêtos*
mundane: *enkosmios*
musical: *mousikos*
myth: *muthos*

name: *onoma*
nature: *phusis*
number: *arithmos*

orator: *rhêtôr, rhêtorikos*
orator, popular: *dêmagôgos*
order: *taxis*

panegyrical: *panêgurikos*
part: *meros, morion*
pastime: *paidia*
people: *dêmos*
perceptible: *aisthêtos*
perception: *aisthêsis*
persuade: *peithein*
phenomenal: *phainomenos*
philosopher: *philosophos*
philosophy: *philosophia*
please: *kharizesthai*
pleasure: *hêdonê*
poetry: *poiêtikê*
political: *politikos*

popular: *dêmôdês*
possessed: *katokhos*
possessed, be: *enthousian*
power: *dunamis*
practice: *tribê*
praise (n.): *epainos*
praise (v.): *epainein*
prayer: *eukhê*
principle: *arkhê*
probability: *to eikos*
probable, the: *to eikos*
propriety: *euprepeia*
proverb: *paroimia*
public speaking: *dêmêgoria*
pupil: *mathêtês*

rank: *taxis*
rational: *logikos*
recollection: *anamnêsis*
refute: *anairein*
remind: *hupomimnêskein*
reminder: *hupomnêma*, *hupomnêsis*
rhetoric: *rhêtorikê*
rhetorical: *rhêtorikos*
rhetorician: *rhêtôr*

saying: *paroimia*
scientific: *epistêmonikos*
seek: *zêtein*
seem: *phainesthai*
self-indulgence: *glukuthumia*
self-moving: *autokinêtos*
sensible: *aisthêtos*
similarity: *homoiotês*
soul: *psukhê*
speaker: *rhêtôr*, *rhêtorikos*

species: *eidos*
speech: *logos*
speech-writer: *logographos*
speech-writing: *to logographein*
sphere: *sphaira*
spirited: *thumikos*
spirited part: *thumos*
spoken: *prophorikos*
subject matter: *hulê*
symbol: *sumbolon*

teach: *didaskein*, *paradidonai*
teacher: *didaskalos*
theologian: *theologos*
thinking: *dianoia*
thought: *dianoia*, *ennoia*, *noêma*
time: *khronos*
truth: *alêtheia*, *to alêthes*
type: *eidos*

united, be: *henoun*
unity: *to hen*, *to hênômenon*, *henôsis*
uttered: *prophorikos*

virtue: *aretê*

whole: *holos*
win over: *paragein*
wing: *pteron*
wisdom: *sophia*
wise: *epistêmôn*, *sophos*
word: *logos*, *onoma*, *rhêma*
write: *sungraphein*
writer on the art: *tekhnographos*
writing: *sungramma*, *sungraphê*

Greek–English Index

References are to the page and line numbers of the Greek text (indicated in the margins of the translation).

adelphos, cognate, 251,13; brother, 272,3; 273,8; 277,10
adikos, unjust, 229,27; 231,5.8.11.15; 236,21
adoleskhês, subtle thinker, 256,10
adoleskhia, subtlety, 256,20
adunatos, impossible, not possible, 234,3.12.17; 257,8.15; 259,23
aêr, air, 226,27; 256,9.31
agalma, statue, 250,5.6; image, 267,29
agapan, love, 269,28
agathos, good, 219,21; 225,10; 229,21, etc.
agnoein, not know, 230,19; 239,23; be ignorant, 230,23; 277,1
agôn, struggle, 264,15
agrupnein, remain, stay, awake, 223,24; 224,4.6
agrupnos, wakeful, 224,21
aïdios, everlasting, 267,11
ainigma, riddle, 245,14
ainittesthai, hint at, 243,17
aiskhros, shameful, 220,2.28; 221,2.5; 228,20; 247,21; 275,22; 276,20; base, 229,28; 239,30
aiskhrôs, in a shameful manner, 227,17
aisthanesthai, hear, 227,30; see, 236,13; 270,23
aisthêsis, perception, 237,4; 244,25; 246,16; 260,23.28
aisthêtos, perceptible, 224,16; 226,6; 241,9; 244,25; 269,2; sensible, 225,26.29.30; 226,12; 244,24; 268,14.20; perceptual, 226,2
aitia, cause, 221,27; 222,22; 241,14; 270,15; reason, 237,25.26; 260,12.13
aitiasthai, hold responsible, 238,18.20.25
aition, cause, 223,14; 230,18
aitios, the cause of, 244,8; responsible, 241,4; 256,9

akinêtos, motionless, 250,4
akoê, hearing, 222,27; 227,26; tradition, 266,15.18; report, 270,11
akolastos, licentious, 246,30
akolouthein, be guided, 260,6; follow, 265,1
akolouthia, conformity, 253,3
akousios, involuntary, 254,22
alêtheia, truth, 228,27.31; 230,10; 233,21, etc.
alêthês, true, 230,14; 232,6; 234,9, etc.; *to alêthes*, truth, 228,28.31; 229,5.15.16.17.20, etc.
alêtheutikos, truthful, 262,19
alêthinos, genuine, 229,21; 231,28; 232,5.17; 234,5; 248,13; 261,28
alogia, irrationality, 279,13
alogos, irrational, 224,2; 227,26.29; 279,13; not rational, non-rational, 246,8; 268,23; unreasoning, 237,19
anagein, carry back, 221,24.27; direct up, 223,13; lead up, 226,17; 244,22.23; refer back, 238,19.22; 241,8.15; 246,5; 266,12; refer, 271,3; collect, 248,7; elevate, 256,12; 265,15; 267,3; 268,30; 269,1
anagôgê, ascent, 224,11.15; 225,1
anagôgos, elevating, 223,19; 245,1
anairein, refute, 253,4; 255,4; abolish, 271,10
anakuklein, recycle, 251,3
analogia, analogy, 259,29
analogos, analogous, 258,7
anamimnêskein, recall, 263,5
anamnêsis, recollection, 244,25
anepistêmôn, without knowledge, 238,3; ignorant, 238,13;274,18; lacking knowledge, 255,26; 271,17
anêr, man, 248,22; 266,20.22.27; 272,25

angellein, report, 260,29
angelos, messenger, 260,28; angel, 268,2
ankôn, bend, 220,23; 221,4.6
anodos, ascent, 224,26
anoia, lack of mind, 256,20.22
anomoios, dissimilar, 236,10.22.24
anomoiotês, dissimilarity, 236,19; 237,11.29
anôpherês, ascending, 223,19
anthrôpinos, human, 244,16.18; 246,26; 247,10; 251,22; 267,4; 271,8; 277,22; 278,1
anthrôpos, human, human being, 222,17; 224,20; 225,6, etc.; man, 220,21; 253,22; 263,15; 264,28; 265,8.22; people, person, 220,17; 226,12.30; 258,5
antigraphê, rebuttal, 246,27; 247,19
antikeimenos, opposite, opposing, opposed, 236,18; 245,26; 261,25.28
antilegein, contradict, 236,7.8
antilogikos, of disputation, 236,27; *to antilogikon*, contradiction, 236,9
antiparaballein, pit against, 219,7; compare, 234,1.5
antiparathesis, comparison, 234,4; 261,24; counter-presentation, 245,22; 246,27
antistrophos, counterpart, 245,23
apagein, lead away, 237,16
apatan, deceive, 237,16
apatê, deception, 237,1.3.12
apeikazein, liken, 235,23.25; 242,19; 248,1; image, 245,1.7; represent, 245,2
aphairein, shorten, 224,5; take, 263,19; rob, 263,23
aphanes, to, obscurity, 269,3
aphanizein, decimate, 267,18.19
aphorizein, distinguish, 271,7
aphrôn, crazed, 247,8.11; foolish, 272,14.24
aphthonon, to, freedom from envy, 269,6
aphthonôs, without envy, 269,8
aplaneis, fixed stars, 227,5
apodeiknuein, demonstrate, 221,7; prove, 250,4; make, 272,5
apodeiktikos, demonstrative, 234,9.10.11; 259,4.6; 260,6.10; convincing, 257,17
apodeixis, proof, 250,1.2; 255,9
apokrinein, answer, 270,9; 272,9; give an answer, 272,13

apokrisis, response, 270,12
apokruptein, hide, 259,11; 262,24; conceal, 263,24
apolausis, enjoyment, 265,19
apoleipein, be wanting in, 249,2.4.8
apologia, defence, 229,30
apoptôsis, perversion, 245,10
apotelein, render, 219,11; perform, 227,7; *to apoteloumenon*, outcome, 255,32
apotelesma, outcome, 253,9
apsukhos, soulless, 271,25.26; inanimate, 272,2.3.7.12.23; 273,8
ardein, moisten, 274,25.26
aretê, virtue, 259,16; 261,18; 264,15.18; 275,2
argia, indolence, 223,29
aristeros, left, 247,14.16.17.19
arithmos, number, 236,1; 268,10.12.14.15.16; *tou arithmou*, arithmetical, 268,13
arkhaios, ancient, 267,17
arkhê, origin, 219,13; 228,24; beginning, 239,6.9.13; 242,28; 277,20; 279,7; starting point, 229,3; 242,14; 243,2; 244,15; principle, 237,27; 267,25; first principle, 221,25.27; 256,32; 257,1; rule, 256,16
arkhein, begin, 219,19; 239,31; 241,16; 242,4.8; 243,3.7; 275,24; 279,6;
arkhetupos, archetype, 222,3
arkhôn, ruler, 259,6
asapheia, lack of clarity, 246,18
asaphês, unclear, 239,30; 243,29
asômatos, incorporeal, 268,13.17
asthenês, weak, 263,15.17.20.25
astronomein, engage in astronomy, 227,23; pursue astronomy, 227,27
astronomia, astronomy, 268,18
ataktos, disorderly, 227,27; 239,31; 242,11; 243,29; all at sea, 238,3
atekhnia, want of art, 266,2
atekhnos, lacking in art, 239,13; without art, 249,30; inartistic, 261,10; that don't fall under the art, 276,21; foreign to the art, 276,22; *to atekhnon*, artlessness, 237,23
atekhnôs, in an unartistic manner, 239,13
atelês, imperfect, 273,28;
athanatos, undying, 267,19; immortal, 272,19; 275,12.13

atomos, individual, 246,9
autokalon, beautiful-itself, 244,26
autokinêtos, able to move self, 272,9; self-moving, 272,19.23; self-moved, 273,12

basileus, king, 221,21; 268,28; 269,22
basilikos, kingly, 248,22; 268,30
bios, life, 224,14; 225,23; 227,10; 231,6; 250,11; way of life, 219,1
blabê, harm, 231,7.8; 238,13
blaberos, harmful, 241,3
blaptein, harm, 253,18

daimôn, daemon, 223,21; 224,17; 225,6.10.13; 226,28; 238,25.28; 239,1; 267,14; 268,1.2.6
daimonios, daemonic, 225,8; 226,23.26; 268,5.8
dêmagôgos, popular orator, 256,6
dêmêgorein, give public speeches, 231,18
dêmêgoria, public speech, 232,10; public speaking, 232,18
dêmiourgein, craft, 256,21
dêmiourgêma, creation, 274,6
dêmiourgia, creation, 274,2; 275,5; creative activity, 277,16
dêmiourgos, Demiurge, 225,28; artificer, 232,20; creator, 269,2
dêmôdês, popular, 229,18.20; 230,14; 231,28; 232,9.16; 233,7.10.12.16; 234,6; 248,11; 261,21.27; 262,5; 263,8
dêmos, people, 221,12; 232,5; 248,24; 254,18; 261,2; deme, 221,13
despotês, master, 245,16.17; Lord, 266,26.27; 267,15; 268,29; 269,20; 273,25; 277,24
despozein, be lord of, 265,8
diairein, distinguish, 239,15; 259,2; 260,22; divide, 240,15.17; 244,16; 246,7.14.25; 247,4.7.13; 248,7; 254,26; 257,2.3; 260,4
diairesis, division, 246,7; 247,5; 248,2; 249,3; 251,13; 276,3
diairetikos, of division, 229,6; 235,9; 240,22; 245,27; 246,3.11; 247,3; 257,21; skilled in division, 229,9; 236,20; 240,1; means of division, 231,2; 245,23; one who practises division, 247,26;

diairetikê, *diairetikon*, division, 247,28.30; 248,26; 252,24; 260,17
diakosmein, regulate, 232,3
diakrinein, work out, 222,6; distinguish, 239,2.28; 248,8; *diakekrimenos*, distinct, 219,12
diakrisis, determination, 238,20
dialektikos, dialectician, 248,5; 250,3; dialectical, 236,4; 247,27; 249,10; *dialektikê*, dialectic, 245,24; 248,27; 254,25.26
dianoêtikôs, in a discursive manner, 260,28
dianoia, thinking, 223,5; thought, 223,29; 273,15; discursive thinking, 223,31; mind, 232,1; 239,22; 247,8
diaphora, differentia, 246,10; difference, 250,25; 252,26; different, type, 276,18
diaphoros, difference, 230,13; different, 240,30; 249,24; 276,11
diaphtheirein, corrupt, 233,10; *diaphtheiresthai*, perish, 279,21
diastasis, extension, 268,18
diatribein, spend time, 225,22; 226,11; occupy self, 256,11
didaskalos, teacher, 260,22.27; 270,6; 271,22
didaskein, teach, 224,6; 228,22; 229,2; 251,12.18; 252,22; 253,12; 269,7.10; instruct, 250,17; 253,10; explain, 261,12
diistanai, have apart, 250,7; have gaps, 252,12.14.18; 253,1
dikaios, just, 229,23; 230,2; 231,5.8.11.15; 236,21; 240,5; 274,9.11; 277,1; *to dikaion*, the just, 229,25.27; 230,10
dikaiosunê, justice, 252,1; 275,2
dikanikos, judicial, 222,14; 229,24.26.27.29; 234,27; 259,4
dikastês, juror, 233,11; 237,25; 251,19
dikê, case, 250,17.19
dioratikos, capacity for clear seeing, 224,12; clear sighted, 240,25
diorizein, specify, 239,30
diplasiologia, diplasiology, 251,7
dogma, doctrine, 272,27
doxosophia, belief in own wisdom, 270,4; supposed wisdom, 270,20; conceit of wisdom, 271,27

dunamis, power, 232,28; 235,5.11; 244,28, etc.; art, 245,26; function, 249,21; force, 252,11

egeirein, stir, 232,22; excite, 251,19
eidôlon, image, 273,14; 276,29
eidos, type, 222,14; 247,2; 259,2.4.25; 276,4; form, 225,23; 236,23; 237,11; 247,1; 248,6; 260,2; kind, 227,17; 240,18; 244,17; 260,19; species, 229,9; 246,9.10.14; 247,4; 255,13.14; nature, 258,22.24; variety, 259,20
eikôn, image, 222,2; 238,9.10; 245,8; 268,26; likeness, 223,17; 251,10
eikonologia, eikonology, 251,10
eikos, likely, 255,30; *to eikos*, probability, 229,1.19; 237,23.27; 249,31; 263,4.6; 264,8.10; 278,27; the probable, 262,21; 263,1.6.12.13; 264,2.5
ekgonos, offspring, 273,13; progeny, 277,10
elenkhein, be critical of, 239,6; criticise, 239,9
elenkhos, criticism, 239,7, 241,24; 243,12
emphainein, indicate, 267,26; 279,11; reveal, 267,28; display, 268,17
emphanes, to, the visible, visibility, 225,27; 269,4
empsukhos, animated, 232,18; animate, 272,2.4
enargês, self-evident, 228,10.11.12
endeiknunai, indicate, 239,8; 243,13; 245,20; 267,12; show, 241,18; 269,7; 271,29; display, 259,10
endiathetos, internal, 272,4; 273,7; 277,18
endoxos, based on common opinion, 220,16; 245,25; generally accepted, 257,17; 262,22
endoxôs, on the basis of common opinion, 220,16.22; 221,7
energeia, activity, 222,24; 224,22; 245,8; 267,24; 269,6.16; 274,8; 277,14; power, 273,18
enkosmios, mundane, 274,2
ennoia, thought, 273,6; conception, 276,29
enthousian, be possessed, 245,3.16
enthousiastikon, to, divine possession, 241,8
epainein, praise, 245,28; 250,8.9; 257,11; 267,5; 269,13.29; 276,27; 278,18.26

epainetos, praiseworthy, 221,2.5; to be praised, 265,23
epainos, praise, 230,1; 231,12; 264,27
ephoros, overseer, 223,13; patron, 227,8; guardian, 245,18; presiding, 267,21; 270,25
epibolê, intuition, 269,15
epideixis, demonstration, 248,20
epikheirêma, argument, 242,16; proof, 245,25
epilampein, radiate, 242,24
epimeleia, care, 226,18; 232,2
epistêmê, knowledge, 248,1; 254,11; 255,23.26; 258,4; 266,6; 271,13.30; 276,2.8; science, 255,31; 261,25 scientific knowledge, 221,26.28
epistêmôn, wise, 270,21; 272,24.25; wise man, 233,13; knowledgeable, 248,25; 274,17; 278,2; with knowledge, 246,12; 271,31; with understanding, 277,10; acquainted with, 238,12; skilled, 248,19; studious, 255,21
epistêmonikos, scientific, 221,25; 223,8; 228,23; 262,19; epistemic, 276,28
epithumêtikos, appetitive, 258,11.13; 260,4.7
epithumia, appetite, 259,7; desire, 268,22
epitropeuein, oversee, 277,23; govern, 279,10
eran, love, be in love, 221,1; 227,13.15; 242,5.6; *ho erôn*, lover, 242,5; 244,7.9.14; *ho erômenos*, beloved, 241,4
erastês, lover, 244,8; 279,3
erôs, love, 227,17; 239,16.19.29, etc.
erôtikos, erotic, 244,27; 245,1; *ta erôtika*, erotic matters, 227,16
êthikos, ethical, 235,14
ethos, custom, 238,21; 272,25
êthos, disposition, 260,20; character, 278,20; *en êthei*, out of tact, 230,5; 248,18; charitably, 249,4; politely, 249,28; 259,12
eukhê, prayer, 279,6.8; 280,3
eukhesthai, pray, 219,4; 279,15
euphrosunê, good cheer, 226,9; merriment, 250,26; 251,1
euprepeia, propriety, 229,12; 266,4.5.13 271,4.5; 275,17.19; 276,23
euprepôs, with propriety, 266,11; appropriately, 271,16; 277,7

exêgeisthai, interpret, 224,25; explain, 246,16; comment on, 267,9
exêgêsis, interpretation, 225,21
exetazein, scrutinise, 222,3; 223,11; examine, 222,14; question, 233,28; test, 249,6

gê, world, 256,14; soil, 273,20.24
genesis, origin, 222,26; generation, 223,28.30; 224,18.19; 226,1; 277,23; coming into existence, 273,25; genesis, 225,28
gennan, produce, 222,17; generate, 275,11
gennêma, offspring, 267,32
genos, genus, 229,8; 238,24.25.28; 247,4; 277,26; class, 240,24
geômetria, geometry, 268,18
glukuthumia, self-indulgence, 223,22.28; 224,13; 225,12; pleasantness, 260,8
gnôsis, knowledge, 228,31; 231,11; 232,19; 233,21; 240,22; 256,32; understanding, 229,1
goês, sorcerer, 237,6

hadros, grand, 259,26; 260,11
hamartêma, failure, 231,22; fault, 243,13.17.18.19; offence, 254,22
harmonia, harmony, 226,7.13; 254,8.9; mode, 259,15.17
harmonikos, harmonic(s), 254,15; 255,12; *harmonikê*, musical theory, 253,4
harmozein, fit, be fitting, 239,27; 241,6; suit, be suited, 240,27; 260,20; be appropriate, 254,5; be applicable, 257,23; match, 272,28; assign, 246,26; apply to, 249,10; 261,4; harmoniously order, 254,12; adapt, 257,6
hêdonê, pleasure, 222,19–223,27; 226,8; 250,26; 267,6; 274,23
hêgeisthai, lead, 226,19
hêgemôn, guide, 245,19
hen, to, unity, 219,10; 257,25; one, 229,6.8.9; 240,17; 246,15; 247,2.3; 248,3.7; 253,29; the One, 242,23.24
henoeidôs, in unitary mode, 269,18.19
henôsis, unity, 242,25
henoun, be united, unified, 219,11; 242,22; *to hênômenon*, unity, 219,10; 242,26
hepesthai, follow, 225,14; 230,15; 244,1.23; be guided, 259,6.7

hêrôs, hero, 223,21; 225,14; 267,14; 268,3
hetairos, pupil, 234,19; friend, 243,9; 278,13.14
heterokinêtos, other-moved, 273,9
holos, whole, 223,2; 245,16; 256,28.30.32; 257,8.9.12.15; wholly, 244,20; completely, 249,21; universal, 225,31
homoiotês, similarity, 236,15.16.18.19.30; 237,9.11.15.17.27.29; 238,2.16; 247,20; 264,9
homologia, concession, 236,14
hôra, season, 253,19
horismos, definition, 229,11; 239,19.21; 240,29.30; 246,14; 249,3; 276,3
horistikos, of definition, 245,22.27; 246,3.11; 247,2; skilled in definition, 236,20; 240,1; someone who practises division, 247,26; *horistikê*, definition, 229,10; 252,24; 260,17; *horistikon*, definition, 248,26
horizein, define, 240,17.19; 241,11.18.19.20.22.27; 242,3; 243,2; 246,14; 252,27; produce a definition, 247,3
hugeia, health, 253,10.11; 258,18
hugiês, sound, 252,19; well, 253,18
hugros, moist, 257,27
hugrotês, moisture, 223,30
hulê, matter, 224,27; 256,22; subject matter, 237,24; 240,6; 245,25
hulikos, material, 256,24
humnein, hymn, 245,15; 265,1
humnos, hymn, 264,24
hupar, waking vision, 276,29.31
huperkosmios, hypercosmic, 225,24
hupodeigma, example, 223,11; 238,1.7.9; 243,26; 246,21; 254,8; 263,13; illustration, 251,11
hupolêpsis, conception, 239,20.29; 240,30
hupomimnêskein, remind, 249,19; 271,14; 276,5
hupomnêma, aide-mémoire, 270,14.15; reminder, 274,16
hupomnêsis, reminding, 270,13; reminder, 271,29
huponoia, conception, 240,28; covert indication, 245,12

iatrikê, medicine, 253,4; 254,14; 256,26; 258,15; 259,29

iatros, doctor, 243,22; 253,8.10.12.15.19; 255,9.10; 256,27
idea, kind, 240,20; form, 246,13; 248,7
idiôma, distinctive characteristic, 227,18; 257,4.5
idiôtês, layman, 253,11
indalma, form, 267,24

kairos, appropriate, right, time, 253,24; 260,21; 261,4
kakos, bad, 219,20.21.24; 220,13, etc.; *to kakon*, badness, 219,22; evil, 230,15; 231,17; 244,8
kallos, beauty, 219,14; 242,25.27; 244,22.24
kalos, fine, 219,21.24; 220,27; 221,5, etc.; good, 239,20; 241,6; 247,6, etc.; noble, 230,2.10; 264,22; beautiful, 234,13; 242,25; 245,18; of value, 249,1.2.4.5; *to kalon*, fineness, 219,22; beauty, 242,23; 244,25; the beautiful, 244,22
kanôn, standard, 222,6; 233,9.10.11; rule, 223,10; straight edge, 228,25.26.28
kataphronein, despise, 226,13; 256,19; disdain, 267,4; look down on, 270,3
katatattein, order, 227,29
katêgorein, predicate, 228,14
katêgoria, prosecution, 229,30
kathairein, purge, 255,10
katharos, pure, 222,21; 245,19; *to katharon*, purity, 245,20
kathêgemôn, leader, 219,1
katholikos, general, 222,9; 223,8.12; 228,23; 235,5
katokhos, possessed, 244,19; 247,10
kêlein, beguile, 223,27; 224,9
kharizesthai, gratify, 244,8.9.14; 265,9.11.12.16.17; please, be pleasing, 264,24.27–30; 266,12.17; 267,5; 271,6
khoreia, dance, 227,2.3.5.6.8.9.15
khoreuein, dance, 227,6.11
khrêma, resource, 232,12; money, 248,21; possession, 279,18
khrêsimos, useful, 249,18; 268,21; *to khrêsimon*, usefulness, 269,11; 274,15
khrêsis, use, 249,24; 253,16; 273,17; practice, 254,11; 260,22
khronos, time, 225,26; 242,5; 273,29; 278,27; *pros tous khronous*, chronologically, 242,4; *para tous khronous*, contrary to chronology, 242,8
khrusos, gold, 237,5; 279,25
kinêsis, motion, 223,29; 227,28
koinos, everyday, 236,28; in common, 280,1; *to koinon*, the state, 232,4; *koinêi*, in public, 234,29
kosmos, cosmos, 224,16; 225,26.29-31; 226,6; 254,12; 256,8.14; 269,2; 274,3.7; 277,16.25
kratein, rule, 223,1; win, 261,7.9; master, 279,13
krinein, detect, 228,25; judge, 228,27; 269,16.17.24; 275,19
krisis, judgement, 241,24; 250,20; 269,14.15.19.20
kritikos, critic, 242,9; discerning, 269,13; *to kritikon*, ability to judge, 269,25
kubernêtês, steersman, 269,17
kubos, dice, 236,1; 274,19
kuklos, circle, 262,17
kurios, proper, 251,13; ordinary, 251,15; valuable, 253,11

lêthê, forgetfulness, 271,15.26; loss of memory, 274,16
logikos, rational, 222,16; 223,25; 246,8; 258,11; 260,4; 268,22; 269,15; 279,12; endowed with reason, 239,1; involving calculation, 268,11; of calculation, 268,12
logios, of language, 277,24
logismos, calculation, 268,16
logistikê, hê, calculation, 268,15
lographein, to, speech-writing, writing speeches, 219,20; 220,7.13.18.19.27; 221,1.5.7.20.22; 279,2
logographos, speech-writer, 219,19.24; 275,27; 278,11.22
logos, speech, 218,27; 219,6.7, etc.; discourse, 219,10.11.12, etc.; account, 221,24; 222,9.12; 228,8, etc.; conversation, 223,17; story, 226,15; 270,25; word, 227,22; 231,8; 234,25, etc.; language, 232,18; 266,26; 267,16.21; 277,25; discussion, 228,24; 270,12; argument, 233,17.26; 234,1.8.11, etc.; statement, 241,6; 261,23; expression, 251,4; composition,

251,16; 276,11; work, 253,30;
description, 267,26; letter, 269,8;
thought, 267,28; 270,3.4.7; 274,23;
reason, 222,19.23; 239,1; 260,6;
reasoning, 262,19; formula, 229,11;
rational forming principle, 248,6;
concept, 254,27
lupê, pain, 222,22.26; grief, 250,11

mania, madness, 244,13.16.17.24; 246,25; 247,9.10.16; 253,22
manthanein, learn, 222,5; 228,13; 232,24; 255,29; 270,7.29; 271,26; 276,18; *ho manthanôn*, pupil, 270,6; 273,6; learner, 271,15; 272,5; 277,7
mathêma, knowledge, 253,6; science, 268,25; 274,24
mathêtês, pupil, 250,15.17.18; 255,1; 263,29; 271,20; 272,5.27; 275,9; 277,11; learner, 270,15
meletê, practice, 255,23.28
merikos, individual, 225,31; particular, 269,18; *ta merika*, parts, 257,8
meros, particular, 221,26; 223,12; part, 224,5; 229,24.25; 247,7; 254,1; 257,2.3.15; 258,10; 260,19; 267,9; branch, 234,27; *ta kata meros*, details, 222,6; 259,25; portion, 256,31
metadosis, distribution, 268,7.8
methodos, method, 229,7; 235,4.9.11.13.15; 240,22; 245,23.27; 246,11; 257,21; 266,2; enquiry, 256,4
metron, measure, 253,24; limitation, 278,2; *meta metrou*, metrical, 222,10; *aneu metrou*, non-metrical, 222,11
mimeisthai, imitate, 243,28
monimon, to, stability, 268,25
morion, part, 219,12; 242,26; 247,14; 259,2; 260,3; component, 256,30
mouseion, gallery, 251,4.5
mousikos, musical, 225,20; 226,14; 254,11; 259,17; musician, 254,8; 259,18; *mousikê*, music, 225,18
mustêrion, mystery, 227,7
muthikos, mythical, 245,11
muthologein, tell stories, 275,2.3
muthos, myth, 223,4; 225,17; 244,29; 245,13.14; 267,9; 268,29; story, 275,4.6

neotelês, newly initiated, 225,32; 245,19
noêma, thought, 268,27; 271,19.23
noeros, intellectual, 222,24; 228,5; 269,16; intellective, 258,5; *to noeron*, intellective part, aspect, 222,16; 228,6; intellection, 223,30
noêtos, intelligible, 218,29; 224,11.15; 225,2.22.23.29; 226,3; 231,29; 241,8; 244,24; 245,5; 248,6; 256,23; 268,13; 277,17
nomizein, believe, 220,11; 231,6.7; consider, 231,8; 232,11; 256,14; take, 237,4
nomos, law, 221,9
nomothetês, lawgiver, 221,21; 277,30
nomothetikos, legislative, 222,13; 277,27
nous, intellect, 226,17; 238,9.10; 239,1; mind, 256,9.20.21; sense, 236,11; 249,12

oikeiotês, relationship, 228,5; kinship, 267,23
oikonomikos, economic, 235,14
onar, dream, 276,29.30.32
onoma, word, 228,18; 239,16; 240,16; 249,14; 250,25; 251,2.11.12.15; 278,4; name, 247,14; 268,1; term, 248,11
onomazein, name, 228,1; call, 252,5
opados, attendant, 224,21; 225,13; 226,21; 266,20
ôpheleia, benefit, 248,21; 269,11; 271,15; advantage, 271,7
ophelos, advantage, 233,2; 238,12
oregesthai, strive, 278,4.7
orektikos, appetitive, 259,3
organon, tool, 229,14; 247,30; instrument, 266,13
orthos, right, 232,11; 246,29; genuine, 240,26; 254,17; valid, 259,6; *orthê*, set square, 228,25; square, 228,26
ouranios, celestial, 227,25.28.29.31
ousia, being, 218,29; 231,29; substance, 272,19; nature, 273,17; essence, 229,15
ousiôdês, substantial, 234,9
ousioun, have substantial being, 222,16.23

paideia, education, 268,23
paideuein, educate, 278,17
paidia, amusement, 238,15.17; 273,19.23; 274,1.19; 275,3; pastime, 266,8; 268,23;

271,15; play, 273,27; 274,8.13; 275,1; 277,5.13; game, 277,15
paidion, child, 232,23; 269,27
palaios, ancient, 219,24; 230,6; 235,18; 256,10; 267,11; old, 267,12; early, 270,27; venerable, 271,11
pan, to, the All, 256,30; the universe, 279,10
panêgurikos, panegyrical, 229,25.26.28; 230,1; 234,28
paraballein, compare, 239,5; 242,15; 256,26; 273,18.23; 274,18; 276,29
paradeigma, example, 230,13; 237,21.22; 238,10; 243,16.19; 253,4.26; 255,8.12; 259,28; 273,19; 276,10
paradidonai, teach, 223,9; 243,21; 254,29; 255,15.16; 256,4; 258,22.26; 259,24; 264,22.23; 266,2; 268,21; 271,13; 273,17; give, 237,26; 259,20; impart, 259,28; 268,24; get across, 261,14
paragein, win over, 237,15; 238,2.16; lead, 240,12
parergon, secondary activity, 265,9.17
paroimia, proverb, 220,24.27.28; 262,2.5; saying, 250,15.21; 280,2; *apo paroimias*, proverbial, 231,10.17
pathos, sensation, 222,29; emotive effect, 232,8.9; emotion, 232,8.10; 233,8; 253,28; 254,10; passion, 245,1; 254,18; experience, 237,12
peira, trial and error, 260,12; 261,22; test, 260,26; trying, 261,20
peithein, persuade, 229,18; 230,12.16.24, etc.; be persuasive, 232,23.24; 237,27; talk into, 230,19; convince, 238,9; 264,8
peithô, persuasion, 230,26; 232,20; 234,26; 236,27; 276,15; belief, 258,17.19
peras, end, 277,21
periagein, bring around, 236,18; 237,10
perilambanein, encompass, 221,26; 229,11; grasp, 235,9
phainesthai, appear, 226,6.7; be seen, 229,29; seem, 236,10; 246,1; 252,13.16; 253,1; 256,16; be clear, 267,27; *phainomenos*, phenomenal, 219,14; 275,5; apparent, 253,3; 270,16; 272,11; 276,32; *phainomenon*, appearance, 224,10; 272,11
phantastikos, imaginative, 259,3; of the imagination, 276,29

pharmakon, potion, 243,22; medication, 253,16.17; 255,10; 258,7.9.15
phaulos, bad, 240,16; 269,27; paltry, 275,1.3
philokhrêmaton, to, love of money, 248,20
philomousos, Muse-loving, 225,14; lover of the Muses, 226,17
philosophia, philosophy, 219,5; 227,21.26; 234,12.16.17.18.20; 237,12; 256,7; 278,16; 279,3
philosophos, philosopher, 218,27; 219,9.15.19, etc.; philosophical, 221,25; 225,15
philotimia, ambition, 271,8
phôs, light, 226,27; 244,1
phôteinos, enlightened, 258,5
phronêsis, soundness of mind, 247,9
phulattein, guard against, 243,22.23.27; carefully consider, 253,19
phusikos, physical, 242,19; natural, 247,4; 269,15
phusis, nature, 229,15; 230,21; 233,3, etc.
pisteutikos, that creates belief, 276,16.17
pistis, credence, 238,10; proof, 249,13.30; 255,6; belief, 257,17
pistôsis, confirmation, 250,1
planasthai, go astray, 227,24; be uncertain, 240,12
plasma, fiction, 245,1.12
plattein, make up, 270,23.24
plêthos, the many, 231,21; 232,9.22; 261,30; 262,6.22.25.27; 263,2.7; quantity, 279,25; amount, 262,11
poiêtês, poet, 274,3
poiêtikos, poetic, 221,24; 277,27; *poiêtikê*, art of poetry, poetry, 253,4; 254,14; 255,12
polemos, war, 224,27
polis, city, 221,19; 231,24; 232,2.3.12; 235,10.15; 248,24; state, 267,18
politikos, political, 222,10.12; 232,3; 235,15; 277,27; politician, 277,30
polueidês, multiform, 258,23
ponêria, vice, 251,10
pragmateia, diligent study, 264,14
praktikos, practical, 254,12
praxis, action, 219,23
problêma, question, 228,23; topic, 242,4; issue, 271,3

pronoia, providence, 238,24; concern, 263,3
proodos, procession, 225,27; 226,6
prooimion, introduction, 239,10.11; 248,16; 249,13.20.23–5; 252,29; 253,5; 255,6
prophorikos, spoken, 264,26; 277,17; uttered, 267,32; 273,7
prosdialegein, address, 236,14.16; 237,10
prosekhês, attentive, 249,21
prosôpopoiia, personification, 232,18
prosphoros, appropriate, 229,12; 246,26; fitting, 232,7
prosphorôs, fittingly, 254,10; as befits, 256,12; appropriately, 258,18; 260,26
prostatês, champion, 262,6
prosthêkê, assistance, 254,12
prothesis, intention, 219,22
psegein, censure, 245,28; 250,8
psektos, blameworthy, 221,2
pseudês, false, 263,2; 276,27
pseudesthai, lie, 263,22
pseudos, false, 239,28; 260,17; 270,29
psukhagôgia, influencing of the soul, 234,25; leading of the soul, 260,1
psukhê, soul, 218,29; 222,16.17.23, etc.
pteron, wing, 244,29; 245,2; 267,26
pur, fire, 256,30

rhapsôdos, rhapsode, 277,30
rhêma, word, 240,27; 259,13
rhêton, literal meaning, 267,9
rhêtôr, rhetorician, 228,28; 230,11; 231,11; 248,24; 262,12; 263,14; 264,26; 266,3; speaker, 231,18; 233,14; 234,2; 237,28; 238,2; 252,23; 255,14; 256,13; orator, 219,25.26; 231,24; 232,5.9.13; etc.
rhêtoreuein, give, make, deliver, speeches, 230,2; 255,20; 256,3; speak, 256,13
rhêtorikos, rhetorical, 249,10.14; 276,14; speaker, 231,14; orator 255,17.19; 256,2; 262,18; *hê rhêtorikê*, rhetoric, 219,13.17.20; 221,23; 223,6, etc.
rhuthmos, rhythm, 227,26

selênê, moon, 228,16
sêmainein, mean, 228,18; indicate, 240,16; *sêmainomenon*, sense, 229,7; 239,17; 241,17.22

skhesis, relationship, 268,15.16
skholê, time, 223,3.14
skia, shadow, 231,10–13
skopein, consider, 240,26; 257,1; 258,28.29; 263,17; examine, 258,22
sôizein, rescue, 227,24; preserve, 230,14
sôma, body, 226,18.21; 242,22; 247,12, etc.
sômatikos, bodily, 222,26; 226,19; of the body, 223,28
sophia, skill, 230,8; wisdom, 270,16; 278,4.8
sophistês, sophist, 250,16
sophistikos, sophistic, 243,21; 260,10
sophos, wise, 230,4.6; 265,2.5; 266,21.24.27; 270,21; 278,1–3.5; 279,23; clever, 248,17.18
sôphronein, be of sound mind, 244,15
sphaira, sphere, 225,25.27.30; 226,8; 228,1.2
spoudaios, serious, 274,7; 277,5
spoudazein, take seriously, 271,15; do with serious intent, 274,14; enthuse about, 276,26
spoudê, seriousness, 273,27; 275,8; 277,15; serious work, 274,8; serious attention, 274,10; serious intent, 274,12; *meta spoudês*, in all seriousness, 238,16; that involves serious engagement, 273,26
stasis, standing still, 268,19
stoikheion, element, 256,28; 257,26
stratêgikê, hê, art of generalship, 235,7
strephesthai, engage with, 231,29; be directed, 232,1; sojourn, 241,8; be concerned with, 245,24
sullogismos, argument, 236,24
sumbainein, result, 229,22; 230,20; be incidental, 265,11; *kata sumbebêkos*, incidentally, 265,10
sumbolon, symbol, 273,15
summetria, due balance, 251,3
sumperasma, conclusion, 233,15
sunagein, bring, gather, together, 219,1; 229,10; 247,2; infer, 263,4
sunaptein, connect, 226,26; link up with, 236,11; join with, 256,8
sunekheia, continuity, 268,19
sunekhês, continuous, 242,20; *to sunekhes*, continuity, 219,10
sunergos, workmate, 227,14; contributor, 277,23

sunêtheia, custom, 220,18
sungramma, writing, 220,8; 221,21; 266,23; 270,14; 271,19; 275,4; composition, 269,29; 277,28
sungraphê, writing, 222,12; 223,7; 276,31
sungraphein, write, 220,22; 228,19.21; 266,5.6.8.9, etc.
sunkrisis, comparison, 272,2
sunopsis, overview, 275,16; 277,8; review, 276,22.
sunousia, conversation, 235,2; 243,12; meeting, 235,19
sunthetos, composite, 228,8.14; 256,28; compound, 251,13; complex, 257,22.25; 258,10.23.24; 260,19
sustoikhia, column, 247,18

taxis, disposition, 238,4; arrangement, 238,27; ordering, 242,21; order, 242,29; 243,6; 254,28; 255,7; 269,25; organisation, 253,29; rank, 267,13.14; 268,30; 269,21; *taxei*, in an orderly manner, 239,24
tekhnê, art, 231,26; 232,15.20.24; 233,3, etc.; artistry, 278,19
tekhnikos, proficient, skilled, in an art, 236,2; 237,14.15; artistic, 241,13; of the art, 249,20; 259,24; belonging to the art, 252,16; *to tekhnikon*, technique, 244,4
tekhnitês, artificer, 232,21; 250,2; practitioner, 254,15
tekhnographos, writer on the art, 252,29
tektôn, carpenter, 230,6; 232,21; craftsman, 233,13.14
teleios, perfect, 273,28.29; mature, 275,10
telestês, priest, 237,6
telos, goal, 229,25; 233,6.8.15; 253,9.12; 261,17; purpose, 234,23; outcome, 231,19; end, 242,4.28; 264,23.24; 265,15; 277,21; final part, 252,3; ending, 279,7
thanatos, death, 226,20; 278,15.18
thea, spectacle, 232,2; vision, 232,3.6
thea, divinity, 277,23
theios, divine, 223,20; 224,18; 225,21, etc.

thelgein, charm, 223,27
theoeidôs, in a godlike manner, 224,19
theologos, theologian, 245,14
theôrein, contemplate, 225,24; study, 257,12.21; develop theories, 261,23; observe, 268,15; watch, 274,18
theôrêma, general principle, 235,4; principle, 259,24; technique, 252,16; 255,16
theôrêtikos, theoretical, 254,11; thoughtful, 258,12
theôrêtikôs, allegorically, 224,25; 246,29;
theôria, contemplation, 223,16; 231,29; 266,14; 279,27; allegorical interpretation, 225,17; 226,16
theos, god, 223,18.21; 224,15.18.21, etc.; deity, 223,13
therapeuein, indulge, 232,8.10; 254,18
thnêtos, mortal, 223,24; 225,23
thumikos, spirited, 258,11; 259,3; 260,4
thumos, spirited part, 260,7
topos, spot, 220,24.26; 221,4
tragôdia, tragedy, 253,28
tribê, practice, 233,22; 237,19; routine, 233,27; 234,4; knack, 261,10.28; experiment, 261,22
trigônon, triangle, 243,7
tukhê, chance, 238,11; 246,5; luck, 268,25; *ek tukhês*, as it happens, 246,3
tupos, framework, 259,14.19; mark, 270,10

zên, live, 222,18; 224,19; 225,12.13; 226,17; 235,24; 259,7; 272,23; 273,11
zêtein, seek, 228,8.17; 230,10; enquire, 228,10.11; look for, 241,26; investigate, 258,25; 261,17; 267,10
zôê, life, 226,19.20; 227,7.10
zôion, living being, living creature, 219,10.11; 242,19; 246,8; 247,13; 267,25; creature, 223,24; animal, 223,25; 230,17; 242,20; living thing, 237,5; figure, 272,8
zôôdês, that resembles a living person, 272,10; animal, 279,12

Subject Index

References in the form 224,25 are to the page and line numbers of the Greek text in the margins of the translation; those listed after 'n.' to the notes.

Adonis 273,23.25
Adrastus 254,13.16
allegory 224,25; 245,8–15; n. 36, 38, 128, 228, 277
Ammon 269,4.20; 271.5.26; n. 253, 257
analysis 229,3
Anaxagoras 234,19; 256,8; n. 181, 185, 247
angels 268,2
Aphrodite 216,17; 244,21.23
Aristotle 228,7; 236,25; 245,23; 262,22; 275,13; n. 9, 20, 21, 62, 64, 93, 95, 99, 138, 140, 149, 205, 247
art (*tekhnê*) 221,24; 231,26; 232,15; 233,4–25; 235,4–12; 236,9.26.29; 237,14–24; 238,21; 239,2.14; 240,14; 246,6–12.24; 248,15; 249,3–19; 251,24
Athena 250,23
Athens
    Assembly 221,12; 261,2
    Council 221,12; n. 15
    law courts 219,26; 235,2.19; 236,6.8.26.28; 262,19

beauty
    beauty-itself 244,22.26
    intelligible beauty 244,23
    perceptible beauty 219,14; 244,23
body 247,12; 256,28.32; 257,14.23.25; 258,8.15.18.28; 263.16–19; n. 188, 195
    care of 226,19
    pleasures of 223,28

Calliope 227,19.21
cicadas 223,20.24; 224,10.18; 225,9.16; 226,14.16; 227,16.22; n. 51, 65, 263
common opinion 220,16–22; 221,7; 245,25; n. 13

cosmos 254,12; 256,9.10.14; 274,2.7; 277,16.25; n. 52, 176, 253
    intelligible 225,30
    sensible 224,16; 225,25–31; 226,6; 269,2; n. 253, 277

Daedalus 250,4; n. 150
daemons 223,20; 224,17; 225,6–14; 226,23–8; 238,25; 239,1.2; 267,14; 268,1–9; n. 51, 106, 107, 248, 297
dance 227,2–11; n. 52
definition 229,10.11; 236,20; 239,19.21; 240,1.29.30; 245,22.27; 246,3.12.14; 247,2.3.26; 248,26; 249,3; 252,24; 260,17; 276,3; n. 176.
Demiurge 225,28; 232,20 ('artificer of persuasion', *Gorg.* 453A2); 269,2; n. 277
Demosthenes 234,19; 251,8; n. 91, 160, 161
desire 267,7; 268,21
dialectic 236,4; 245,24.28; 246,3; 247,29; 248,5.25.27; 249,10; 250,3; 254,24–6; 275,7; n. 95, 142–4, 179, 261, 273
division, method of 229,6.9; 235,9; 236,20; 240,1.22; 245,23; 246,7–10; 247,3–7.26–30; 248,2.26; 249,3; 252,24; 257,21; 260,17; 276,3; n. 138

Egypt/Egyptians 220,24; 266,25; 267,16–21; 269,3.22; n. 243, 253, 264
Erato 227,13–15
Eros (*see* love/Love)
etymological explanations 220,24–221,5; 227,13–17.21.31; 250,15; 269,3
experience (*empeiria*) 233,28; 234,4; 260,13; 261,14; n. 75, see also routine (*tribê*)

Subject Index

forms 225,23; 236,23; 237,11; 247,1; 248,6; 260,2; n. 143

gods 221,18; 223,20; 225,6–8.21; 226,19; 227,7; 238,20–6; 245,14; 251,23; 265,8; 267,7.14.23; 268,30; 269,19; 270,25; 271,5; 279,6–8; n. 245, 246, 257
   connection of humans to 226,25
   gifts of 224,15.20; 225,3.10–14; 247,30; 264,14.15; n. 142
   heavenly or celestial 227,5; n. 53
   hypercosmic 225,24
   laughter of 274,3–8; 277,16; n. 277
   souls that attend upon 225,3.10–14; 266,20–2
   what is pleasing to 264,24.30; 265,13.16; 266,11–14; 267,3; n. 222
good, the 230,10; 233,8.18.19.24

Hephaestus 274,5; n. 277
Hermes 266,26.27; 267,15.21; 268,4.9.12.29; 269,21; 271,4.11; 277,24; n. 239, 248
heroes 223,20; 225,14; 267,14; 268,2
Hippocrates 253,19; 257,9.10.16–27; n. 173, 192, 195
Homer 277,26; n. 164
   Iliad 224,25; 230,6; n. 277
   Odyssey 224,26; n. 38

Iamblichus 225,21
ibis 267,20–7; n. 241, 243, 244, 246, 247
Isocrates 278,14–24, n. 292

Kronos 228,1

Laconian 233,23.24
language 232,18; 251,4.14; n. 163
   god of 266,21; 277,24
   invention of 266,26; 267,15
Licymnius 251,4.12
love/Love
   ambiguous notion 235,15–31; 240,15–19; 247,22
   as god 225,5; 227,13; 244,21–3; 245,16.19; 246,2.21; 278,5; n. 39
   defining of 241,17–22.28; 242,5–7; 243,2; 245,28

   noble or correct love 240,26; 241,4–6; 247,29
   of money 248,20
   of Muses, wisdom or philosophy 226,17; 278,5; n. 290
   of speech-writing or language 220,23; 221,1; 279,4
   shameful love 227,13; 246,30; 247,31; n. 141
   speeches about 244,3.7–15

madness 244,13–19.24; 246,25–8; 247,9.10.16.21; 253,22; n. 140
matter 224,27
medicine 243,22; 253,4–19; 255,9.10.14; 256,26; 258,15; 259,29; n. 188, 203
Muses 223,14; 225,17–226,20.29; 227,19.20; 228,5; 246,5; 271,3; n. 42, 45, 176
music (more broadly, 'culture') 225,18–20; 226,15; 227,19.31; 253,4; 254,7–12; 259,15–19; n. 34, 54, 59, 60, 176, 202
myth 244,29; 245,10–14; 267,9; 268,29; n. 48, 65, 129, 251, 263, 264, 281
mysteries 227,7

Nestor 235,21–3; 236,5; n. 95
number 236,1; 268,10.12–19
Nymphs 241,11–14; 246,4; 277,22; n. 287

Odysseus 224,13.29; 235,22–5; n. 38
Olympiodorus n. 75, 172, 177, 188, 213, 298, 292
One, the 242,24; n. 66
Orpheus 271,11

Palamedes 235,22; 236,1–3, 267,20
Pan 246,4; 279,9–10
Pericles 220,20; 232,13; 234,18; 254,16; 256,7; n. 13, 75
philosophy 219,9; 227,21.26; 234,12–20; 237,12; 256,7; 278,16; 279,3; n. 55, 131, 237
Platonic dialogues
   Alcibiades 256,15; n. 172, 194
   Charmides 266,24; n. 237
   Gorgias 232,14; 265,3
   Philebus 247,27; n. 26, 138, 142

Republic 224,6; 233,12; 247,28; n. 2, 32, 84, 119, 129, 142, 169, 174, 256, 294
Sophist 235,6; 247,30; 266,21; n. 138, 178, 234
Statesman 247,28; n. 138, 141
Symposium 220,9; 225,5; 226,23; 267,29; 278,5; n. 11, 49, 245, 291
Theaetetus 226,11; n. 46, 100, 115
Timaeus 256,29; 266,25; 267,16; 274,22; n. 31, 52, 53, 57, 107, 178, 187, 189, 237, 240, 279
pleasure or taking pleasure 220,7; 222,19–223,2.22.27; 226,9; 238,7; 250,26; 259,7–8; 260,6; 267,6; 274,21–4; 276,10; n. 26, 34, 38, 157, 222
Plotinus 275,13; n. 52, 143
Polemarchus 218,6; 219,4; n. 2
Polemo 272,6
Polus 251,5.13; 262,11; 265,3.5; n. 158, 162, 205
probabilities 229,1.19; 237,24.27; 249,27.31; 262,21.25; 263,1–9.11–15; 264.2–10; n. 221, 222
Proclus, n. *passim*
Prodicus 250,24; 251,1; n. 154, 157
proverbial sayings 220,24–7; 231,10.17; 262,2.5; n. 72, 212
providence 238,24; n. 203, 277
Pythagoras 220,21; 227,31; 247,18; 265,2; 272,25; n. 140, 236, 237

recollection 244,25
rhetoric, *passim*
   and action 264,20
   and dialectic 255,25
   and psychology 257,1–6; 258,7–13.15–26; 259,2–8
   and truth 236,10–25; 237,23–238,3; 240,15; 263,3–8; 264,6–10
   branches of 229,24–5; 234,27–8
   kind intermediate between popular and true 231,27–232,14; 253,16–20
   pleasing gods versus pleasing men 264,20–265,2
   popular versus true 229,18–23; 230,13–15; 232,17; 233,6–19; 234,5; 248,10–15; 252,21–7; 261,26–31
   preliminaries to true rhetoric 248,15–17; 249,13–16; 253,5–7; 255,6–17
   purpose of 234,24–235,1; 264,22–5
   subject matter of 229,24–231,2; 234,4–15; 240,6.7.9–14
routine (*tribê*) 233,27; 234,4; 237,19; 261,28

sensible or perceptible things (opp. intelligible) 224,16; 225,26.29.30; 226.2.6.12; 241,9; 244,24.25; 268,14.20; 269,2; n. 277
similarity 236,15–19.30; 237,11.29; n. 176
Sirens 224,9.16.28; n. 34
Solon 221,18; 277,26; n. 45
sophists 220,15; 243,21; 250,16; 260,10; n. 261
soul, *passim*
   divine 223,20; 224,18; 227,4; 277,23
   harmonies in 226,7
   human
      ascent 224,25–225,2
      become attendants of gods 225,11–14.22–5
      communion with gods mediated 238,22–5
      different natures persuaded differently 259,2–8; 261,2–6; 276,9–12
      led by words 234,25–8; 260,1
      newly initiated 245,19
      parts of 257,1–5; 258,22–5; 260, 2–4
      words in soul of learner 268,26; 270,5; 272,2–5; 273,5–14; 277,5–8; n. 285
   immortal 218,29; 272,19
   rational 222,16–18.23–4; n. 26
   self-moving 272,19
   world soul 225,31
Sparta, *see* Laconian

Terpsichore 227,1.8.14
Thamus 268,28; 269,5.12.20; n. 257
Themistocles 220,20; 232,14; n. 13
theologians 245,14
Theuth 268,1.6.8; 269,12.22; n. 244, 246
Thrasymachus 235,25; 248,17; 251,8;

256,3; 258,21
Tisias 250,14; 263,9.10.15.27.28; n. 154

unity
   of body 257,25; n. 195
   of discourse 219,10; 242,26; n. 118

virtue 259,16; 261,19; 264,15.18; 275,2

writing
   animate words written in the soul 272,2-7; 273,11-14
   conditions for propriety 266,5-9
   origins of 266,28; 268,10.26
   piety and 266,11-14; 271,5-9; n. 232
   Plato's writings lost in shipwreck 271,18-23
   purposes of 270,14-16

Xenocrates 272,6

Zeno of Elea 235,25; 236,2; 250,3
Zeus 219,1; 235,17; 241,10; 269,2; n. 253

'Syrianus'

Introduction to Hermogenes On Styles

Conventions – 'Syrianus'

[…]   Square brackets enclose words or phrases that have been added to the translation for purposes of clarity.

(…)   Round brackets, besides being used for ordinary parentheses, contain transliterated Greek words.

The page and line numbers of Rabe's 1892 edition are printed in the margins of the translation and the page numbers of his 1931 edition in bold round brackets in the text.

Abbreviations – 'Syrianus'

Brinkmann	'Phoibammon *peri Mimêseôs*', *Rheinisches Museum für Philologie* 61 (1906), 117–34.
Lampe	G. W. H. Lampe (ed.), *A Patristic Greek Lexicon*, Oxford: Clarendon Press, 1961.
LSJ	H. G. Liddell and R. Scott (comps), *A Greek-English Lexicon*, rev. H. Jones, with a New Supplement, 9th edn, Oxford: Clarendon Press, 1996.
TLG	*Thesaurus Linguae Graecae* (CD ROM and online at https://stephanus.tlg.uci.edu)

Introduction

1. The Preface to Hermogenes' *On Types of Style* (*Peri Ideôn*) attributed to Syrianus

When it became clear that Hermias' *Phaedrus Commentary* could not be divided into two volumes in this series, we realised that the third and final volume would be short. We wished to complement Hermias' exegesis of Plato's discussion of rhetoric and composition with the first English translation of some of Syrianus' commentary activity in relation to the standard canon of rhetorical theory in late antiquity: the works of Hermogenes of Tarsus. After all, Syrianus was the teacher of both Proclus and Hermias. Moreover, his commentary *On Hermogenes On Types of Style* (*Peri Ideôn*) is more thematically connected to the *Phaedrus*' alleged theme (*skopos*) of 'beauty at every level' than Syrianus' other Hermogenes commentary – the work dealing with *On Issues* (*Peri Staseôn*). The latter deals with 'stasis theory' which, as we explain below, concerns strategies of argument that a rhetorician can pursue in the juridical or deliberative contexts. The question of styles, by contrast, was said to concern how one might produce *logoi* that were beautiful. Finally, Syrianus' work on Hermogenes' *On Types of Style* has had no modern language translation, while his commentary *On Hermogenes On Issues* has recently appeared in a French translation.[1]

This plan for locating a related and relevant companion to the concluding section of Hermias' *On Plato's Phaedrus*, however, faces two unfortunate obstacles. First, Syrianus' commentary *On Hermogenes On Types of Style* is very long. The work, in two books, occupies 95 pages in Rabe's Teubner edition of 1892.[2] So a translation of the entire thing was not feasible within the word count allowed for volumes in this series. Nor is it easy to identify extracts that seem to be especially philosophically salient. While most Plato and Aristotle commentaries are prefaced by an extensive discussion of the theme, style, setting, etc., Syrianus' commentary on Hermogenes' *On Types of Style* is very brief. After a mere 26 lines, Syrianus begins to interpret Hermogenes' text lemma by lemma. The task of selecting parts of the commentary that would complement the themes of Hermias' *Phaedrus Commentary* was too daunting.

Now, it might *appear* that there is an easy solution at hand. Rabe's 1892 edition of Syrianus' *On Hermogenes On Types of Style* also contains a second introduction which he calls the *Preface* (or *Praefatio*) to *Hermogenes On Types of Style*. At 17 pages, the *Preface* was roughly the right size for our purposes. Moreover, the content of the work is of a more general and philosophical nature since it concerns itself with answering sceptical objections to the very possibility of a theory of the types of styles and with the utility of such a theory even were it possible. But this happy solution is only apparent: the *Preface* – or at least most of it – is certainly *not* the work of Syrianus, the teacher of Hermias.

Left with a choice between rounding out this volume with a short essay on rhetorical theory that is relevant to the concerns of Hermias' *Phaedrus Commentary* and extracts from a too-long commentary on the types of style that is more plausibly assigned to the teacher of Hermias we have opted for thematic unity over personal connection. The *Preface* records doubts of a philosophical nature about the possibility of a genuine *tekhnê* for one of the key concepts of rhetorical theory in late antiquity – types of style – but it is not by Hermias' teacher.

Let us review the content of the *Preface* before turning to more detail about its likely authorship. In sections 2 and 3 we shall provide a broader context and discussion of rhetorical theory and the concept of types of style, as well as the features of rhetorical theory that prompted philosophers to write commentaries on Hermogenes.

(a) Overview of the content of the *Preface*

The author of the *Preface* records a number of sceptical objections to the project of describing types of style and of the utility of this project for the emulation of ancient writers. These sceptical considerations include the impossibility of knowing particular things and, by extension, the specific characteristics of particulars. Curiously, however, the sceptical arguments rehearsed in the *Preface*, do not name Hermogenes as a target, but rather earlier theorists of types of style: Dionysius of Halicarnassus, an otherwise unknown Hipparchus, and Demetrius (99,18–100,2).

Even if a theory of styles were possible, the sceptical arguments continue, they would not facilitate the imitation of the ancient paradigms of good style, since

Introduction 157

every writer will 'shape (*methodeuein*) the language (*logos*) in the direction of his own nature' (99,14–15). Moreover, any such imitation would have to come about either by nature, by chance, or through art. The sceptical arguments attempt to eliminate the first two possibilities and then revert to the claim that imitation through art would always involves an element of individuality which must be dominant (102,8–9). So even if a theory of styles were possible, its utility would be questionable.

The author of the *Preface* begins his replies to this barrage of sceptical arguments at the start of page 103. The case for the knowability of styles occupies him from there to 104,11, where he turns to his arguments for the possibility and usefulness of emulation, which run to 105,21. At this point he asserts that the sceptics' arguments have now been fully answered – although it must be said that many of his arguments have been poor, sometimes consisting of mere dismissal or counter-assertion – but he will continue the argument, making use of an analogy between a living creature and a style. What follows reveals some awareness on the part of the author of the *Preface* that the sceptic has something of a point. The grasp of the elements that make up a style does not straightforwardly give one an understanding of the style itself; any more than an understanding of the parts of a living creature gives one an understanding of that living creature as a whole. It is as if the master painter were to explain to the apprentice about the colours, the brushwork, but could not explain the *logos* or *morphê* that governs the whole work (107,5–9). So, one might say that the author of the *Preface* registers that each type of style is an 'organic unity' that does not emerge from its components in accordance with any formula that can be easily specified.

Confronted with this problem of the organic unity of styles, the author of the *Preface* reports that some people resort to a kind of account that he calls 'symbolic'. He insists, however, that such symbolic accounts cannot illuminate the component parts or their concomitants. So the person who has a *tekhnê* concerning styles will not settle for merely symbolic names for the styles, but will instead aim to call styles by names that are expressively vivid (*emphantikos*, 107,17). But our author concedes that the standard of expressive vividness is problematic 'for the reason mentioned earlier' (107,18–19) – a remark whose *specific* reference is far from clear. As a result, he falls back on names metaphorically (rather than symbolically) derived from paradigms of the various types of style, 'as though the discourses themselves were subjected to visual perception like the forms of the individual [components]' (107,23–4).

At 108,4 we have another abrupt transition and our author takes us on to the standard questions about a text that we find regularly in commentaries by

Ammonius, the son of Hermias, and by his students: (1) its objective or *skopos*; (2) its utility; (3) what its title is; (4) whether it is genuine and the work of an ancient author; (5) in what order it should be read within the Hermogenean corpus; and (6) its division into parts. These standard questions, however, are postponed for a moment while the author of the *Preface* deals with two different questions: 'What is a style?' and 'Why hasn't Hermogenes defined it?' These are questions that are familiar from the longer commentary on Hermogenes' *On Types of Style* that is generally accepted as being by Syrianus. In that longer work Syrianus immediately moves to this question after his very brief introduction. There Syrianus writes:

> A type [of style] is a quality of discourse that is in harmony with both the personalities and the subjects at hand in terms of thought (*ennoia*), diction (*lexis*), and the whole framing of the structure [of the discourse]. A species (*eidos*) differs from a type (*idea*) as a genus differs from a species and a whole from a part. For the species is inclusive of the types and the types are subordinated to the species. For it is impossible for the juridical, deliberative, or panegyric species of speech to be composed without a mixture of multiple types [of style].
>
> (Syrianus, *in Herm.* I. 2,16–3,3, our translation)

But in the *Preface*, no definition matching that of Syrianus is given and the whole discussion is muddled by the fact that our author runs together the question of *what a style is* with the replies to critics who say that the book – *On Types [of Style]* (or *Peri Ideôn*) – is not accurately titled. We may reasonably suppose that our author takes these critics to be philosophers since his first response is that one ought not to blame a rhetorician if he fails to use the term *idea* exactly as the philosophers do (108,20). But the *Preface* concedes that they have a point that the title should perhaps have been simply *On Styles* (*Peri Kharaktêrôn*) rather than *On Types* [*sc. of Styles*]. The author offers us (at 110,5–14) a differentiation between types and styles that is very opaque and contrasts poorly with the treatment of this distinction that we find in the longer commentary that is attributed to Syrianus. We also find in the *Preface* corresponding epistemic distinctions which reflect the difference between wholes whose features emerge from their parts in a discursively specifiable manner and those that do not. But the matter is by no means clear. After discussing the authenticity of Hermogenes' work and its relation to the rest of his works, our author gets tangled up again with the distinction between styles and their types and offers nothing much clearer than his earlier remarks. The *Preface* then abruptly ends.

(b) Authorship of the Preface

The *Preface* has the same opening paragraph (96,3–97,6) as the preserved commentary on Hermogenes' *On Types of Style* of Syrianus (1,4–2,11).[3] There are, however, two fairly strong arguments against Syrianian authorship of the rest of the work. The first is the inclusion of answers to the six questions (objective, utility, title, authenticity, position among the author's other works, and textual division) posed by our author at 108,4. These aren't known to have been posed in exactly this form prior to Ammonius, the son of Hermias, which would suggest an author later than Syrianus.[4] In itself this is also not entirely conclusive, as it is supposed by Mansfeld and others that these preliminary questions about a text were informed by Proclus' now lost introductory work and, in fact, Ammonius begins the commentary on *On Interpretation* by noting his debt to Proclus' interpretation of Aristotle's difficult treatise.[5] So it is not impossible that the six questions were posed in the lost Aristotelian commentaries of Proclus or even those of Syrianus. That said, if the author's description of the six questions as '[matters] that it is *customary* to investigate in the case of every book' at 108,6 is at all accurate, he was presumably writing after both Syrianus (d. 437) and Proclus (d. 485) and perhaps even after Ammonius (d. 517–526), for even if these standard questions *might have originated* in the Athenian school around Syrianus, Hermias, and Proclus, their use would not accurately be described as 'customary' at that time.

Another argument for regarding the *Preface* as not by Syrianus is simply the ramshackle nature of the work. The other works that are generally accepted as genuine Syrianus are more carefully constructed. Malcolm Heath has observed that Syrianus was not really a natural when it comes to rhetorical analysis.[6] (It was perhaps lucky for him that he 'made it' as a philosopher!) But in both his (genuine) rhetorical and philosophical works he's at least generally coherent, if not always very subtle. The *Preface* is just not as well organised and regularly lacks smooth transitions between its parts. It feels like the work of a compositor.

It looks then as though the introductory paragraph from Syrianus' commentary has been joined to the introductory material from someone else's commentary on Hermogenes' *On Types of Style*. Just why and how this fusion occurred is a mystery. Syrianus' introduction is quite specific to his own commentary and his own circumstances (see in particular the mention of his son or grandson Alexander, 96,7) and the other material makes a rather awkward fresh start at 97,7. Perhaps some teacher of rhetoric felt the need to insert something on the possibility or usefulness of the theory of styles and the appropriateness of Hermogenes' title into Syrianus' commentary. Perhaps this expanded introduction then somehow became detached from the rest of Syrianus' commentary into which it had been inserted and took on a life of its own in the manuscript tradition.

As it happens we have another candidate for authorship of the non-Syrianian part of the *Preface*. The clue comes from John of Sicily (Ioannes Sikeliotes, mid-tenth century.)[7] who wrote a commentary on Hermogenes' *On Types of Style* in which he uses much of the material in the [Syrianus] *Preface* and twice (at 405,15 and 412,23) attributes it to a certain *Phoebammon*.[8] Further, *Preface* 111,9–11 shows that its author also wrote a commentary on Hermogenes' *On Issues* and Christophorus, an eleventh-century monk, cites such a commentary half a dozen times under the name Phoebammon in his own commentary on *On Issues*. On its own this would not be evidence that the author of the *Preface* was called Phoebammon, but it does lend support to the evidence from John.[9]

So who and when was Phoebammon? Stegemann puts the relevant Phoebammon, or Phoebammons, in the fifth or sixth centuries, Brinkmann in the latter part of the fifth at the earliest, Kennedy, on the ground of a tentative identification with a sophist who lived in Antinoöpolis, in the sixth.[10] On the basis of the evidence reviewed above, we are inclined to put him some time after Syrianus and Proclus. How long after is less clear. Because the name Phoebammon is Egyptian and because of his consideration of the six questions that we find clearly articulated in Ammonius, as well as the philosophical nature of some of his content, it is not unreasonable to suppose that he had some connection with the Alexandrian school, which would mean that he flourished no later than the middle of the sixth century.

The identity of the sceptical opponents whose arguments Phoebammon/ [Syrianus] summarises and attempts to answer must also be a matter of speculation. Brinkmann's article on Phoebammon suggested that they were 'rhetorically active Neoplatonists or Neoplatonist-influenced rhetors, such as Marinus' and Damascius' biographies of Proclus and Isidorus present in such large numbers'.[11] This would perhaps make sense given Phoebammon's/ [Syrianus]'s defence of the title of Hermogenes' work (108,11–25) – his claim that one cannot blame a rhetorician for not using the word 'type' (*idea*) as philosophers would. This is perhaps not *wildly* speculative, but it is speculative – as is the hypothesis about the motives of the compositor who conjoined material from Phoebammon with the first few lines of Syrianus' *Peri Ideôn* commentary. This seems to be as far as the evidence can take us.

2. The context for the *Preface*: Hermogenes and rhetorical theory in late antiquity

In the following sections, we provide some wider context for the [Syrianus] *Preface*. Some readers will find this superfluous, but we suspect that many readers of the Commentators series will not. The history of late antique philosophy is a subfield within the disciplines of Philosophy and Classics and there are a growing number of specialists. There is also a growing community of specialists in the history of rhetoric and rhetorical theory in late antiquity. Our limited exposure to the literature in this field suggests that the practitioners of these specialisations belong to largely non-overlapping sets. This is a shame, because rhetoricians and philosophers in late antiquity were more intertwined with one another than are the specialists in these areas today. We suspect that the study of late antique Platonism in particular would benefit from a wider appreciation of the background in rhetorical studies that most philosophers of the period shared.

In the first volume of our translation we noted the role of training in rhetoric in the advanced education shared by the elites of the late Roman Empire.[12] This advanced education or *paideia* constituted a common point of reference for the wealthy, as well as officials and politicians, from the various Roman provinces. It was part of the glue that held together the educated elite, since exhibiting oneself as one of the 'friends of the Muses' – as the educated called themselves – was sometimes sufficient to enter into systems of patronage and the exchange of mutual favours.[13] As well as being a form of social capital, *paideia* also constituted a kind of insurance policy, since there were social norms that, to some extent, limited the ways in which an educated person could be treated.

The studies that were regarded as essential to being an educated person or *pepaidoumenos* centred on rhetoric. By the time of Syrianus, Proclus, and Hermias, the course of education revolved around an initial, practically-oriented set of preliminary exercises in composition (the *progumnasmata*). These were followed by more theoretical treatments of specific aspects of the rhetoric. We shall discuss just two of these: the *stasis* theory or the theory of 'issues' (in a technical sense that we shall clarify in a moment) and the theory of the types of style. At the centre of this curriculum were works by – or at least attributed to – Hermogenes of Tarsus.

Hermogenes of Tarsus was discussed briefly by Philostratus in his *Lives of the Sophists* (2.7). He was a child prodigy in declamation and the Emperor Marcus Aurelius travelled to see him perform. Philostratus informs us that the Emperor took pleasure in the fifteen-year-old's *dialexis*, but was amazed at his ability to improvise. Now, one meaning of *dialexis* in rhetorical texts is that of a philosophical discourse, though it can also mean the informal introduction to the main declamation or *meletê*.[14] So it is possible that Hermogenes developed a theoretician's talent early in life. But his gifts in declamation, Philostratus tells us, deserted him 'through no obvious illness'. Apart from cruel jests at the expense of a young man who lost his gift, Philostratus tells us no more about him. But it seems that when he ceased to be an oratorical performer, he took to writing treatises on rhetorical theory.[15] Or at least this appears to be the case. Four works – all attributed to him, but only two of which are likely to be genuine – formed the core texts on rhetorical theory in late antiquity. These were:

1. Hermogenes, *On Issues (Peri Staseôn)*[16]
2. Ps.-Hermogenes, *On Invention*[17]
3. Hermogenes, *On Types of Style (Peri Ideôn)*[18]
4. Ps.-Hermogenes, *On the Method of Forceful Speaking*[19]

The fact that the genuine works of Hermogenes were the subject of commentaries attributed to Syrianus, the teacher of both Hermias and Proclus, is not as surprising as it might seem given the general antagonism between rhetoric and philosophy that is depicted in Plato's *Gorgias*. Nearly every Platonic philosopher of late antiquity was a beneficiary of education in rhetoric. While it became a conventional part of philosophical biographies that the subject of the biography turned his back on rhetoric to pursue philosophy,[20] in fact philosophers engaged regularly with works of rhetorical theory. For their part, rhetoricians came to adopt more philosophically sophisticated approaches to their craft than one might have expected from the *Phaedrus*' depiction of the haphazard techniques that Phaedrus and Socrates describe as mere preliminary matters to the business of genuine rhetoric. It is therefore worthwhile to consider the mutual influence of rhetoric and philosophy upon one another in late antiquity.

3. Philosophers and rhetorical theory

In his book on Greek rhetoric under the Christian emperors, Kennedy identifies several features that distinguish rhetorical theory in late antiquity from that in earlier periods.[21] In addition to the centrality of stasis theory and theories of the types of styles, Kennedy identified the influence of Neoplatonic philosophers:

... few things emerge more clearly than the role of the Neoplatonic philosophers, beginning with Porphyry, in reorganizing the discipline on a philosophical basis as an introduction to dialectic. The logical process of definition and division, fundamental for all philosophical understanding, is given a preliminary presentation to the student through stasis theory.[22]

Both stasis theory and the theories of the types of style posed an attraction for Platonic philosophers and this helps to explain Kennedy's claim about the role of Neoplatonic philosophers in organising rhetoric as a suitable introduction to dialectic.

Stasis theory was initially developed as a part of judicial rhetoric and its point was to isolate the basic issues in a dispute. Hence works on the varieties of stasis titled *Peri Staseôn* are often translated as 'On Issues'.[23] In its most basic form, it serves to help the legal advocate decide what ground he will argue on. It does this by dividing the issue into the 'heads of argument'. These provide strategies for the advocate to pursue. So, for instance, one might wonder if it is clear or not whether the accused person in fact did what was alleged. If it is not clear, then the stasis is one of fact (*stokhasmos*). If, however, it is clear that the accused did do what was alleged, then one might argue that this action was not, in fact, something that the law actually forbids because the description of the action is incomplete (*atelês*). In this case, the stasis or head of argument is definition (*horos*). Alternatively, one might concede that the description is complete, but argue the case by appeal to specifically legal considerations (*nomikê*). There are several issues under the 'legal' heading: one might defend one's client by arguing that the wording of the law does not adequately express the intent behind it (*phêton kai dianoia*) or that the law is ambiguous (*amphibolia*) or that there is a conflict among laws (*antinomia*). Alternatively, one could appeal to wider, extra-legal considerations that we might characterise as 'natural justice' (*logikê*). Perhaps one might decide to base one's argument on the claim that the action was unintentional (the stasis of *antilêpsis*) or that, even though illegal, it was beneficial to the city (*antistasis*) or actually caused by one's opponent (*antenklêma*). While stasis theory had its primary home in the practice of rhetoric in the courts – so-called judicial rhetoric – works in stasis theory sought to apply a parallel system to deliberative rhetoric. That is to say, one could structure speeches intended for a deliberative assembly along similar lines. The issues of deliberative rhetoric were categorised under *pragmatikê* and included things such as the lawful, the just, the expedient, etc.

It is not as if rhetorical theory in the Classical or Hellenistic periods was completely silent on these issues. One can find some discussion of these sorts of considerations in Aristotle's *Rhetoric*, but attempts to classify them much more systematically really began in the second century BC. By the late-second century AD, however, we find that the issues (in a now technical sense) have been multiplied and a consensus reached that there are 13 of them. Two second-century rhetorical theorists stand at the origins of this professional consensus around the 13-stasis theory: Minucianus and Hermogenes of Tarsus. Minucianus was an Athenian who flourished in the reign of Antoninus Pius (136–161), while Hermogenes, as we noted above, was a young man in the reign of Marcus Aurelius (161–180). While both men wrote treatises on stasis theory, Hermogenes' book eventually became the canonical one on the subject.

There are features of Hermogenes' *On Issues* that make the book attractive to philosophers of a Platonic bent. First there is the systematicity and the way in which that systematicity seems to coincide with the practice of *dialectic* as it is described in the *Phaedrus*. At 266B5–C1, Socrates equates this with the method of collection and division. At the outset of *On Issues*, Hermogenes describes what he is about to do as a division of political questions into what he calls 'heads' (1,10, Rabe). Moreover, Hermogenes immediately seeks to define what it is that is being divided by saying what counts as a 'political question' (1,13–17). Finally, having established that a political question is 'a rational dispute on a particular matter, based on the established laws or customs of any given people, concerned with what is *considered* just, honourable, advantageous, or all or some of these things together', Hermogenes insists that it is not the task of rhetoric to investigate what *is truly and universally* noble, just, etc. Whatever Hermogenes might have intended by this restriction, a Platonist philosopher might admire the manner in which he both begins with a division of a defined whole (i.e. political questions) and seemingly knows the subordinate relation of rhetoric to philosophical dialectic that, as Hermias says, 'divides the *intelligible* forms into many and collects them into one' (*in Phaedr.* 248,6–7).

The other work in the standard rhetorical curriculum that is both widely accepted as a genuine work of Hermogenes and also the subject of a commentary by Syrianus is *Peri Ideôn* or *On Types of Style*. If one were to contrast style with content, then one might say that the elements of style are things like diction, figures of speech, word order, clauses, and cadence or rhythm. But, in fact, Hermogenes offers a typology of styles that considers these elements in essential relation to different kinds of content (*ennoia*) and approach (*methodos*) (Hermogenes, id. 218,18–19).[24] So, as Hermogenes understands 'types of style', they apply primarily to an *author's* style because this type is the one that is predominant in his writings. As Hermogenes says:

Thus every type of style is created out of the elements discussed above. But it is very difficult, nearly impossible in fact, to find among any of the ancients a style that is throughout composed of elements such as thought, approach, diction, etc., characteristic of only one kind of style; it is by the predominance of features belonging to one type that each acquires his particular quality.

(Hermogenes, id. 222,1–6, trans. Wooten)[25]

The exception is Demosthenes who, Hermogenes insists, is master of all the types of styles. Yet even he favours one style above others – the one that Hermogenes calls 'abundance' (*peribolê*). So his book on styles is useful for anyone who wants to *evaluate* the style of writers, ancient or contemporary, or to *produce* speeches of their own, modelled on the best of the ancients (Hermogenes, id. 213,7–14).

Like the material about argumentative strategies that is codified in stasis theory, theoretical observations upon style go back to the origins of rhetoric as a would-be *tekhnê*. Hermogenes' types of style are continuous with Aristotle's virtues of style in *Rhetoric* 1404b1–4. In both Aristotle and Hermogenes, 'clarity' (*saphêneia*) holds pride of place. It is a necessary condition for speech to achieve its purpose that it be clear. But clarity is not enough: the language must exhibit propriety for its subject matter, as well as striking the mean between too much and too little ornamentation. Theophrastus seems to have added a fourth virtue (correctness of language), while Stoic philosophers added 'brevity' (*suntomia*). But, running alongside this proliferation of virtues for written or spoken language considered in relation to the task at hand, there was also a tradition of regarding different Homeric heroes as having different styles. Menelaus was credited with the 'plain style', while Odysseus' words – 'like snowflakes on a winter's day' (Homer, *Il.* 3.212–24) – embodied the 'grand style'. This tendency to treat styles as applying principally to paradigmatic authors lies behind the system of Demetrius' *On Style* with its classification of plain, grand, elegant, and forceful (*deinos*) styles. Hermogenes' *On Types of Style* goes yet further in both adding styles and in creating relations of subordination among them. In all there are seven basic types of style, but these admit of subdivisions so that the full system involves the description of 20 types. Wooten (1987, xii) provides a useful diagram (see Figure 1).

In the tradition of Aristotle's *Rhetoric*, Clarity plays a special role. But the admixture of other styles prevents the clear presentation of the content from tipping over into banality or triteness.[26] Moreover, Force (*deinotês*) seems to be something of a universal mastery of other styles to good effect.[27] Hermogenes

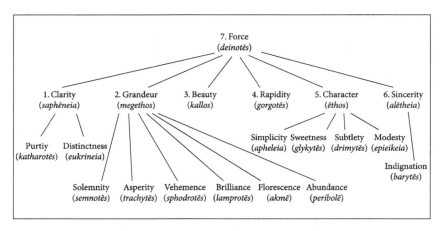

Figure 1 Hermogenes' types and subtypes of style.

revisits the earlier tradition of assigning styles to Homeric speakers with an extended argument that Force is the defining feature of Odysseus' speeches.[28]

As with stasis theory, there is much in Hermogenes' theory of the types of style to attract the attention of a Platonic philosopher. First, Platonic philosophers were concerned with the various ways in which Plato was thought to communicate and with the role of style in these modes of communication. Thus in the first volume of our translation we saw Hermias defending Plato's style in the *Phaedrus* as suitable to his purposes (*in Phaedr.* 11,11–20) by adverting to the manner in which he mixes the plain style of Lysias' speech with the more dignified or solemn (*semnotês*) style that Hermogenes discusses as a means of achieving Grandeur. (Examples could be multiplied from Proclus' discussions of Plato's styles in various dialogues.) Second, the method that Hermogenes employs throughout *On Types of Styles* has a strong affinity with the method of analysis, as Platonists understood it. This, of course, was the complement to division or *diairesis* and one of the essential tools of *dialectic*. The parallel with analysis emerges clearly when Hermogenes says:

> Moreover, since it is not possible to understand or appreciate a mixture, in reference to style or anything else, and it is certainly not possible to create a mixture until we recognize the various elements out of which the mixture was created (to understand gray, for example, we must first understand black and white), we must ignore the style of individual writers such as Plato, Demosthenes, and Xenophon and proceed to examine separately the most basic elements of style itself. One who starts from this point can then easily go on to appreciate

and describe individual authors, detecting their careful combinations, whether he wants to study and emulate one of the ancients or someone more recent.

(Hermogenes, id. 224,12-23, trans. Wooten)

So, from a Platonist's point of view, *On Types of Style* is an application of the method of analysis to the constituents of styles and a study of the manner in which these elements combine in various ways to yield various effects.

Porphyry was the first well-known Platonic philosopher to contribute to stasis theory. Our sources attribute to him a work 'On the Art' or 'On the Art Dealing with Stasis' (depending on how the title is reported), as well as a commentary on a now lost treatise on stasis theory by Minucianus.[29] Malcolm Heath has argued that Porphyry introduced an innovation that was subsequently adopted by teachers of rhetoric who did not also identify as philosophers: the detailed commentary on works in rhetorical theory.[30] The adoption of this innovation, Heath notes, is easily explained by the common educational culture shared between rhetoric and philosophy in late antiquity:

> Commentary on a standard teaching text provides specialists with an excellent vehicle for exploring (and debating) technical doctrine in depth and detail. So it is not surprising that an innovation in the form of rhetorical technography should have disseminated rapidly from philosophers to sophists. In a culture in which philosophy was part of general advanced education, many rhetoricians who were not professional philosophers would in any case have had some philosophical training, and been familiar with both the formats and the language of philosophical writing. ... Conversely, one would expect philosophers to have studied rhetoric in the course of their schooling, given the place of rhetoric in ancient education.[31]

Porphyry was not alone among Platonic philosophers who wrote commentaries on rhetorical teaching texts. Syrianus tells us that other, less known Platonist philosophers also dealt with the canonical works of the rhetorical teaching curriculum. These include Evagoras and Aquila, the latter of whom likely wrote a commentary on Aristotle's *Categories* in the early fourth century. But the commentaries on the works of Hermogenes in the standard curriculum that were undertaken by philosophers seem to have their own agenda. Russell observed forty years ago that:

> This philosophical intervention may be judged unhelpful. The commentators on Hermogenes, among whom Syrianus was particularly influential, seem much more concerned with the arrangement of their own material than with any utility the system might offer either for the potential speaker or for the reader of Demosthenes.[32]

Syrianus *says* that philosophers are more precise in their definitions of the *staseis*. Thus at 56,16 in his commentary on Hermogenes' *On Issues* Syrianus switches from a close reading of Hermogenes' text to somewhat different divisions and definitions for stasis theory found in the philosophers Evagoras and Aquila. These philosophers come later than Hermogenes and Syrianus regards their definitions as supremely scientific (*epistêmonikôtata*). They are precise, according to Syrianus, while Hermogenes dealt with the definitions of the issues only in outline.[33]

Apart from the primacy of theoretical tidiness and clarity over practical application, are there other differences in the manner in which a philosopher, like Syrianus, dealt with the material in Hermogenes and the manner in which rhetoricians who were not philosophers did? Surveying the differences between Syrianus and Hermogenes, as well as the differences between philosopher-rhetors and non-philosophers, Heath finds no vast differences between their techniques and methods. All of them are in love with the method of division. The doctrinal differences over questions about these divisions between philosophers writing on rhetoric and non-philosophical rhetoricians are minor. Heath does suggest one difference, though it is subtle: the scholia on acknowledged rhetorical exemplars, like Demosthenes, by pure rhetoricians evince no scruples over the use of sophisms or over the fact that Demosthenes was likely to have bribed a witness in the case under consideration.[34] Other scholia on the same speech, which may have originated with a Platonist philosopher, are more circumspect and reserved about such underhanded rhetorical tricks.

4. Conclusion

Plato's *Gorgias* famously challenged the status of rhetoric as a *tekhnê*. The *Phaedrus*, just as famously, held out the possibility of a genuine *tekhnê* of rhetoric, but one far removed from the actual theory, teaching, and practice of rhetoric. By the time of Syrianus and Hermias rhetoricians themselves had adapted philosophical methods like collection and division to produce theories that defined (*inter alia*) styles or enumerated the dimensions along which to arrange the content of juridical or deliberative oratory. The *Preface* of [Syrianus] shows us that there were critics who were still not sufficiently impressed with the technical pretensions of the philosophical rhetoric of late antiquity. But the Hermogenes commentaries of Syrianus treat rhetoric as a matter worthy of serious intellectual engagement.

5. The translation

Rabe in fact edited Phoebammon's prolegomenon twice, the first edition, as already mentioned, appearing in 1892, the second in 1931. In the second edition he took a rather different view of the manuscript tradition and, largely as a result of this, the text differs from that of the earlier edition at some points. Because this later edition represents Rabe's final thoughts on the text we have decided to base our translation on it. Unfortunately from our point of view the two editions are paginated differently. Our first thought was to give the page and line numbers of the edition we are translating in the margin of our translation, but because the *TLG* text gives those of the 1892 edition, we decided it would be more useful to provide them. We do, however, include the page numbers of the 1931 edition in bold and round brackets in the text of the translation, and for anyone with the 1931 edition to hand it provides the page (but not line) numbers of the 1892 edition in the margins of the text.

The following table lists the significant differences between the two editions:

Line and page numbers in 1892 and 1931 editions	1931 text	1892 text
98,9 (376,3)	*mnêsin*	*mimêsin*
98,18 (376,12)	*gar*	*de*
99,8 (376,26)	*ho ean*	*hos' an*
100,3 (377,15)	<*eis*>	
100,9 (377,21)	<*eti*>	
100,10 (377,22)	*huperebê*	*huperbebêke*
100,11 (377,24)	*oikeian*	*idian*
100,15 (378,2)	*probasin*	*prosbasin*
100,16 (378,3)	*taxin*	*mixin*
100,18 (378,5)	*toutous*	*toutôi*
101,19 (378,28)	<*adunatousa*>	
102,3 (379,4)	*ektelesai, rhast' an poioiê;*	*rhasta poiein, ektelesai*
102,3 (379,4)	<*an*>	
102,4 (379,5)	*hoion ei*	*hoionei*
102,13 (379,14)	*pros, menomen*	*prosmenomen*
102,21 (379,22)	*kai mê [te] ton*	*mê ti ge kai ton*
104,4 (380,25)	*ê tên toiande*	*ê toiande*
104,6 (380,27)	*einai*	*meinai*
104,20 (381,12)	*kai mê*	*mê kai*
104,22 (381,15)	<*dê*>	

(*continued*)

105,12 (381,27)	*asumphora*	*asumphoron*
105,15 (382,3)	*kan* (no accent)	*kan* (grave accent)
105,20 (382,8)	*kai eis*	*eis*
106,12 (382,24)	*logôi*	*logos*
107,7 (383,14)	*meta*	*kata*
107,17 (383,24)	*poiein*	*poiei*
108,7 (384,10)	<*kai*>	
108,9 (384,13)	<*tis*>	
108,10 (384,14)	<*kai tou khrêsimou*>	
110,16 (386,12)	*tên idean*	*tas ideas*
111,5 (386,26)	*eirêtai*	*lekteon*
111,6 (386,28)	*men gnêsion*	*men gar gnêsion*
111,9 (387,2)	*peri staseôn*	*peri tôn staseôn*

Notes

1   Patillon 2021.
2   Rabe 1892.
3   The only significant difference between the two texts as edited by Rabe is the absence of *theois* after *logiois* at 2,10 in the *Preface* – in fact it only appears in one of the two MSS of the genuine Syrianus text known to Rabe and in none of the seven [Syrianus] MSS known to him. It is plausible, however, that the omissions are due to Christian writers. The two manuscript traditions even share many of the same variants.
4   cf. Ammonius, *On Aristotle On Interpretation* 1,12–20, trans. Blank 1996.
5   Brinkmann 1906, 118.
6   Heath 1995, 181.
7   On John see Roilos 2018 and Papaioannou 2019.
8   cf. John 405,13 ff. with [Syr.] 109,4 ff. and John 412,26–413,10 with [Syr.] 102,24–103,15; in the latter case in particular there is considerable verbal agreement between the two texts. Fuhr 1893 seems to have been first to draw attention to these passages. In fact John seems to have had access to the whole of our author's commentary on *On Types* and not just the introductory material preserved in the *Praefatio*, since later in his commentary (at 124,21) a comment on Hermogenes 219,6 ff. is described as coming from 'Syrianus and Phoebammon'. The fullest treatment of Phoebammon is Stegemann 1941, a Pauly article. Brinkmann 1906, where the parts of the *Praefatio* that deal with imitation are edited along with related passages from John, and Kennedy 1983 are also useful.

9   On Christophorus' commentary see Rabe 1895. There are other works, extant or not, going under the name of Phoebammon, notably one on figures of speech (*Peri Skhêmatôn*), but, as Stegemann, 1941 points out, there may well have been more than one 'sophist' named Phoebammon working in the relevant period, and further questions of authorship need not concern us here.
10 Stegemann 1941, 326; Brinkmann 1906, 118; Kennedy 1983,121.
11 Brinkmann 1906, 121.
12 Baltzly and Share 2018, 31–3.
13 The classic work on the subject is Brown 1992. See also Browning 2000 and Connolly 2001.
14 cf. Miles and Baltussen 2023, 623.
15 Or at least this appears to be the case. Patillon 1985, 13–17 doubts that even the works accepted as genuinely by Hermogenes should be assigned to the Hermogenes of Tarsus who figures in Philostratus.
16 Translation and commentary in Heath 1995.
17 Kennedy 2005, Patillon 2012.
18 Heath 2009, Patillon 2009.
19 Kennedy 2005, Patillon 2014.
20 cf. Marinus, *Life of Proclus* §11 and for Damascius' turn from rhetoric, see his *Philosophical History*, fr. 137b Athanassiadi 1999. For commentary, see Caluori 2014.
21 Kennedy 1983.
22 Kennedy 1983, 53.
23 The disputed origins of 'stasis' as the name for this theory, as well as general overview of its complexities are provided in Russell 1983, 40–71.
24 Rabe 1913.
25 Wooten 1987.
26 'It is only natural to discuss Grandeur after the discussion of Clarity, for it is necessary to interject Grandeur and a certain amount of majesty and dignity into a clear passage. This is because the very clear can seem trite and commonplace, which is the opposite of Grandeur.' (Hermogenes, id. 241,11–15, trans. Wooten)
27 'In my opinion Force in a speech is nothing other than the proper use of all the kinds of style previously discussed and of their opposites and of whatever other elements are used to create the body of a speech. To know what technique must be used and when and how it should be used, and to be able to employ all the kinds of style and their opposites and to know what kinds of proofs and thoughts are suitable in the proemium or in the narration or in the conclusion, in other words, as I said, to be able to use all those elements that create the body of a speech as and when they should be used seems to me to be the essence of true Force.' (Hermogenes, id. 368,23–369,9, trans. Wooten)
28 Hermogenes, id. 370,19–372,6.

29 There were other rhetorical works by Porphyry, as well, including a response to rhetoricians criticising Plato. There was a work in six books entitled *Against Aristides* which was likely a reply to Aristides' criticisms of Plato's *Gorgias* and we can discern traces of this Porphyrian work in Olympiodorus' commentary on that dialogue. For an overview of works on rhetoric by Porphyry, see Heath 2003. For *Against Aristides* in particular, see Behr 1968.
30 For an overview of the genre of commentary, see Pepe 2018.
31 Heath 2009, 148.
32 Russell 1983, 42.
33 cf. Syrianus, *On Hermogenes On Issues* III.1.6 (Patillon 2021).
34 Heath 2009, 150–1.

'Syrianus'[1]

On Hermogenes' On Types [of Discourse][2]

Translation

Virtually all of the treatises of Hermogenes, the writer on the art (*tekhnographos*) [of rhetoric], that have come down to us are admirable and full of political wisdom. I am referring to his treatise *On Issues*, which many others, indeed both sophists and Platonic philosophers, have found not unworthy of commentary, to the *On the Method of Forcefulness*,[3] and to the *Notes on Public Speeches*, of which he himself makes mention;[4] but his treatise *On Types* is above all the rest deserving of admiration as the best and most proficient in the art (*tekhnikos*) and as in no respect lacking in the most accomplished critical skill on the subject of speeches (*logos*). Since, however, much that is contained in it is not easy for everyone to understand and to this day we have not come across anyone who has written a commentary on it, I thought it necessary, Alexander, dearest of my children,[5] to put together to the best of my ability some brief [notes] to help with a more accurate reading of the book. But should anyone be able to produce something yet better than these [notes] to assist with the task, we shall be very grateful to him for showing us [an instance of] 'Common Hermes!'[6] by actions rather than words (*logos*). Finally, (*to peras*), after calling on the [gods][7] of eloquence (*logios*) to grant a good [outcome] to us and these efforts [of ours], let's get on with the task.

(375) If it is altogether desirable for a political man to learn the virtues (*aretê*) of discourse[8] (*logos*) and to wish not only to distinguish the [various] styles (*kharaktêr*) of the ancients but also, I assume, to produce more or less similar ones as well, he must investigate their methods and work hard on their discovery. For a thing so very difficult to grasp would not come very easily to anyone even if he were to have great faith in [his own] nature, since without the art natural advantages are of no benefit, as the rhetorician (*tekhnikos*) also says;[9] but in the case of someone for whom knowledge of the discipline is added [to natural ability], it [sc. natural ability] contributes a lot, even when the person trained in the art is blessed with [only] moderate facility. But the enterprise would perhaps be difficult if we were endeavouring to perceive the types of speeches (*logoi*)[10] on our own, but as it is the rhetorician has freed us from these labours; in fact, even with much effort one would probably unearth nothing [new] of value, just as those before him [sc. Hermogenes] also seem to have worked in vain. But if the hard part does not remain, I mean making discoveries and presenting what has been discovered with clarity, what is left other than to zealously come to grips with the present treatise, if indeed we care about speeches[11] (*logoi*), we who intend to differ from the unlettered[12] (*alogos*) in just this respect? For I think that those who concern themselves [solely] with bodily matters and expect (376) to be remembered not so much for their words (*logoi*) as through the succession of

children are extremely foolish. A short time obliterates them, but someone who has worked with discourse (*logos*) leaves behind for readers[13] an everlasting memory (*mnêsis*)[14] even after death. Accordingly, in line with Plato's words,[15] one must honour the offspring of the soul rather than those of the body, not only as being more worthy but also, I think, on account of our self-determining control (*dioikêsis*) in [the area of] speeches (*logoi*); for in the case of children, the shaper of their characters (*tropoi*) also has the power of decision,[16] but we govern our discourse (*logos*) and shape[17] (*methodeuein*) it just as we wish. And let no one find fault with us before clearly understanding what we have said; for the treatise (*logos*) on types [of discourse] is analogous to a living creature and the thought has the status (*taxis*) of its soul, the style of its body.[18]

But someone versed in [the art] must not only have accurate knowledge of the number of styles but also of the particular character (*idiotês*) [of each] and their imitation of the ancients. People who repudiate this and say that it is impossible to grasp these should not concern us. 'Just[19] as it is not possible to know exactly the number of particular things, so too', they say, 'is it impossible [to know the number] of styles, if, as you claim, they are entirely (*holôs*) analogous to a living creature'.[20] And [they further say] that 'it is not possible to describe the particular characters of individual things, for the result of this would reveal yet another [such character]. Besides, even if you grasped [them], the cause that explains a particular character[21] [would remain] unclear'. And they say that 'particular things alter whatever they lay hold of (*lambanein*) to their own nature; (377) for instance, nothing is prejudicial to anything in good condition even if it is harmful, but for something in a bad state, on the other hand, everything is prejudicial even if everything is [in itself] beneficial (*epôphelês*), for [such beneficial things] are changed to the make-up (*krasis*) of that thing. So this being so', they say, 'for anyone attempting to imitate the styles of the ancients the effort is also futile; in every case he will shape (*methodeuein*) the language (*logos*) in the direction of his own nature, not that of his [intended] treatment. And if some have thought to name (*epigraphein*) the styles and to limit their number, they have done so in vain. One such is Dionysius. This man says that there are three styles: the plain, the intermediate, the grand. Hipparchus adds the graphic and the florid. Demetrius rejects the graphic[22] while approving of the [other] four.[23] But even if these men have', they say, 'limited the [number of] styles and assigned [them], as they see it, to a definite number,[24] they are nonetheless still (*palin*) not to be grasped. In fact, we shall find many plain [styles], in one direction allowing of intensification, in the other, in turn, of diminution. For when the plain style moves towards the grand without the mix becoming balanced,[25] it rejects [all] three styles. It is not the natural plain style any more,[26] since it has leant more towards its opposite; nor the intermediate, since it has gone past that, nor, again, the grand, since it hasn't altogether changed its own nature. And the same goes for the others: just as the plain style, when the mix becomes unequal, is neither **(378)** intermediate nor, on the other hand, grand, in the same way the grand style, when moving progressively (*kata probasin*) towards the plain but not being blended with [it] in the prescribed manner (*kata taxin*),[27] does not become plain, but goes past the intermediate, in that it[28] alone has received intensification. 'These styles', they say, 'allowing [as they do] now of intensification, now of diminution to a greater or lesser degree, it is impossible to grasp. And even if we accept that they are able to be grasped, we need [to put in] hard work and much effort to gain knowledge [of them]; and after understanding [of them is achieved] the knowledge is again useless. That understanding is not [gained] by way of the styles, we shall know from the following. Things that are accomplished by us in emulation of others come to be either (1) naturally or (2) by chance or (3) through an art. For either (1) nature distributes its gifts more or less equally. For instance, it may have given one person a clear voice and another [the ability] to speak [with] the same [kind of voice] so that they didn't differ from one another in any respect (I mean as regards voice). Or (2) the same [outcome] does not come about naturally but two people are found to have performed the same action by some chance. And (3) if it is neither naturally nor by chance [that this comes about], then at all events, employing a particular method and the same equipment, we imitate, [say,] an artist, producing a painting of a like appearance. But when the similar thing has been produced either naturally or by chance or by art, such things avoid [any] difficulty, but when the situation changes and we want to grasp by art a thing produced naturally or by chance, then the understanding [of it] becomes very difficult, and, one might almost say, cannot be subject to knowledge.[29] To take a hypothetical case. **(379)** Someone has thrown a stone. Landing (*piptein*), and being randomly (*kata tukhên*) shattered, this has produced [pieces of] many [different] shapes. Well, if someone were to ask a sculptor, even Phidias himself, to make these shapes, would he produce them with any ease (*rhasta*)? He wouldn't be able to. And similarly in the other cases[30] – if, for instance, one were to want to emulate offhand someone with a naturally clear voice or a drawing produced by Zeuxis.[31] So what comes about naturally or by chance', they say, 'is difficult to grasp by art. And even should we grasp it, the knowledge is useless for the nature of the individual is dominant (*epikratesteros*). Moreover, it is impossible to emulate the styles of the ancients because of the restraints imposed by our time of life, at one time (*pêi men*) because of our youth, at another (*pêi de*) because of the passage of time. For until we are sixteen, or a little before that, we remain of the same nature and have no aptitude for emulation of another style. And if we are approaching forty, old age in its turn prevents imitation. And in the period between sixteen and forty we have the aptitude for emulation, but how many turns of events do you think will be found to stand in the way of such an attempt? And so it turns out that we are denied such a nature, and do not grasp the style (*tupos*) of the ancients due to the circumstances prevailing in the period between [sixteen and forty].'

That then is what those who raise difficulties have to say. In reply to them this can be said. We know everything there is either in (*kata*) theory or in practice (*praxis*). The same then goes for styles. But if you want to grasp them in theory, you have avoided the [issues of] uselessness and difficulty **(380)** and so it is only necessary to consider [the question of] impossibility in its case; [and] when this has becomes quite clear, you will of course also refer to [your findings] in your remarks (*logoi*) on practice, [although] the question of uselessness and difficulty is retained there. So let's return briefly to theory, where we shall first show[32] that styles are capable of being grasped as far as [their] number goes, if indeed even the followers of Dionysius, limiting them at the outset, assigned them a definite number. For taking the intensification and the diminution of plainness as amounting to separate styles – that was nonsensical: [plainness], being defined at the outset, whether it receives augmentation or diminution, is not a whit less plain. And the same goes for the other [styles].

And their number being capable of being grasped, the particular character [of each] of them is clear to those who consider the matter accurately and don't get sidetracked among the attributes (*parakolouthêma*) of the styles, for it is not the case here too, in the way it is with substance, that an attribute (*to parakolouthoun*) is one thing and the entity (*huparxis*) [itself] another – thanks to which, the specific character is hard to grasp there [i.e. in the case of substance], since it is impossible to have accurate knowledge of variations in the attributes (*parakolouthêma*), whereas in the case of style, the attribute (*to parakolouthoun*) itself is also a component [of the style], because of which it can be very easily grasped. For instance, in the case of substance Socrates remains [Socrates] even if whiteness or snubness or darkness or any other of his characteristics (*idiôma*) is taken away, but in the case of styles if you take away an attribute, [their type of] figurative expression or the like, for example, you destroy the whole. And so [the circumstance] that the entity is one thing and the attribute another has made the particular character of individual things hard to grasp, whereas [their] specific properties (*idiôma*) themselves constitute the styles, for [in their case] **(381)** if you grasp the entity, you know the attributes, and if you learn the specific properties, you know the entity.

That it is possible to know the specific properties of the styles has, in my opinion, [now] also been made abundantly clear and we must now move on to the third difficulty. What was this? 'It is not possible', they say, 'to emulate the styles (*tupos*) of the ancients, for nature, falling back on its own predisposition (*diathesis*), changes the whole ordering of the composition (*logos*) in the direction of its own particular character'. And this is close to the truth, for to emulate the style of Demosthenes or of Plato with accuracy is impossible, except perhaps imperfectly. However it will be graspable in part by those who work hard [at it]. One should be pleased with coming close to other [writers] even, let alone Demosthenes or Plato. So don't give up [composing] speeches (*logos*) because you can't immediately become a Demosthenes to us, but keep at it (*spoudazein*), and think of all the other speakers (*rhêtôr*), who would have kept silent from the start if with them too the wish that their speeches (*logoi*) should in no respect seem to depart from the style (*tupos*) of Demosthenes had prevailed.

To enquire about the uselessness, the difficulty, and the rest, and especially about the vexatiousness (*duskherês*), is superfluous. It is characteristic of lovers of [mere] pleasure to say that fine (*kalos*) things are not easily grasped because these are [indeed] hard to grasp and it is their nature to become available to men as a result of their other efforts.[33] And, further, that after knowledge [of them has been acquired] they are not useless **(382)** is clear from the following. It is possible at the same time to both maintain one's own nature and emulate an ancient style (*tupos*). For someone with an aptitude for the plain [style] and properly trained in it, at the same time both keeps his own nature intact and emulates the style of Lysias.[34] And the same goes for the other [styles]: whenever a person sees his own nature weighing more heavily in the balance, he will, by working above all on this, certainly be brought [back] down towards[35] an ancient style (*tupos*) and [at the same time] not depart from his own forte (*dexiotês*).

These things having [now] been clearly established and the number (*plêthos*) [of styles] being definite[36] and [their] particular character and [their] imitation being as far as is possible accurately understood, we must take up (*ekhesthai*) the example[37] and advance by way of that. It will help us in many ways because of its similarity to the styles; for, just as with animate bodies, it is possible to grasp their component material even in a part (*kata meros*) but impossible to fully describe their mixing and such a combination verbally. For that a human being is composed of four elements is plain to everyone, but it is impossible to say what is the productive cause of such a circumstance (*khrêma*), [a cause] that has also made [individual] characteristics different. And in fact the completed [product] (*to teleion*) is discerned by sense, and [by sense] alone, for one could not present the whole as a whole verbally (*logôi*) other than symbolically.[38] And such knowledge does not grasp the attributes, much less the underlying substance, but being imposed from outside **(383)** is able to indicate [who a person is] when [the identity of] the person is agreed, but if it is at the outset unknown, it cannot describe [the person] in that it does not grasp [the person's] substance or its attributes (*episumbebêkota*); that is to say, the name assigned to each person is symbolic, and only succeeds in identifying (*dêlôsis*) [them] when the person is not unknown.[39] And if we grasp the variations in individual things[40] and the form (*morphê*) produced from the parts by sense and [sense] alone, then the mix of the [various] styles too is unclear and it is not difficult to recognise that the language (*logos*) of Demosthenes is produced by means of a particular kind of diction or thought, but it is extremely difficult to describe the whole, or the mix produced from the components (*meros*), in words. For just as the painter passes on (*paradidonai*) to the learner the colours that contribute to a mixture but, beyond (*meta*) the panel (*pinakion*) and the sketching (*graphê*), is at a loss to explain the scheme (*logos*) in accordance with which this particular configuration (*morphê*) [of paint] was blended together, in the same way the [elements] that create the types [of discourse] are obvious, but it is not possible to give an account of the finished product, unless one wishes to do so in the symbolic mode, which cannot illuminate any of the components or attributes. And if, as we have shown, it is impossible to describe (*exeipein*) the product (*to poioumenon*) verbally in that it is complete, [it is] much more so to identify (*exeipon*) it by a name. It is characteristic of someone who is a master of his craft (*tekhnitês*) and highly skilled not to assign names that are symbolic but [names that are] indicative of the subject matters. The rhetorician, being keen to do this but being, for the reason mentioned earlier, at a loss to do so, has fallen back on the resemblance of examples and, transferring the nomenclature for the individual aspects that perception has drawn from [their] actual appearance to the completed work (*logos*), has named [its] type by transferring (*metaphorikôs*) [that name], as though **(384)** the works (*logoi*) themselves were subjected to visual perception like the forms of the individual components; for it is starting out from this point that the ancients have called styles grand or plain or florid and have transferred to styles more or less as many configurations as they have observed in bodies.

But enough of these things. Let's come to grips with the business in hand, after first saying a little by way of preface to the book.[41] For at this point we must enquire into [those matters] that it is customary to investigate in the case of every book, and especially a technical (*tekhnikos*) one. These are: its objective, its utility, what its title is, whether the book is a genuine [work] of an ancient [writer], what the order of reading[42] [should be], what its division into parts is.

Well, deferring investigation of [its] objective and [its] utility, let's deal with those who object to the title. [These people] say that the rhetorician has failed to understand the meaning of the term [*sc. idea*], for philosophers want the *idea*[43] to be more generic and embracing of the individuals. 'And not only in this', they say, 'has he erred, but he more or less immediately overturns his own position by contradicting himself. For if the whole, as being complete, cannot be subject to teaching, how is it, given that he is dealing with complete [things], that he has given the book this title?' Well, in the first place it is silly to criticise the rhetorician for not understanding the meaning [of the term] as the philosophers do seeing that he is discussing political styles, albeit – to concede one point – this [present sense of the term] too is no less embracing; for in the same way that according to the philosophers the species (*eidos*) embraces the individuals, solemnity embraces the [styles] of Demosthenes **(385)** and, say, Antiphon, and the rest. But the solution to this is immediately obvious. The difficulty raised next, on the other hand, is very much an open question.

'Why on earth' [they ask] 'has he, neglecting the appropriate title, used (*lambanein*) the one that is applied to wholes, [thereby] explicitly contradicting what was said earlier?' And because there was a need to formulate a title with an eye to the teaching that forms the subject of the book, we would agree [with them] if its objective were to deal with the ingredients (*ta poiounta*) and not with the [works] produced through [their] mixture. But since as it is (*nun*) the plan (*proairesis*) of the rhetorician has to do with the wholes and concerns the understanding of the [works that are] produced, we need to look more to this [*sc.* the plan] and not to the immediate [question] (*to katepeigon*);[44] for although he has for the moment (*kata peristasin*) left aside completed (*apotelein*) [works], he hasn't abandoned the objective, even if he has turned to the partial aspects. 'And yet', they say, 'according to the plan of the rhetorician the title should have been *On Styles* (*kharaktêr*). For he himself at the beginning of the treatise[45] suggests that those with a knowledge of it can be producers of speeches (*logoi*) and judge the [efforts] of others as to whether they are of good quality and hit the mark (*akribôs ekhein*) or not – [and] clearly we do create and judge *styles*, for just as some bodies are manly, some effeminate,[46] some in between, in the same way we shall find with styles that some are florid, say, some middling, some harsh and austere. And if in the preface he promises to teach [us] about these, why on earth didn't he make the title of the book accord with his own plan?' [Well,] he has quite admirably disregarded them as being more generic and not able **(386)** to be grasped through the factors that create (*ta poiounta*) [them].[47] For just as the type [of discourse] is embracing of the thought, the method, the diction, and everything else, by which [things] it is also produced,[48] in the same way the styles also embrace the types [of discourse], from which they derive their structure, but the [factors] that create the type [of discourse], inasmuch as they are partial and accessible to teaching, are also grasped by reason, whereas those that produce the styles evade knowledge based on reasoning (*logos*) as being complete (*teleios*)[49] and encompassing the thought, the method, and everything to do with diction. And if, as we have learned, the factors that produce the styles, being wholes, are not grasped by reason, while the factors that produce a type [of discourse] are accessible to teaching and knowledge, the rhetorician has appropriately rejected that title in whose case both what creates and what is created are unclear and preferred the one in whose case what produces the type is capable of being grasped; for if he had used the title *On Styles*, it would from the outset have been impossible to describe them [*sc*. the styles] in words (*logos*) as having something of the nature of wholes[50] (*holikôteros*). But perhaps it would have been possible to distinguish them through their ingredients (*ta poiounta*). Indeed they too are for their part (*palin*) capable of being grasped in so far as they are complete and embracing of diction and thought. But as it is (*nun*), taking the middle path, he has rejected the more generic, I mean the styles – for these cannot be grasped, even if you consider their ingredients – and entitled it *On Types*, which [*sc*. the types of discourse] are known at the outset through their components.

What the order of reading [should be] and whether the book is a genuine [work] of an ancient [writer] has been stated in the work (*logos*) *On Issues*, but nothing prevents [us] from also saying a little [about them] now.

That it is genuine all agree. Its precision, **(387)** its limpid style, and its diction cry out, so to speak, that the work is Hermogenes', and moreover he himself mentions[51] the present composition in the *On Staseis*, as we have also pointed out there.

The [correct] order of reading is likewise clear, for the subject matter (*pragmata*) coming first, comment (*logos*) on it necessarily then follows.[52] There are two things that frame discourse (*logos*), [namely,] power and pleasure, and power shows itself in the topics and the arguments, and pleasure draws its strength from the expression, for the figures of speech, the types (*eidos*) [of style], and other such things are productive of pleasure.[53]

The next thing would be to learn about the [work's] division into parts. Or [perhaps] this too is superfluous, for the rhetorician himself will teach [us about this] further on. But it will be stated, [albeit] obscurely, in the present [work] too – for perhaps it will contribute towards a more accurate understanding of the title on our part. The book, then, is divided into the [factors] that produce the styles – I mean of course the types [of discourse] – and the thing that is produced itself, which he presents both as though by genus and by the man (*anêr*) [sc. the author]; for he is at pains to not just present the type[54] (*idea*) [of discourse] of Plato or that of Demosthenes but to first teach [us] what solemnity is, what purity is,[55] and finally, after such instruction, to come to the styles (*kharaktêr*) of the ancients.

But according to some we have, without realising it, introduced the topic of the title; for in the present passage we have assumed that the styles too are accessible to teaching, something we denied in what went before. **(388)** 'If it is actually possible to grasp them in thought (*logos*), why on earth hasn't he used the title *On Styles*?', [they ask]. But the earlier argument was nevertheless valid, for he didn't undertake to teach what the whole is but what produces [it]. It would have seemed to clash with what went before if, after the combination (*suneleusis*) of the types [of discourse], he had also attempted to describe the compositions (*mixis*) of the styles. As it is, he first presents the types [of style] by themselves (what solemnity is or what purity is, for instance), then what it is that is produced through [their] mixture, which [is something it] is not possible to articulate clearly in words unless symbolically. Thus he gives no account of the whole but, after first presenting [each of] the [factors] that produce the whole on its own, also teaches what kind of style they produce after their combination, but does not explain how you should understand it in so many words.[56]

Notes

1. As explained in the Introduction, the greater part of what follows is clearly not by Syrianus. In his 1892 edition Rabe brackets Syrianus' name and in 1931 supplies the title <Phoebammonis Prolegomena in Hermogenis Περι Ιδεων>. We translate what appears to have been the title in all but one of the manuscripts known to Rabe.
2. The Greek is *Peri Ideôn*. It isn't clear how best to translate *idea*. Hermogenes uses it both of the styles of individual authors and of the 20 types, or qualities, of style that he identifies. The author of the present work, on the other hand, normally, but not always, prefers *kharaktêr*, or occasionally *tupos*, for the former and *idea* for the latter. It would in fact be possible to render all three terms 'style' (for this see for example LSJ *idea* 4.b, *kharaktêr* II.5, and *tupos* VI.3), but it seems best to distinguish them in translation and we follow Wooten (1987) in using 'type' for *idea* and add the transliterated Greek after 'style' for the few cases of *tupos*. Wooten's full title for his translation is *On Types of Style*, but both Hermogenes and the author of the present work frequently talk of *ideai logou* (indeed Rabe chooses *Peri Ideôn Logou* from among the various titles in the manuscripts for his edition of Hermogenes' treatise) and it seems to us that 'discourse' is a better supplement than style and we frequently translate *ideai* 'types [of discourse]', as we have in the title. 'Speech' would be another possible rendering of *logos* in these contexts, but that properly speaking refers to oral communication whereas 'discourse' is used of both written and spoken communication.
3. This is not thought to be the work of Hermogenes.
4. cf. the similar reference in Syrianus' commentary on Hermogenes' *Peri Staseôn,* 3–7, which shows that the reference is to *Peri Staseôn* 53,12–13. The 'Notes' themselves have not survived.
5. Or perhaps 'descendants'.
6. The Greek is *ton koinon Hermên, koinos* ('common' presumably in the sense 'shared') being an epithet of Hermes. Diodorus Siculus (5.75.1 ff.) claims he has the epithet as the patron of heralds, who benefit all parties in common during a war, which would certainly be in accord with his role as a messenger or intermediary in a variety of other contexts. Whatever the origin of the epithet, the phrase was, it seems, used in quite other contexts: when someone was present when another person made a lucky find, they might call out *koinos Hermês*! to claim an equal share in the discovery. Here of course the situation is rather different. The discoverer himself is imagined as

invoking the phrase and doing so by acting on it rather than merely uttering it. (Interestingly, the paroemiographer Michael Apostolius gives *hermaion koinon* as an alternative to *Hermês koinos*, which would be easier, the first sense of *hermaion* in LSJ being 'gift of Hermes, i.e. unexpected piece of luck, godsend, wind-fall, treasure-trove'.)

7   The version of this introductory paragraph that introduces Syrianus' commentary actually has 'gods' at this point.
8   *sc.* the qualities of good writing or speaking.
9   The *tekhnikos* is Hermogenes, 7–17 being inspired by *Peri Ideôn* 213,4–214,12. LSJ suggests 'artistic, skilful, workmanlike' for the relevant sense of *tekhnikos* and 'the grammarians' for *hoi tekhnikoi*. After considering and rejecting renderings such as 'the expert', 'the technician', the master of the art [of rhetoric]', we have opted for 'the rhetorician' on the analogy of 'the grammarians'.
10 Although the plural *logoi* suggests this rendering, 'types of speeches' isn't an obvious description of Hermogenes' subject matter in *Peri Ideôn* and we were initially inclined to translate 'types of discourse'. However, Hermogenes thought that one or another style of composition dominated in the speeches of most orators (Demosthenes was an exception) and so perhaps he could at a stretch be said to be writing about types of speeches.
11 Or perhaps 'words' in view of 98,5–9 below.
12 *logôn* in line 2 suggests something like 'the unlettered' for *tôn alogôn*, and that is what we have opted for, but passages like *Prolegomena* 276,5–6, where it is said that when we call humans 'rational (*logikos*) living beings' we do so to distinguish them from non-rational (*alogos*) animals (cf. too *Rhetores graeci* vol. 7, 869,26–7, where an anonymous scholiast on Hermogenes' *Peri Ideôn* makes a similar statement), suggest that animals may after all be in question here.
13 See Lampe *entunkhanô* B for *entunkhanôn* in this sense.
14 Rabe has adopted Brinkmann's emendation *mnêsin* ('memory') for *mimêsin* ('imitation', 'representation', 'portrait'), the reading of all the manuscripts. In fact *mnêsis* is difficult. It is only listed in the supplement to LSJ and only on the authority of an inscription. However (1) *mimêsis* is difficult too and *mnêsis* gives much better sense, and (2) it is easy to see how *mimêsin* could have replaced the rare word *mnêsin* in a text which will go on to discuss *mimêsis* and we have translated *mnêsin*.
15 *Symposium* 208E ff. (cited by Hermias at 220,7–8).
16 One might think that a parent would have an important role here, but to provide the necessary contrast with what follows, the author presumably has in mind others such as their teachers or their peers or the children themselves.
17 cf. Lampe s.v. 2.c.
18 cf. Porphyry (Smith 416F): 'if discourse is thought of as having a soul and a body, the discovery of ideas would rightly be considered the soul, their expression the

Notes to pp. 176–7

body'. The passage is quoted by Syrianus both in his commentary on Hermogenes' *Peri Staseôn* 14,9 ff., where he says that it comes from a treatise on *staseis*, and in his commentary on Hermogenes' *Peri Ideôn* 93,9 ff., as well as by an anonymous commentator on Hermogenes' *Peri Staseôn* (Walz 1832, 1086, l. 13 ff.). cf. too the passages cited by Rabe in his note at *Prolegomenon Sylloge* 205,1–4. The likening of a piece of writing to a living creature goes back at least to Plato, *Phaedrus* 264C.

19 Although we have followed Rabe in enclosing what follows and some later passages in inverted commas, it seems unlikely that they are really direct quotation.
20 If the reference is to 98,17–19 above, it is actually the treatise on styles that is compared to a living creature there, not the styles themselves.
21 The Greek is *adêlon to aition to* (*kai* rather than *to* in Sikeliotes) *sêmantikon tês idiotêtos* and we aren't sure that we have understood it correctly.
22 Although he does use the term *graphikê lexis* in his discussion of the plain style at *de Elocutione* 193,2 (on which see the next note), where it is said to be 'easy to read' and seems to be descriptive of the plain style. (In his translation of 193,2 Roberts 1902 renders *graphikê* 'literary'. We have preferred 'graphic', in the sense of 'descriptive' or 'lively', for which cf. LSJ, s.v. II.3.)
23 Dionysius of Halicarnassus lived from *c.* 60 BC to after 7 BC. He used the terminology in the text in his essay on Demosthenes (at *Dem.* 33,23, for example), but in his treatise *On Literary Composition* (at 21,15–18, for example) uses the terms *austêros, glaphuros*, and *eukratos* – austere or rough; polished or smooth; well-blended. Hipparchus is unknown. Demetrius, the otherwise unknown author of a work *Peri Hermêneias* (commonly referred to as *de Elocutione* or *On Style*) was probably active in the late Hellenistic or early Roman period. See *de Elocutione* 36,1–2 for the four styles. It may be significant that no later author is mentioned.
24 Following Brinkmann, Rabe, comparing 103,10–11 below, adds *eis* ('to') before *hôrismenon* at 100,3 in his 1931 edition. The text without *eis* (as in Rabe's 1892 edition) would translate 'and, as it seems, assigned a definite number to them', which would in some ways be easier.
25 i.e. an equal mixture of plain and grand elements, which would constitute the intermediate style.
26 Comparing Sikeliotes 1834, Rabe adds *eti* after *estin* at 100,9.
27 Or 'according to the recipe', (cf. LSJ *taxis*, II.3.b.). The alternative manuscript reading *kata mixin* perhaps points in the same direction.
28 *ate monos autos dexamenos tên epitasin* (100,17–18) is difficult. The best we have been able to do is to take it that *autos* refers back to the plain style (*iskhnos*), which has increased in intensity, whereas the intermediate style, overall at least, has not. However, this doesn't seem very satisfactory and something may have gone wrong with the text.
29 Following Brinkman, Rabe has added *adunatousa* after *pesein* at 101,19. Perhaps *adunatei*, giving 'it cannot be subject to knowledge', with 'it' looking back to *to kata*

phusin apoteloumenon, would be a better addition. (A more literal translation of *hupo gnôsin pesein* in lines 18–19 would be 'cannot fall under knowledge'.)

30 *sc.* for anything produced naturally or by art.
31 Rabe punctuates with a question mark.
32 Presumably this means at 103,10–15.
33 *sc.* understanding and appreciation of what is worthwhile in a field isn't immediately available but only arises with hard-won mastery of the field. cf. Hermogenes, *Peri Ideôn* 214,17–18.
34 The prime exemplar of the plain style.
35 The metaphor is that of a balance. A person's natural tendencies weigh down one pan, his attempted emulation of a style of one of the ancients the other.
36 *hôrismenou ontos* could be translated 'has been defined', but the author has not argued for any particular number of styles but only that there is not an indefinitely large number of them. cf. the similar passages at 100,2–4 and 103,11–15, where no particular number is stated but it is being claimed that there is a definite (*hôrismenos* again) or limited number of styles.
37 Perhaps this and what follows look back to 99,24 ff. where an analogy is drawn between styles and a living creature, although there a living creature is quoted as a parallel rather than as an example.
38 As what follows shows, this means that one can assign a name to it that will serve to identify it to someone who already knows what you are talking about but not name it or describe it in a way that would identify it or explain it to anyone without full knowledge of it. Such a name will be a *sumbolon* in something close to the sense at LSJ s.v. A.2: 'token serving as a proof of identity'.
39 Strictly speaking this is only true when the person is being referred to in their absence.
40 Or perhaps 'individuals'.
41 'About the preface to the book' would be the obvious translation, but that doesn't fit what follows.
42 This means relative to the other treatises attributed to Hermogenes.
43 *idea*, which we normally translate 'type', was one of the terms for a Platonic Form. Because its meaning is the issue here we have left it untranslated in this sentence.
44 *sc.* the issue raised by the question at 109,4–6. 'What is pressing' would be a more literal rendering of *to katepeigon*.
45 Hermogenes, *Peri Ideôn* 213,6–12.
46 'Effeminate' doesn't appear to be attested for *malthakos*, but *malthakôdês* and *malthakôn* in Lampe and *malthakiazô* in the supplement to LSJ suggest that it should be a possible sense for it and it provides the right kind of contrast with 'manly'.
47 A reference to the rule that if definition is by genus and differentiae a *summum genus*, having nothing above it, cannot be defined.

48 With this first part of the sentence, cf. Syrianus' commentary on Hermogenes' *Peri Ideôn* 2,16–19.
49 Another way of describing their generic nature.
50 Again, another way of saying that they are generic in nature.
51 Hermogenes, *Peri Staseôn* 35,7.
52 We'd expect our author to describe the order in which the texts of the standard rhetorical curriculum (*sc.* in his day basically those attributed to Hermogenes) should be read, but, if we understand him correctly, he begins by stating that speeches, and other texts, should be read before comment on them.
53 Perhaps this means that among the works rightly or wrongly attributed to Hermogenes the *Peri Ideôn* and *On Method* should be read after the *Progymnasmata*, *Peri Staseôn*, and *On Invention*.
54 This actually amounts to their style and *idea* and *kharaktêr* are virtually synonymous in this sentence.
55 With 112,2–4 cf. Hermogenes, *Peri Ideôn* 214,22 ff.
56 'In so many words' translates *logôi*.

Bibliography

Athanassiadi, Polymnia (1999), *Damascius*: *The Philosophical History*; *Text with Translation and Notes,* Athens: Apamea Cultural Association.

Baltzly, Dirk and Michael Share (2018), *Hermias*: *On Plato's* Phaedrus *227A–245E,* London: Bloomsbury.

Behr, C. A. (1968), 'Citations of Porphyry's *Against Aristides* Preserved in Olympiodorus', *The American Journal of Philology* 89(2), 186–99.

Blank, David (1996), *Ammonius*: *On Aristotle* On Interpretation *1–8,* London: Duckworth.

Brinkmann, August (1906), 'Phoibammon *peri Mimêseôs*', *Rheinisches Museum für Philologie* 61, 117–34. (cited as Brinkmann)

Brown, Peter (1992), *Power and Persuasion in Late Antiquity*: *Towards a Christian Empire,* Madison: University of Wisconsin Press.

Browning, Robert (2000), 'Education in the Roman Empire', in A. Cameron, B. Ward-Perkins, and M. Whitby (eds), *The Cambridge Ancient History*, vol. 14: *Late Antiquity*: *Empire and Successors, AD 425–600*, Cambridge: Cambridge University Press, 855–83.

Caluori, Damian (2014), 'Rhetoric and Platonism in Fifth-Century Athens', in R. Fowler (ed.), *Plato in the Third Sophistic*, Berlin: De Gruyter, 57–72.

Connolly, Joy (2001), 'Rhetorical Education', in M. Peachin (ed.), *The Oxford Handbook of Social Relations in the Roman World*, Oxford: Oxford University Press, 101–18.

Fuhr, Karl (1893), 'Syriani in Hermogenem commentaria edidit Hugo Rabe. Vol. 1. B.G. Teubner, 1892', *Deutsche Literaturzeitung* 31, 967–8.

Heath, Malcolm (1995), *Hermogenes,* On Issues: *Strategies of Argument in Later Greek Rhetoric*, Oxford: Clarendon Press.

Heath, Malcolm (2003), 'Porphyry's Rhetoric', *Classical Quarterly* 53 (1), 141–66.

Heath, Malcolm (2009), 'Platonists and the Teaching of Rhetoric in Late Antiquity', in P. Vassilopoulou and S. R. L. Clark (eds), *Late Antique Epistemology*: *Other Ways to Truth*, London: Palgrave Macmillan, 143–59.

Jackson, Robin, Kimon Lycos, and Harold Tarrant (1998), *Olympiodorus, Commentary on Plato's Gorgias*: *Translated with Full Notes*, Philosophia Antiqua 78, Leiden: Brill.

Kennedy, George A. (1983), *Greek Rhetoric Under Christian Emperors*, Princeton: Princeton University Press.

Kennedy, George A. (2005), *Invention and Method*: *Two Rhetorical Treatises from the Hermogenic Corpus*, Atlanta: Society of Biblical Literature.

Lampe, E. W. H. (1961) (ed.), *A Patristic Greek Lexicon*, Oxford: Clarendon Press. (cited as Lampe)

Liddell, H. G. and R. Scott (1996) (comps), *A Greek–English Lexicon*, rev. H. Jones, with a New Supplement, 9th edn, Oxford: Clarendon Press. (cited as LSJ)

Mansfeld, Jaap (1994), *Prolegomena: Questions to be Settled before the Study of an Author, or a Text*, Philosophia Antiqua 61, Leiden and New York: Brill.

Miles, Graeme and Han Baltussen (2023), *Philostratus* Lives of the Sophists; *Eunapius* Lives of Philosophers and Sophists, Loeb Classical Library 134, Cambridge Mass.: Harvard University Press.

Papaioannou, Stratis (2019), 'Ioannes Sikeliotes (and Ioannes Geometres) Revisited, with an Appendix: Edition of Sikeliotes' Scholia on Aelius Aristides', in André Binggeli and Vincent Déroche (eds), *Mélanges Bernard Flusin*, Travaux et mémoires 23, Paris: Association des Amis du Centre d'Histoire et Civilisation de Byzance, 659–92.

Patillon, Michel (1985), *Théorie du Discours chez Hermogène le Rhéteur: Essai sur les Structures Linguistiques de la Rhétorique Ancienne*, Paris: Les Belles Lettres.

Patillon, Michel (2009), *Corpus Rhetoricum*, tome II, *Hermogène*, Les États de Cause, Paris: Les Belles Lettres.

Patillon, Michel (2012), *Corpus Rhetoricum*, tome III, 1re partie & 2e partie: *Pseudo-Hermogène*, L'Invention - *Anonyme*, Synopse des Exordes - *Anonyme*, Scolies au traité sur l'Invention du Pseudo-Hermogène, Paris: Les Belles Lettres.

Patillon, Michel (2014), *Corpus Rhetoricum*, tome V, *Pseudo-Hermogène*, La Méthode de l'Habilité; *Maxime*, Les Objections Irréfutables; *Anonyme*, Méthode des Discours d'Adresse, Paris: Les Belles Lettres.

Patillon, Michel (2021), *Syrianus*, Sur les États de Cause, Paris: Les Belles Lettres.

Pepe, Cristina (2018), 'The Rhetorical Commentary in Late Antiquity', *AION: Sezione di Filologia e Letteratura Classica* 40, 86–108.

Rabe, Hugo (1892), *Syriani in Hermogenem Commentaria*, vol. 1: *Commentarium in Libros peri Ideôn. Accedit Syriani quae fertur in Hermogenem Libros peri Ideôn Praefatio*, Leipzig: Teubner.

Rabe, Hugo (1893), *Syriani in Hermogenem Commentaria*, vol. 2: *Commentarium in Libros peri Staseôn*, Leipzig: Teubner.

Rabe, Hugo (1895), 'De Christophori commentario in Hermogenis librum peri Staseôn', *Rheinisches Museum für Philologie* 50, 241–9.

Rabe, Hugo (1913), *Hermogenes Opera*, Leipzig: Teubner.

Rabe, Hugo (1931), *Prolegomenon Sylloge*, Leipzig: Teubner.

Roberts, Rhys (1902), *Demetrius on Style: The Greek Text of Demetrius de Elecutione Edited after the Paris Manuscript*, Cambridge: University Press.

Roilos, Panagiotis (2018), 'Ancient Greek Rhetorical Theory and Byzantine Discursive Politics: John Sikeliotes on Hermogenes', in T. Shawcross and I. Toth (eds), *Reading in the Byzantine Empire and Beyond*, Cambridge: Cambridge University Press, 159–84.

Russell, D. A. (1983), *Greek Declamation*, Cambridge: Cambridge University Press.

Sikeliotes, John (1834), 'Exêgêsis eis tas Ideas tou Hermogenou', in C. Walz (ed.), *Rhetores Graeci*, vol. 6, Stuttgart: Cotta, 56–504. (cited as Sikeliotes)

Smith, Andrew (1993) (ed.), *Porphyrii Philosophi Fragmenta: Fragmenta Arabica David Wasserstein Interpretante*, Leipzig: Teubner.

Stegemann, Willy (1941), 'Phoibammon 5', in *Paulys Realencyclopädie der classischen Altertumswissenschaft*, Neue Bearbeitung, Band XX, 1, Stuttgart: Druckenmüller, 326–43.

Walz, C. (1832) (ed.), *Rhetores Graeci*, vol. 7, Stuttgart: Cotta.

Wooten, C. W. (1987), *Hermogenes' On the Types of Style*, Chapel Hill and London: University of North Carolina Press.

English–Greek Glossary

ancient: *arkhaios, palaios*
animate: *empsukhos*
aptitude: *epitêdeiotês*
argument: *enthumêma*
art: *tekhnê*
artist: *zôgraphos*
attribute (n.): *to episumbebêkos, to parakolouthoun, parakolouthêma*
augmentation: *auxêsis*
austere: *austêros*

balanced: *isorropos*
beneficial: *epôphelês*
blend (v.): *sunkerannunai*
bodily: *sômatikos*
body: *sôma*
book: *biblion*

chance: *tukhê*
change: *metaballein*
characteristic: *idiôma*
clarity: *eukrineia, to akribes*
commentary: *hupomnêma*
complete, completed: *teleios*
configuration: *diatupôsis*

defined: *hôrismenos*
definite: *hôrismenos*
difficult: *duskherês*
difficulty: *aporêma, to duskheres*
diction: *lexis*
diminution: *meiôsis*
discourse: *logos*
discovery: *heuresis*
drawing: *graphê*

emulate: *zêloun*
emulation: *zêlos*
entitle: *epigraphein*
entity: *huparxis*
everlasting: *aïdios*
example: *paradeigma*

expression: *lexis, phrasis*

figurative: *tropikos*
figure of speech: *skhêma*
find: *heuriskein*
florid: *anthêros*
forcefulness: *deinotês*

generic: *genikos*
genuine: *gnêsios*
genus: *genos*
grand: *hadros*
graphic: *graphikos*
grasp: *katalambanein*
graspable: *katalêptos*

hard to grasp: *duskatalêptos*
harmful: *blaberos*
harsh: *trakhus*
human being: *anthrôpos*

imitate: *mimeisthai*
imitation: *mimêsis*
individual: *to atomon*
intensification: *epitasis*
intermediate: *mesos*
issue: *stasis*

knowledge: *epistêmê, gnôsis*

limit (v.): *sustellein*
living creature: *zôion*

man: *anêr*
master of his craft: *tekhnitês*
meaning: *sêmasia*
method: *methodos*
mix (n.): *mixis*

name (n.): *onoma, onomasia*
name (v.): *onomazein*
nature: *phusis*

note: *hupomnêma*
number: *arithmos, to poson, posotês*

objective: *skopos*

painter: *zôgraphos*
part: *meros*
partial: *merikos*
particular character: *idiotês*
perception: *aisthêsis*
philosopher: *philosophos*
plain: *iskhnos*
pleasure: *hêdonê*
political: *politikos*
precision: *eukrineia, to akribes*
preface: *protheôria*
produce: *apotelein*
producer: *ergatês*
proficient in the art: *tekhnikos*
public: *dêmosios*
purity: *katharotês*

reading: *anagnôsis*
reason: *aitia*
resemblance: *homoiotês*

sculptor: *plastourgos*
sense: *aisthêsis*
shape (n.): *diamorphôsis, diatupôsis*
shape (v.): *methodeuein*
shaper: *dêmiourgos*
similarity: *homoiotês*
sophist: *sophistês*
soul: *psukhê*

speaker: *rhêtôr*
species: *eidos*
specific property: *idiôma*
speech: *logos*
style: *kharaktêr, tupos*
substance: *ousia*
symbolic: *sumbolikos*
symbolically: *sumbolikôs*

teach: *didaskein*
teaching: *didaskalia*
technical: *tekhnikos*
theory: *theôria*
thought: *ennoia*
title: *epigraphê*
train: *engumnazein*
treatise: *pragmateia, sungramma, suntagma, logos*
truth: *alêtheia*
type: *idea, eidos*

understanding: *katalêpsis*
unlettered: *alogos*
useless: *asumphoros*
utility: *to khrêsimon*

variation: *exallagê*
virtue: *aretê*

whole: *to holon*
word: *logos*
writer on the art: *tekhnographos*

Greek–English Index

References are to the page and line numbers of the Greek text (indicated in the margins of the translation).

agnoein, be unknown, 106,17.21; understand, 108,12
aïdios, everlasting, 98,7
aisthêsis, sense, 106,11.23; perception, 107,20.24
aitia, reason, 107,19
aition, cause, 99,7; 106,8
akatalêptos, not (able) to be grasped, 100,4; 110,27; cannot be grasped, 111,1
akribês, accurate, 111,7; *to akribes*, precision, 111,22
alêtheia, truth, 104,18
alogos, unlettered, 104,18
anagnôsis, reading, 96,18; 108,9; 111,4.11
analogein, be analogous, 98,17; 99,3
anatrepein, overturn, 108,16
anazêtein, investigate, 97,10
anêr, man, 112,2
anisos, 100,13, unequal
anoêtos, foolish, 98,3; futile, 99,14; silly, 108,20
anthêros, florid, 99,21; 107,26; 109,25
anthrôpos, human being, 106,8
antilambanein, come to grips with, 98,1
apagoreuein, deny, 112,10
apaitein, ask, 102,2
aparneisthai, reject, 100,8
apartizein, produce, 107,3
aphairein, take away, 104,1.3
aphanizein, obliterate, 98,7
aphoran, think of, 105,3
apodidonai, assign, 100,4; 103,11
aporein, be at a loss, 107,8.18
aporêma, difficulty, 104,13
apotelein, accomplish, 101,2; produce, 101,13.14.16.20; 102,5; 106,22; 107,4; 109,10.14; 110,7.11.16.20; 112,19; *to apoteloumenon*, finished product, 107,10; component, 111,3

apotelesmatikos, productive, 106,8
aretê, virtue, 97,7
arkhaios, ancient, 97,9; 99,14; 102,10.22; 104,14; 105,14.20; 108,8; 111,4; 112,6
arrenôpos, manly, 109,23
askein, train, 97,16
asumphoros, prejudicial, 99,9.11; useless, 101,1; 102,8; *to asumphoron*, uselessness, 103,3.7; 105,7.12
atomon, to, individual, individual thing, aspect, component, 99,4; 104,5; 106,22; 107,20.24; 108,14.25
austêros, austere, 109,26
autoproairetos, self-determining, 98,12
auxêsis, augmentation, 103,14

biblion, book, 96,19; 108,5.7.9.19; 109,7; 110,3; 111,5.23
blaberos, harmful, 99,10

deinotês, forcefulness, 96,9
dêlôsis, identifying, 106,21
dêmiourgos, shaper, 98,13
dêmosios, public, 96,9
dexiotês, facility, 97,17; forte, 105,21
diadokhê, succession, 96,9
diaginôskein, discern, 106,11; recognise, 107,3; distinguish, 110,23
diakrinein, distinguish, 97,8
dialattein, depart from, 105,5
diamerizein, distribute, 101,20
diamorphôsis, shape, 102,1
dianoein, think, 99,16
diaphtheirein, destroy, 104,4
diaporein, raise difficulties, 102,24; 109,3
diathesis, predisposition, 104,16
diatupôsis, shape, 102,1; configuration, 108,1
didaskalia, teaching, 108,17; 109,7; 110,10.17; 112,9; instruction, 112,5

didaskein, teach, 110,1; 111,21; 112,4.13.23
diexerkhesthai, describe, 106,6
dioikêsis, control, 98,13; ordering, 104,17
doxa, position, 108,16
dunamis, ability, 97,1; power, 111,14.15
duskatalêptos, hard to grasp, 103,21; 104,5; 105,10
duskherês, difficult, 107,3; ***to duskheres***, difficulty, 103,3; 105,8

eidos, species, 108,24; type, 111,18
ekballein, reject, 100,1
ekgonos, child, 96,17; offspring, 98,10
ektelein, make, 102,3
emphantikos, indicative, 107,17
empodizein, 102,19, stand in the way
empsukhos, animate, 106,4
engumnazein, train, 105,16
enkalein, find fault, 98,16
enkheirêsis, attempt, 102,20
ennoia, thought, 98,19; 107,2; 110,6.13.25
enthumêma, argument 111,16
epeisagein, produce, 97,1
epideiknunai, show, 97,4
epignôsis, knowledge, 100,23
epigraphê, title, 108,8.11.19; 109,5.8.17; 110,3.18; 111,22; 112,7
epigraphein, name, 99,17; use a title, 110,21; 112,12; entitle, 111,2
epikheirêma, enterprise, 97,17
epistêmê, knowledge, 97,15
epistêmôn, versed in, 98,20; with knowledge, 109,19
episumbebêkos, to, attribute, 106,19
epitasis, intensification, 100,5.18.20; 103,12
epitêdeiotês, aptitude, 102,14
epôphelês, beneficial, 99,11
ergatês, producer, 109,20
errômenos, intact, 105,16
euektein, be in good condition, 99,10
eukrineia, clarity, 97,24; precision, 111,8
exallagê, variation, 103,22; 106,22

genikos, generic, 108,13; 110,3.26
genos, genus, 112,1
gnêsios, genuine, 108,8; 111,4.7
gnôsis, knowledge, 97,15; 101,19; 102,9; 105,12; 106,13; 110,13.17

graphê, drawing, 102,5; sketching, 107,8
graphikos, graphic, 99,21; 100,1
gumnazein, work on, 105,20

hadros, grand, 99,20; 100,7.11.14.15; 107,25
hêdonê, pleasure, 111,15.16.18
heuresis, discovery, 97,11
heuriskein, find, 100,5; 101,9; 102,19; 109,25
holikos, having the nature of wholes, 110,22
holos, to holon, whole, 104,4; 106,12.13; 107,4; 108,17; 109,5.12; 110,15; 112,14.21
homoiotês, similarity, 106,3; resemblance, 107,19
homologein, agree, 106,16
horatikos, visual, 107,24
horizein, hôrismenos, defined, 103,13; definite, 100,3; 103,11; 105,22
hulê, material, 106,4
huparxis, entity, 103,20; 104,6.8.10
huperbainein, go past, 100,10
hupoballein, be subject to, 107,23
hupomnêma, note, 96,9; commentary, 96,16
hupomnêmatizein, comment on [but paraphrase used], 96,8
hupothesis, kath' hupothesin, to take a hypothetical case, 101,19
hupotithenai, suggest, 109,19; assume, 112,8

idea, type, 96,1.11; 97,18; 98,18; 107,10.22; 108,13; 110,5.9.10.16.20; 111,2.24; 112,3.15.18
idiôma, characteristic, 104,2; specific property, 104,7.9.11
idiotês, particular character, 98,21; 99,5.7; 103,17.21; 104,5.16; 105,23
iskhnos, plain, 99,20; 100,5.7.9.13.15.17; 103,15; 105,15; 107,26; ***to iskhnon***, plainness, 103,12
iskhuein, succeed, 106,20
iskhus, strength, 111,17
isorropos, balanced, 100,7

kalos, fine, 105,10
katalambanein, grasp, 98,24; 99,6; 100,20; 101,17; 102,8; 103,3.24; 104,8; 105,9;

Greek–English Index

106,5.23; 110,5.11.15; 112,11;
understand, 105,23; 112,23
katalêpsis, understanding, 100,23;
101,2.18; 109,13; 111,23
katalêptos, able to be grasped, capable of being grasped, graspable, 100,21; 103,9.16; 104,21; 110,20.24
katalimpanein, leave behind, 98,8
katamanthanein, clearly understand, 98,17
kataphanês, quite clear, 103,5
katapherein, bring down, 105,20; ***katapheresthai***, fall back, 104,15;
katêgorein, apply to, 109,5
kathaptesthai, grasp, 106,14.18
katharotês, purity, 112,4.18
kephalaion, to, topic, 111,15
kharaktêr, style, 97,9; 98,19.21; 99,2.14.17.19; 100,3.8.18; 101,1; 102,10.15; 103,2.9.13.18.23; 104,3.7.12.18; 105,17; 106,3; 107,1.26; 108,2.4.22; 109,18.22.24; 110,8.15.21; 111,1.24; 112,9.11.16.23; characteristic, 106,10
khrêsimon, to, utility, 108,7
khrôma, colour, 107,6
khronos, time, 98,7
krasis, make-up, 99,12; mix, 100,8; combination, 106,6
krinein, judge (v.), 109,20.22
kritikos, critical, 96,13
kubernan, govern, 98,15
kurios, have the power, 98,14

lamprophônos, with a clear voice, 102,4
lexis, expression, 104,4; diction, 107,2; 110,7.14.25; 111,8
lithos, stone, 101,19
logios, of eloquence, 97,5
logos, speech, 96,13; 97,18; 98,2.13; 105,1.6; 109,20; word, 97,3; 98,5.10; 107,5; 110,21; 112,19; discourse, 97,8; 98,7.15; 111,14; treatise, 98,18; remark, 103,6; language, 99,15; 107,3; scheme, 107,8; way, 108,24; reason, 110,11.16; reasoning, 110,12; work, 107,22.23; 111,5; composition, 104,17; topic, 112,8; thought, 112,11; argument, 112,13; account, 112,21; comment, 111,13; ***logôi***, verbally, 106,6.12; 107,15; in so many words, 112,24

lusis, solution, 109,26
lusitelein, assist, 97,2

mallon, mallon kai hêtton, to a greater or lesser degree, 100,19
malthakos, effeminate, 109,23
manthanein, learn, 110,15; 111,19; ***ho manthanôn***, learner, 107,7
meiôsis, diminution, 100,6.20; 103,12.14
merikos, partial, 110,10
meros, part, 104,20; 106,5.23; 108,9; 111,19; component, 107,4; ***kata meros***, partial, 109,16
mesos, intermediate, 99,20; 100,10.14.17; in between, 109,24; middling, 109,27; middle, 110,25
metaballein, alter, 99,9; change, 99,12; 100,12; 104,16
metakheirisis, treatment, 99,16
metapherein, transfer, 107,22; 108,2
metaphorikôs, by transferring, 107,22
methodeuein, shape, 98,16; 99,15
methodos, method, 96,8; 101,11; 110,6.14; means, 97,10
mimeisthai, imitate, 99,13; 101,12
mimêsis, imitation, 98,22; 102,17; 105,24
mimnêskein, mention, 111,10
mixis, mix, 100,13; 107,1.5; mixing, 106,6; mixture, 107,6; 109,11; 112,19; composition, 112,16
mnêmoneuein, remember, 98,6
morphê, appearance, 101,13; form, 106,23; 107,25; configuration, 107,9

onoma, name, 106,20; 107,15; term, 108,13
onomasia, name, 107,17; nomenclature, 107,20
onomazein, name, 107,22
opsis, appearance, 107,21
organon, ta organa, equipment, 101,12
ousia, substance, 103,20.25; 106,15.18

pais, child, 98,6.13
palaios, ancient, 98,22; 107,26
paradeigma, example, 106,1; 107,19
paradidonai, pass on, 107,7; present, 112,1.17.24

parakolouthein, to parakolouthoun, result, 99,5; attribute, 103,20.23; 104,3; 107,13
parakolouthêma, attribute, 103,18.22; 104,6.9; 106,14
paraphthengesthai, repudiate, 98,23
parektikos, productive, 111,18
paristanai, present, 97,23; 106,12; 112,2; describe, 99,4; 106,18; 107,5; 110,22; explain, 107,8; 112,22
periekhein, embrace, 108,25; 110,8.13
periektikos, embracing, 108,14.23; 110,6.25
peristasis, turn of events, 102,19; circumstance, 102,23; time being, 109,14
peritunkhanein, come across, 96,16
philêdonos, lover of pleasure, 105,9
philosophos, philosopher, 96,7; 108,13.21.24
phônê, voice, 101,6.8
phrasis, expression, 111,16
phronêsis, wisdom, 96,5
phulattein, maintain, 105,14; keep, 105,17
phusikôs, naturally, 101,13
phusis, nature, 97,13.14; 99,9.15; 100,12; 101,4; 102,9.14.21; 104,15; 105,14.16.19; *tês phuseôs,* natural, 97,14; 100,9; *kata phusin, têi phusei,* naturally, 101,3.8.10.16; 102,4.7
pinakion, painting, 101,12; panel, 107,7
piptein, be subject to, 101,19; 108,17; land, 101.20; be accessible to, 110,11.17; 112,9
planan, get sidetracked, 103,17
plastourgos, sculptor, 102,2
pleonektêma, advantage, 97,14
politikos, political, 96,5; 97,7; 108,21
ponein, work hard, 97,10; 104,20
ponos, effort, 97,5; 105,12; labour, 97,19
posos, to poson, number, 99,17; 103,9.16; 105,23
posotês, number, 98,21; 99,1
pragmateia, treatise, 98,1; 109,18; composition, 111,10
praxis, matter, 98,4; action, 101,10; practice, 103,1.6
proäiresis, decision, 98,14; plan, 109,11.17; 110,2

probainein, move, 100,7; advance, 106,1
probasis, kata probasin, progessively, 100,15
prokeimai, to prokeimenon, task, 97,2
prophainein, be obvious, 109,2
prosôpon, person, 106,16.21
protheôria, preface, 108,5; 110,1
psukhê, soul, 98,10.20

rhêtôr, speaker, 105,3

sêmainein, indicate, 106,15
sêmantikos, that explains, 99,7
sêmasia, meaning, 108,12.21
semnotês, solemnity, 108,25; 112,4.18
skhêma, figure of speech, 111,17
skopein, consider, 103,17
skopos, objective, 108,7.10; 109,9.15
sôma, body, 98,11.19; 106,4; 108,1; 109,23
sômatikos, bodily, 98,4
sophistês, sophist, 96,7
spoudazein, endeavour, 97,19; concern oneself, 98,4; keep at, 105,2
stasis, issue, 96,6; 111,5.10
stoikheion, element, 106,7
sumbainein, turn out, 102,20; prevail, 102,22
sumballein, understand, 96,15; put together, 96,19; contribute, 97,15
sumbolikos, symbolic, 106,20; 107,10.16
sumbolikôs, symbolically, 106,13; 112,20
suneleusis, combination, 112,15.22
sungramma, treatise, 96,4.6
sunistanai, know, 104,7; frame, 111,14
sunkeisthai, be composed, 106,7
sunkerannunai, blend, 100,16; 107,9
sunkhôrein, accept, 100,21; concede, 108,22
sunomologein, agree, 109,8; 111,7
suntagma, treatise, 96,11; work, 111,9
suntelein, help, 106,2; contribute, 107,6; 111,22
suntithenai, put together, 96,19
sustasis, structure, 110,9
sustatikos, (is a) component, 103,24; 106,4; 107,12
sustellein, limit, 99,18; 100,2; 103,10

taxis, status, 98,19; order, 108,9; 111,4.11
tekhnê, art, 97,13.16; 101,4.14.17; 102,8

tekhnikos, proficient in the art, 96,12, technical, 108,7; **ho tekhnikos**, the rhetorician, 97,14; 107,18; 108,12.20; 109,11.17; 110,17; 111,20
tekhnitês, master of his craft, 107,15
tekhnographos, writer on the art, 96,3
teleios, complete, completed, 106,11; 107,14.22; 108,17.18; 110,13.23
temnein, divide, 111,23
theôria, theory, 102,25; 103,2.8
tomê, division, 108,9; 111,19
trakhus, harsh, 109,27

tropikos, figurative, 104,3
tropoi, character, 98,14
tupos, style, 102,22; 104,14; 105,5.14.20
tukhê, chance, 101,4.9.11.14.17.20; 102,7

zêlos, emulation, 101,3; 102,15.18
zêloun, emulate, 102,6.10; 104,14.18; 105,14.17
zêtêsis, question, 103,6
zôgraphos, artist, 101,12; painter, 107,5
zôion, living creature, 98,18; 99,3

Subject Index

References in the form 109,12 are to the page and line numbers of the Greek text in the margins of the translation; those listed after 'n.' to the notes.

Alexander, son (?) of Syrianus, 96,7; n. 5
Antiphon, 109,1

Demetrius, 99,21; n.23
   de Elecutione, n. 22, 23
Demosthenes, 104,19.22; 105,1.5; 107,2; 109,1; 112,3
Dionysius of Halicarnassus, 99,18; n. 23
   Demosthenes, n. 23
   On Literary Composition, n. 23

Hermogenes, 96,4; 111,8
Hipparchus, 99,20; n. 23

imitation, *see* styles

Lysias, 105,17

Phidias, 102,2
philosophers, 96,7; 108,13.21.24
Plato, 98,10; 104,19.22; 112,3
   Symposium, n. 15
Platonists, 96,7

six preliminary questions, 108,5–10
   the title, 108,11–111,3; 112,6–24
   is the work genuine?, 111,6–11
   the order of reading, 111,11–18
   the parts of the work, 111,18–112,6
Sophists, 96,7
styles
   kinds of
      plain, 99,20 ff.; 103,11–15; 105,15; 107,26
      grand, 99,20 ff.; 107,25
      intermediate, 99,20 ff.; 109,26
      graphic, 99,21; 100,1; n. 22
      florid, 99,21; 107,26; 109,25
      austere, 109,26; n. 23
      polished, n. 23
      well-blended, n. 23
   origin of names for, 105,24–108,2
   of individual authors
      Demosthenes, 104,17–105,6; 107,2–5; 108,25; 109,1; 112,3
      Plato, 104,17–22; 112,3
      Lysias, 105,17
      Antiphon, 109,1
   number of, 99,18–100,2
      arguments for impossibility of knowing, 98,24–99,4; 99,16–18
      rebuttal of these arguments, 103,8–15
   characteristics
      arguments for impossibility of knowing, 99,4–7; 100,2–21
      rebuttal of these arguments, 103,16–104,10
   imitation of styles of 'ancients'
      desirability of, 97,7–11
      difficulty of, 97,10 ff.
      value of rhetorical training in, 97,13–17
      of Hermogenes' commentary in, 97,17–98,1
      arguments that successful imitation impossible or useless, 99,7–102,23
      rebuttal of these arguments, 102,24–105,21

types (*ideai*)
   meaning, 108,11–14; 108,20–109,3
   examples of
      solemnity, 108,25; 112,4.18
      purity, 112,4.18
   arguments that title *On Types* inappropriate, 108,10–19; 112,6–12
   defence of the title, 108,19–111,3; 112,12–24

Zeuxis, 102,5